THE PLAINS INDIANS

NUMBER 19

*Elma Dill Russell Spencer Series
in the West and Southwest*

TEXAS A&M UNIVERSITY PRESS College Station

Paul H. Carlson

The Plains Indians

Copyright © 1998
by Paul H. Carlson
Manufactured in
the United States of America
All rights reserved
Second printing, 1999
The paper used in this book
meets the minimum requirements
of the American National Standard
for Permanence of Paper for Printed
Library Materials, z39.48-1984.
Binding materials have been
chosen for durability.
∞

Library of Congress
Cataloging-in-Publication Data
Carlson, Paul H., 1940–
    The Plains Indians / Paul H.
    Carlson. — 1st ed.
        p.   cm.
    Includes bibliographical
    references and index.
    ISBN 0-89096-828-4 (cloth). —
    ISBN 0-89096-817-9 (pbk.)
    1. Indians of North America—
Great Plains—History.   2. Indians
of North America—Great Plains—
Social life and customs.   I. Title.
E78.G73C38   1998   98-13697
978'.00497—dc21   CIP

For

Karen M. Bouley

David R. Carlson

Jean M. Forrest

JoAnn E. Krejca

Contents

Illustrations

Preface

American Indians of the plains are members of dynamic societies, capable of change and full of growth. As a result their societies have evolved. The social organizations, political structures, economic patterns, ethnic compositions, and to a lesser extent worldviews of two hundred years ago have changed. Perceptions, attitudes, and judgments have changed. Much, however, does indeed remain the same. The Plains Indians retain several older customs, myths, ritual procedures, folkways, and traditions as well as much of their early art, cultural identity, music, and life patterns. Nonetheless, their societies today reflect contemporary concerns and ideals that are quite different from earlier ones. In short, modern-day Plains Indian people are unlike their early-day counterparts in enough ways to suggest that there is a fundamental difference between Plains Indian societies of past and present eras.

This book seeks to examine Plains Indian societies of an earlier era—the traditional period. The traditional era is defined as the period from the time when horses and material goods, diffused from an alien Western culture, radically enhanced the complexity of Plains Indian life and society to the time when intensive contact with that same Western culture destroyed that complexity. Ironically, many of the same influences that created the complexity were those that ultimately led to its decline.

Following Raymond J. DeMallie, Alice B. Kehoe, Alvin M. Josephy, Jr., Eldon Johnson, and others, this book defines Plains Indians in a broad sense. Thus, it looks at both the horticultural communities of the western prairies and the hunting groups of the high plains from the Saskatchewan River Basin in western Canada to the Rio Grande Valley in northern Mexico.

Although it lasted only a few generations, the traditional era claims a vivid place in the collective memory of people over much of the world. The Plains Indians of the period (roughly speaking, 1750–1890) enjoyed compelling lifestyles, highly attractive to most who came in contact with them. Both whites and contemporary non-Plains Indian peoples admired and copied them. The Plains Indians of the period were not all alike, of course, and the differences were considerable, but in terms of equestrian, bison-hunting economies, cultural traits offer a pattern for both plains and prairie societies of the late eighteenth and early nineteenth centuries.

This book argues that the plains and prairie societies of the period came into being after extensive contact with Europeans. Horses and firearms, Western trade goods, shifting migration patterns, disease pandemics, and events associated with white contact created channels through which those societies evolved to a peak of influence in the early nineteenth century. Shortly after mid-century most Indian people of the plains were living on reservations.

Thus, an important theme of the book stresses the essentially ephemeral nature of the period. Many of the Plains Indians came to the region late. Their societies developed in the second half of the eighteenth century, reached ascendancy in the early nineteenth century, and changed rather quickly afterward. In 1850 the Plains Indians could ride over much of the western high plains. Twenty years later they were living on reservations, where without abandoning their cultural base they adopted sedentary lifeways and shifted toward new life patterns, new sodalities, and different characteristics of community; new social events and contexts shaped their cultures.

A related theme in this study is the idea of change and cultural adaptation. Plains Indian societies were in a constant state of flux. While granting a basic timelessness to their societies, the peoples of the plains and prairies adapted in constructive and positive ways to changing circumstances. They were neither passive recipients nor helpless victims of new cultural and social forms, and while core elements of their cultures endured, the deep edges evolved to keep pace with an ever-changing present.

The book is not environmental history, but another theme stresses the role of the environment. On one level the effective ecological exploitation of bison helped to create the distinct societies that characterized the Plains Indians of the period. Dependence on bison provided unity to the region. On another level complex interactions with the environment occurred. Although environmental adaptation was difficult at best, people of the plains and prairies to some extent adjusted their hunting practices, their religious ceremonies, and their social organizations to the seasons, to the migrating patterns of bison, and to other environmental factors, such as the grazing requirements of their horses. The Plains Indians, however, did not live in perfect harmony with the environment, which, never static, changed over time. Moreover, such historical factors as migration, diffusion, disease, and contact with whites were important influences shaping the societies.

Finally, the study is designed for a wide audience. In a focused narrative it seeks to examine Plains Indian history and culture and to provide understanding for a key segment of the Plains Indian experience.

Acknowledgments

In working on this book I have received help and support from many people. Staff members at Texas Tech University's fine Southwest Collection were particularly helpful. They provided information and photographs, asked questions, shared ideas, challenged assumptions, and offered encouragement. I am indebted to them, especially Janet M. Neugebauer, Tai Kriedler, Freedonia Paschall, and former director David J. Murrah.

The government documents and interlibrary loan staffs at Texas Tech University's library were always courteous and resourceful. Library personnel at the University of Texas at Austin, Texas Lutheran University, the Texas State Archives, Sinte Gleska University on the Rosebud Reservation, and the Newberry Library likewise helped. At the Nebraska State Historical Society Martha Vestecka-Miller assisted me with the acquisition of several photographs.

Museum personnel provided all kinds of assistance. I am particularly grateful to the staffs at the Museum of Texas Tech University, the Panhandle-Plains Historical Museum, the Fort Robinson Museum, the Buechel Memorial Lakota Museum, Bent's Old Fort, the Akta Lakota Museum, and the Smithsonian Institution's Anthropological Archives—especially James Glenn. The Minneapolis Institute of Arts provided important information on the material culture of the Plains Indians.

I have relied heavily on the work of others, as the notes and bibliography make clear, but I have received other kinds of assistance too. Thomas A. Britten, Susan Dickey, Elise Fillpot, Sean Flynn (Lakota), Monte Monroe, and Sharon Toney offered opinions, perspective, and insight. Janice Ansorge, Earl H. Elam, Robert M. Utley, and the late John C. Ewers read an early version of the manuscript and offered many useful suggestions. Siva Chambers produced the maps from base drawings by Dale Snider. Kenneth D. Yeilding, Harlen Opperman, Frank Day, Frank Temple, John Becker, Sharon Kohout, Leslie J. Cullen, Monroe Tahmahkera (Comanche), Fred Cowart, Elmer "Buzz" Whitepipe (Lakota), Boyd Trolinger, and the late Ernest Wallace each aided in one way or another. I am indebted to all of them.

Pat Opperman, my father-in-law, for years regaled me and other members of his Keya Paha kin with tales of growing up on "the reservation," trading for dogs and horses, attending powwows, and otherwise fussing over beaded moccasins, red-trimmed leggings, and similar paraphernalia of the Lakotas. For that I am grateful.

I owe much to my colleagues. I completed a draft of the book while on leave from Texas Tech University, and I am grateful to the College of Arts and Sciences for the time it allowed me to research and write. Joan Weldon and Peggy Ariaz aided in many ways. Members of the history department, especially Alwyn Barr, Brian L. Blakeley, James W. Harper, Joseph E. King, and Allan J. Kuethe, provided assistance, encouragement, and good humor. I am indebted to them, but I alone accept responsibility for any errors of fact, difficulties of interpretation, or problems of emphasis that might exist.

Most of all I am indebted to my wife, Ellen. Not only did she tolerate my long hours spent in completing the work, but also she took her own valuable vacation time to travel with me to distant archives and libraries. Sometimes the trips had special rewards. One quiet evening in October we sat silently on a grassy knoll at Wounded Knee, South Dakota, watched a golden sun with arching rays set on the famous hilltop grave site, and as darkness descended on the sacred land felt the mystic spirituality of the place wash over us. Haiya! Nahktan, ohmik? (Oh! Why gone, those times?)

THE PLAINS INDIANS

1 : THE PEOPLE AND THE PLAINS

The Plains Indians lived on the broad expanse of open land stretching from the Saskatchewan River basin in Canada southward to the Rio Grande in southern Texas and lying between approximately the ninety-fifth meridian and the Rocky Mountains—the Great Plains of the North American West. People of many tribal groups occupied the rolling prairies and high plains of the region and used them for hunting, farming, trading, and other purposes. Often regarded as the quintessential American Indians, the Plains Indians have been the subjects of dozens of movies, scores of novels, and thousands of books and articles. Their societies have so captured popular imagination as to burn their image deep into the American consciousness. Indeed, their unique societies became so colorful and attractive that during the ascendent years of their development, approximately 1750–1890, neighboring peoples adopted several of their traits and features.

The more than thirty different Indian groups that occupied the Great Plains may be divided into two broad classifications or subclusters: horticulture village people of the eastern prairies and nomadic hunting people of the western high plains. The latter group many scholars judge as the more characteristic Plains Indians, for they possessed in high degree the most distinguishing traits of plains societies in the eighteenth and nineteenth centuries.

Although there is disagreement on a strict definition for Plains Indian culture and about which Indian peoples constituted such a grouping, some pioneering studies list eleven bison-hunting communities of the western high plains as the most characteristic: Arapaho, Assiniboin, Blackfeet, Cheyenne, Comanche, Crow, Gros Ventre, Kiowa, Kiowa Apache, Lakota, and Sarsi.[1] To this list many scholars add the Plains Cree, but some do not include the Sarsis. Others count the Tonkawas of Central Texas and the Lipan Apaches, although they admit that the Lipans possess few of the cultural characteristics that generally denote Plains Indians.[2] Arguably others could be added. By 1830, for example, the eastern Shoshonis had taken on many traits of the Plains Indians.[3]

Nonetheless, the most characteristic hunters of the high plains numbered perhaps fourteen tribal groups. In the far north lived the Blackfeet, Assiniboins, Plains Crees, and Sarsis. The Blackfeet (Nitzitapi, a confederation of

1

Blackfeet proper [Siksika], Piegan [Pikuni], Blood [Kainai], and Small Robes) ranged through northwestern areas of the high plains and the bordering aspen parkland in Saskatchewan and Alberta and the upper reaches of the Missouri River in Montana. Assiniboin people (Nakota Sioux, sometimes called Stoney) moved north from the forests of Minnesota, allied with the Plains Crees, and pushed westward onto the northernmost reaches of the plains lying above the Missouri River. The Plains Crees (Natimiwiyiniwuk) separated from forest-dwelling Crees in Manitoba and pressed southwestward into Saskatchewan. From the subarctic, the Sarsis moved south to settle around the upper Saskatchewan and Athabasca rivers. Few in number, they attached themselves to the Blackfeet and assimilated the ways of other northern Plains Indians.

Along and below the present-day U.S.–Canada border lived the Gros Ventres, Crows, and Lakotas. The Gros Ventres (A'ani', or Atsina) first allied with the Blackfeet along the upper Missouri River, but later they associated with the Assiniboins and a legally unrecognized Métis community at the Fort Belknap reservation in Montana. The Crows (Absaroka), an offshoot of the Missouri River Hidatsas, occupied rich game land near the headwaters of the Yellowstone River at the foot of the Rocky Mountains. They split in two broad divisions: Mountain (or Up Stream) and River (or Down Stream) Crows; but some modern scholars have suggested a third division, the Kicked in the Bellies, a subgroup of the Mountain Crows.[4] Lakotas (Pte Oyate, Titonwan, Teton, or Western Sioux) took possession of the plains west of the Missouri River, north of the Platte River and around the Black Hills. Seven divisions existed among the Lakotas: Oglala, Brule (Sicangu), Miniconjou, Hunkpapa, Sans Arc (Itazipacola), Two Kettle (Oohenunpa), and Sihasapa (Blackfeet).

The Cheyennes and Arapahos occupied the central plains. Once on the plains the Cheyennes (Tsctschastahase) split into northern and southern branches. The northern group hunted west of the Black Hills. The southern group occupied the short-grass plains between the Platte and Arkansas rivers. The Arapahos (Inunaina), who had separated from the Gros Ventres, associated with the Cheyennes and like their allies divided into two branches, a northern one in Montana and Wyoming and a southern one on the plains between the Platte and Arkansas rivers.

The Comanches, Kiowas, Kiowa Apaches, Tonkawas, and Lipans inhabited the southern plains. The Comanches (Nuhmuhnuh), whose people split into several independent divisions, dominated the region below the Arkansas River, west of the Cross Timbers, and east of the upper Rio Grande. The Kiowas (Gaigwa) and Kiowa Apaches, who spoke separate languages but remained closely associated, established themselves between the upper Arkansas and upper Canadian rivers, and after an alliance forged about 1790

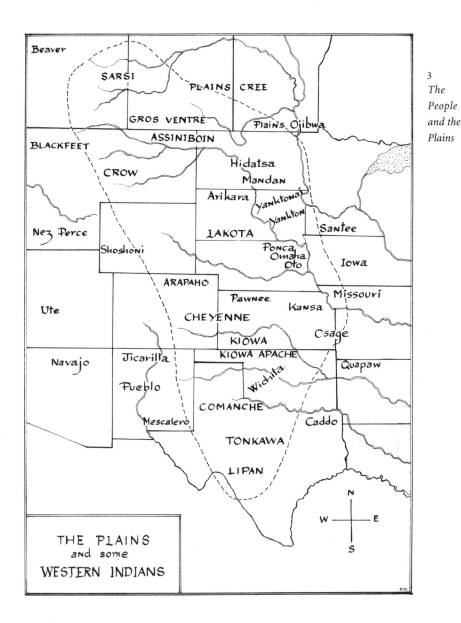

THE PLAINS
and some
WESTERN INDIANS

with the Comanches, they shared the rich bison range with their more numerous neighbors. Central Texas from the Red River to below San Antonio
became the sixteenth-century homeland of a number of autonomous bands
of people who spoke a common language. Over the years these bands declined in population, and by the beginning of the nineteenth century the
survivors had united to become the Tonkawas, a people fairly typical of
southern Plains Indians, except for their clanlike organization and perhaps
their occasional ceremonial cannibalism. One of several Apache divisions,

the Lipans, under both Spanish and Comanche pressure, moved into South Texas below and west of San Antonio and into northern Mexico.

Again, the list of nomadic peoples given here is selective. Because a classification based on culture and geographical lines contains an element of arbitrariness, no implication is intended here that this inventory is all inclusive. Some observers, for example, might include bands of Shoshonis or Pawnees who were nomadic. Perhaps few would include the Sarsis, Tonkawas, or Lipans. But on the high plains the fourteen tribal groups enumerated here exhibited a large measure of cultural homogeneity and commonality.

Several cultural traits stand out. Nonhorticultural, the nomadic peoples hunted large game on horseback and depended on bison for food and for much of their material culture. They maintained warriors' societies, lived in portable tipis, and adopted the vision quest. Most, but not all, practiced the Sun Dance. In addition, such features as the use of a warrior society as "police" (marshals) for a march or hunt, the use of sign language and beasts of burden (dogs and horses), the absence of pottery and basketry, and an emphasis on military honors represented common and usual characteristics.[5]

Although they shared a large measure of cultural affinity, the nomadic peoples of the plains were not identical. Each of the various groups retained many distinguishing characteristics. Most of them sustained much of their preplains culture and many elements of their preplains experience. Moreover, once on the plains they adapted differently to the high, open country and by varying degrees adopted traditional plains cultures. In addition, during the period of their ascendency, they came under progressively severe pressures from the Europeans and Americans who entered their country, which prompted responses that impacted their individual societies in different ways.

The second group of American Indians who occupied the Great Plains included a number of semisedentary farming and hunting peoples who lived on the prairies at the eastern edge of the region or in the middle Missouri River Valley. Although such people did not always possess plains traits to the same high degree as the western groups, many scholars argue that several of them are properly considered Plains Indians, or at least prairie-plains people. In fact, people in a number of the prairie communities abandoned farm crops and made bison hunting the basis of year-round economic and social life rather than a mere complement to horticulture.[6]

In the lake and forest areas of the far north in modern Canada, Wisconsin, and Minnesota lived the Crees and Ojibwas (Chippewa, Anishinaabe, Bungi, or their historic offshoot Saulteaux). Neither of these peoples should be properly included with the plains and prairie groups, but at least one division of the Ojibwas moved to the edge of the plains in Canada, where they became known as Plains Ojibwas. Also a growing population of Métis (Slotas)—French-speaking descendants of fur traders and American Indians (Cree and Ojibwa)—lived along the lower Red River in Canada, and they traveled to the plains to hunt bison.

Below them in the prairie-plains region between the upper Mississippi and the Missouri rivers lived the Santee (Isanti), Yankton (Ihanktonwan), and Yanktonai (Ihanktonwanna) peoples. Dakotas (as they called themselves) or Sioux, they formed part of the larger Oceti Sakowin, or the Seven Council Fires, a group of distinct peoples who under pressure from the Ojibwas in the 1600s separated into three broad divisions. The eastern or Santee division, living on the prairies and woodlands of Minnesota, included four groups: the Mdewakantonwan, Wachpekute, Wachpetonwan, and Sisitonwan (Sisseton). The middle division included two groups: the Yankton and Yanktonai who lived on the prairies and plains stretching west to the Missouri (and who are sometimes called Nakota). The western division included only the nomadic Lakotas (Tetons), but representing about half the Oceti Sakowin population, it was the largest, with some of its subgroups (Oglalas and Brules) having populations larger than most of the other council-fire peoples.

In the tall-grass prairie country of the lower Missouri River basin lived the Ponca, Oto, Omaha, Iowa, Missouri, Kansa (Kaw), and Osage peoples. North and west of them, the Arikaras (Sahnish), Mandans, and Hidatsas (Nuxbaaga, as one division called themselves, and sometimes Atsinas or Minnetarees [Minitaris]—the same names as the Gros Ventres) resided along the middle Missouri River. Quapaw (Arkansa) people lived in Arkansas. The Pawnees (Chahiksichahiks) inhabited Nebraska and divided into four groups: Chaui (Grand), Pitahawirata, Kitkahahki (Republican), and Skiri (Skidi, sometimes called Panismaha). Farther south in Kansas, Oklahoma, and northern Texas, people of the Wichita (Kichais, Taovayas, Tawakonis, Wacos, and Wichita Proper) and Caddo confederations ranged over a large territory. The Caddos were indigeneous to the region, and some of them (called Prairie Caddos) ventured out to the plains to hunt.

The semisedentary, or horticultural village, peoples displayed a prairie-plains culture. Most of them lived on or near the plains in permanent villages, practiced horticulture based on corn growing, engaged in bison hunting, and possessed several traits of the nomads farther west. Many eastern influences, including dress, use of pottery, tribal organization, and certain rituals, marked their lives. Their household items included basketry and woven bags. The northern peoples used carefully made birchbark canoes, and to navigate the large rivers of the Missouri Valley the middle Missouri people used round, skin boats. Maize ceremonies played a more common role than the Sun Dance.

Clearly, then, the plains and prairie people represented a mixed bag of varying societies. Some of the horticultural groups, such as the Métis and Quapaws, and some of the hunting groups, such as the Tonkawas and Lipans, possessed only the narrowest traits of the more characteristic Plains Indians.

Shared traits, particularly dependence on bison, provided unity to people of the plains. They helped to create distinctive native societies and ways of life that varied from section to section and changed over time, but remained sufficiently homogeneous to speak of a Great Plains culture area.

A *culture area* may be defined as a geographic region whose residents are thought to have more cultural affinities with one another than they do with people in other regions. As with most similar concepts, it has its short-comings, for sometimes the differences might outnumber the similarities and Plains Indian societies never remained static. Nonetheless, plains people, for all their significant cultural differences, created societies on the Great Plains that mirrored one another more than they resembled American Indian societies in the eastern woodlands, the western plateau and basin country, or the desert Southwest. To some extent the plains peoples shared in a greater culture area that included everyone east of the Rocky Mountains. The sharing occurred in religion, personality, and worldview.

On the Great Plains, however, there remained far more cultural diversity than the concept of a plains culture area suggests. The plains and prairie groups were, in fact, distinct and different communities. They were separate peoples with different descent and political systems, diverse economic structures, and varied cosmologies. Their historic backgrounds and the plains environment both contributed to the differences, particularly in kinship arrangements and the uniqueness in how plains peoples organized their contrasting summer and winter lifeways. The plains and prairie peoples did not meld into one large and identical society, and they retained their disparity through the reservation period and afterward.

In short, the Plains Indians differed from one another within a broader plains culture area in much the same way that eighteenth-century European peoples differed from one another within a broader western culture. Comanche people, for example, were not like Lakotas, nor Gros Ventres like Kiowas. Blackfeet men in a relative sense were free and easy, concerned with the material pleasures of life; Cheyenne men were far more austere and serious, concerned with the ideals of responsible behavior and virtuous living. Many plains peoples' names for themselves translated loosely as "principal people" or "most human of people," or simply "the people," suggesting further dissimilarities. Custom, tradition, belief, religious and ceremonial differences, and other factors, including an environment that changed over time, made life on the plains varied.

Individual personality varied, too. There were skilled warriors who thrilled in a worthy fight, but there were also peace-loving wise men. There were buffoonish braggerts and cowards, but there were also patriots and heroes willing to risk all for the safety of the village or band. There were women who were healers and some who were warriors. There were homosexuals and male chauvinists. There were industrious folks and dullards, statesmen and fools. There were young men who sang songs of love. There were spinsters, and there were women who cried for the safety of their children. In short, there were considerable differences.

Languages reflected the differences. Several linguistic groups existed on the Great Plains, but none were limited to the region. Arapaho, Blackfeet, Cheyenne, Gros Ventre, and Plains Cree peoples spoke various *Algonquian* languages. People of the Kiowa Apache, Lipan, and Sarsi groups spoke various *Athapaskan* languages. The Assiniboin, Crow, Dakota, Lakota, Hidatsa, Iowa, Kansa, Mandan, Missouri, Omaha, Osage, Oto, Ponca, and Quapaw people spoke various *Siouan* languages. Other languages spoken included *Caddoan* by the Arikaras, Pawnees, and Wichitas; *Kiowan* (with relationships to *Tanoan*) by the Kiowas; and *Uto-Aztecan* (or *Shoshonean*) by the Comanches and Shoshonis. The Tonkawas spoke an unknown tongue, but it may have been related to *Coahuiltecan* and/or *Karakawan* linguistic stock.[7]

Despite the language differences, communication barriers seldom proved insurmountable. The Mandans and Lakotas, for example, spoke mutually unintelligible languages within the Siouan linquistic family, but after some difficulty they could make themselves understood. Among recently separated peoples, such as the Crows and Hidatsas or the Gros Ventres and Arapahos, and among closely related peoples, such as the Yanktons and Yanktonais, members of different tribal groups conversed easily with one another. Moreover, on the Comanche-dominated southern plains, an area of linguistic diversity, many people used the Comanche language when discussing matters of trade or diplomacy. On the northern plains the Lakotas to a lesser extent enjoyed a similar linguistic hegemony, or lingua franca. Besides, many Indian people were bilingual.

People on the plains also developed a universal sign language. They employed symbolic gestures to designate various ideas, not words, and people throughout the plains understood the system. The sign language, not identical to the modern system used by hearing-impaired people but comparable to it, evolved out of the need to communicate over long distances with members of the same band or tribal group. From such practice it developed into intertribal use. The Plains Indians made wide gestures, using arms and hands in such a way that they extended beyond the body and could be seen against a background of light, and they repeated the signs often. They have been called "airpictures—pure pantomine [*sic*]."[8]

Although they had no written language, the Plains Indians enjoyed something akin to it. People of several groups used written "signs" to record famous deeds and time counts on bison skins or tipi walls. Some people painted bison robes in such a way as to produce pictoral histories or calendars— "wintercounts" some people called them—with a significant picture or symbol for each year. Not only were the designs works of art, but also they were a chronicle in pictographs of the band or tribal group. In one of the best-known examples several Kiowa people, using mnemonic devices painted on hides, pictorially identified each year from 1832 to 1892.[9]

While they disagree somewhat about language, scholars vigorously argue about Indian demography. A recent estimate suggests a pre-Columbian population of just over five million people for all of America north of Mexico. Some studies, however, suggest a much greater population.[10]

In either case, Indian depopulation began at an early date. On the southern plains, Indian people may have suffered a measles epidemic as early as 1531, and when Francisco Vásquez de Coronado, the Spanish explorer, reached the central plains in Kansas in 1541, a disease epidemic may have already passed through the area. Smallpox, measles, rubella, and cholera caused the worst havoc to American Indians, who had little or no immunity to the diseases, but scarlet fever, tuberculosis, yellow fever, chicken pox, typhus, and other diseases, as well as alcohol, also brought devastation.[11]

All Indian groups suffered; on the Great Plains many sustained heavy losses. The Mandans, for example, enjoyed a large population of perhaps 15,000 people before the arrival of French explorers in the late 1730s. Their numbers decreased rapidly thereafter. They had nine villages with an estimated 9,000 inhabitants in 1750. Twenty-five years later they lived in five villages. Severe smallpox epidemics in 1780–81 and again in the 1830s further devastated the Mandan population. After 1837 only 138 people remained.[12]

European diseases, the pressures of armed conflict, the uprooting of their people, and other factors all affected Indian populations. Some people, such as the Sarsis, Poncas, Otos, and Tonkawas, remained small in tribal numbers and faced constant pressures from outsiders, both white and Indian. Others, such as the Lakotas, managed to expand both their range of territory and their population. Until the end of the nineteenth century there was no national census information available for American Indians. The conjectures, estimates, and guesses of travelers, traders, and other observers about population figures varied even for approximately the same date, but using data offered by several scholars one can summarize several findings for different periods (see Tables 1 and 2).

The numbers for the early years may underestimate tribal populations, but there is not much agreement among demographers.[13] The Comanches, for example, during the apex of their influence may have numbered 14,000 or more people. They ranged widely over the extreme southern plains, sometimes riding deep into Mexico to hunt or raid. Moreover, until the late 1830s bison thickly populated the heart of their territory, providing ample support for a Comanche population larger than the figures suggest.[14]

Whatever their numbers, the Plains Indians occupied the rolling prairies and high plains of the North American West. Representing more than one million square miles of territory, this enormous country contained varied surface features.

On the central and southern high plains, characteristic landforms included rolling hills interspersed with seemingly endless smooth, flat surfaces, broken washes, and wide streams. The phenomenally flat high plains of western Kansas and eastern Colorado, or the Llano Estacado of West Texas and eastern New Mexico, perhaps best exemplified the broad, flat uplands. In several localities, large and prominent sandy areas, sometimes called sandhills, also existed. By far the largest and most important were the sandhills of central Nebraska. Covering some 20,000 square miles, they contained grassy, rolling hills and active dunes interspersed with low-lying wetlands. Here Indian people gathered small amounts of wild rice and hunted several species of game birds.

On the northern Great Plains, above the Platte River, an area physiographically referred to as the Missouri Plateau, changes occurred. The rolling features of the central and southern plains gave way to a series of terraced plains and scarped ridges, such as Pine Ridge of southern South Dakota and northern Nebraska. Some of the wide river valleys of this section were indefinitely set off from upland areas. Here also, however, several streams of the Missouri River system cut deep into the gravelly soil, leaving a maze of eroded river beds and creating a country of bluffs, gulches, buttes, and washes.[15]

Several groups of domed mountains dotted the plains. They include the Black Hills, the Bear Paw Mountains, and the Sweetgrass and Cypress hills, survivors of the erosive process that cut down the rest of the countryside. Among them the Black Hills, or *Paha Sapa* to Lakota people, became a sacred land where rocks at night turned into spirits who talked like humans, where needle-shaped spires were the home of mighty beings known as thunderbirds, and where clear stream waters held powers to cure many illnesses.

Northwest of the Black Hills spread the great hunting grounds of the

TABLE 1. *Populations of Selected Nomadic Peoples*

People	Year	Population
Arapaho	1780	3,000
	1910	1,419
	1930	1,241
	1980	3,500
Assiniboin	1780	10,000
	1829	8,000
	1920	2,800
	1980	4,000
Blackfeet Confederation	1780	15,000
	1801	9,000
	1855	7,600
	1932	4,600
	1980	22,000
Cheyenne	1780	3,500
	1910	3,055
	1930	2,695
	1980	10,000
Comanche	1690	7,000
	1930	1,423
	1937	2,213
	1980	9,000
Crow	1780	4,000
	1930	1,674
	1937	2,173
	1980	7,000
Gros Ventre	1780	3,000
	1910	510
	1932	809
Kiowa	1780	2,000
	1910	1,126
	1930	1,050
	1980	7,400
Lakota and Dakota	1780	25,000
	1904	27,175
	1930	25,934
	1980	35,000
Plains Cree	1835	4,000
	1858	1,000

Shoshoni		
(Wind River)	1820	1,500
	1878	1,250
(all Shoshoni)	1980	10,000

Note. The larger numbers for 1980 indicate natural population growth, but they also reflect changes in census procedures (self-enumeration after 1960, for example) as well as a growing pride in Indian heritage and some legal advantages of being American Indian. Sources: Robert H. Lowie, *Indians of the Plains,* Lincoln: University of Nebraska Press, 1982), pp. 10–11; Alice B. Kehoe, *North American Indians: A Comprehensive Account,* 2d ed. (Englewood Cliffs, N.J.: Prentice-Hall, 1992), pp. 299–300, 304–310, 393; United States Department of Commerce, Bureau of the Census, *1980 Census of Population: American Indians, Eskimos, and Aleuts on Identified Reservations and in the Historic Areas of Oklahoma,* PC 80-2-1D, Part I, Table 4, pp. 16–31; Table 13, pp. 99–101.

TABLE 2. *Populations of Selected Semisedentary Hunting and Farming Peoples*

People	Year	Population
Arikara	1780	3,800
	1804	2,600
	1937	616
	1980	1,500
Iowa	1760	1,100
	1804	800
	1937	112
	1980	950
Kansa	1780	3,300
	1820	1,850
	1937	515
	1980	677
Omaha	1780	2,800
	1802	300
	1930	1,103
	1980	3,100
Osage	1780	6,200
	1937	3,649
	1980	7,000
Oto	1780	900
	1805	500
	1980	1,500
Pawnee	1780	10,000
	1856	4,686
	1879	1,440

		1937	959
		1980	2,500
Ponca		1780	800
		1930	939
		1980	2,100
Wichita		1780	3,200
		1937	385
		1980	700

Note. The large numbers for 1980 indicate natural population growth, but they also reflect changes in census procedures (self-enumeration after 1960, for example) as well as a growing pride in Indian heritage and some legal advantages of being American Indian. Sources: Robert H. Lowie, *Indians of the Plains* (Lincoln: University of Nebraska Press, 1982), pp. 10–11; Alice B. Kehoe, *North American Indians: A Comprehensive Account,* 2d ed. (Englewood Cliffs, N.J.: Prentice Hall, 1992), pp. 299–300, 304–310, 393; United States Department of Commerce, Bureau of the Census, *1980 Census of Population: American Indians, Eskimos, and Aleuts on Identified Reservations and in the Historic Areas of Oklahoma,* PC 80-2-1D, Part I, Table 4, pp. 16–31; Table 13, pp. 99–101.

northern Plains Indians. Here the rich, green valleys of the Powder, Tongue, and Bighorn rivers supported enormous numbers of bison, deer, elk, pronghorns, and other game, both large and small. Along the banks of such streams grew occasional clumps of trees, most numerous among them the cottonwood with its silvery leaves that were sacred to several Indian groups.

East of the high plains and Missouri Plateau lay the central lowlands, a region from Canada to Texas that varied in topography. In the north it was a low drift plain or gently rolling prairie covered with luxurious tall grass. It extended westward from the woodlands of Minnesota through the Red River Valley to the Missouri.

Southward in the western Iowa, eastern Nebraska, and northern Kansas area a thick blanket of wind-deposited loess obscured the high plains–central lowland relationship. Although a gently rolling prairie country, the area contained such surface features as the Drift Hills along the Missouri River and the rolling Loess Hills east of the Nebraska Sandhills. South of the Platte River the loess covering extended far to the west as a flat plain, intruding onto the high plains and continuing southward into northern Kansas. Rich soils in the loess area encouraged many Indian groups to take up semipermanent residence there along the valleys of the Loup, Platte, Republican, Kansas, and Smoky Hill rivers, where they could practice horticulture, collect wild plants, and hunt.[16]

From Kansas to Texas the central lowlands varied in character. Erosive action of rain and wind gave rise to a series of eastward-facing escarpments, of which the flint Hills—faulting the loess in northern and central Kansas—provide an excellent example. The scarped landscape continued south through eastern Oklahoma, but gave way westward to the Red Beds Plains, a gently rolling lowland in the central part of the state, and to the Gypsum Hills, a zone of subdued escarpments, low hills, and plains.

Below the Red River in Texas various landforms dominated the central prairies. On the north occurred the Rolling Plains, an area of highly eroded terrain interspersed with spacious prairies. Farther south the Edwards Plateau, a broken tableland of shallow soil, was in its eastern portions covered with cedar brakes. Still farther south, stretching to the Rio Grande, the South Texas Plains were a territory of eroded brushlands and chaparral-lined savannahs.[17]

Grasses dominated the natural vegetation. Several hundred species grew on the plains, but they can be separated into three broad divisions: tall grass, or prairie; short grass, or plains; and desert shrub. Desert shrub grasses grew near the Rio Grande in southwest Texas and in southern New Mexico. On the Great Plains the dividing line between tall-grass prairie on the east and short-grass plains farther west was roughly the hundredth meridian but closer to the ninety-eighth in the north. The tall grass was luxuriant with deep roots and rank growth. The short grass formed a thick sod, but its roots were shallow. Farther west, because the climate could not support heavy growth, the sod gave way to more widely spaced tufts or bunchgrass.[18]

But grass cover never remained stable. In rainy years tall grass encroached on the short-grass area, and the short grass pushed into bunch grass. In dry years the process reversed, with short grass intruding on the tall grass.[19] Moreover, the arrival of horses (and later cattle and sheep) brought seeds of European weeds and grasses that thrived on the plains and competed with native species. The European varieties, species that had evolved with horses and cattle, could more easily adapt to the heavy trampling and grazing of horses and the close herding of cattle than could native grasses. In addition, horses (and cattle) competed with bison and other native animals for forage, gradually changing the grassland ecology.

Although grasses dominated, the plains were not without trees. Forested areas existed in the Black Hills, the Bear Paw Mountains, the Rawhide Buttes in Wyoming, and other isolated masses of elevated land. Mesquite thickets grew in the south, and a belt of oak savannah, the Cross Timbers, stretched northward through central Texas and across Oklahoma. In the north a few limited stands of pine and juniper dotted the otherwise monotonous landscape. In Canada the northern border of the plains contained a poplar (aspen) parkland of groves and meadows. Toward the north it gave way to pines and spruces of the subarctic boreal forest. In the eastern prairie regions, long, branching belts of trees extended up the rivers. Some of the belts reached perhaps ten miles wide, covering the valley bottoms and hugging the bluffs. They narrowed toward the west and beyond the hundredth meridian almost disappeared, although cottonwood, willow, elm, ash, hackberry, box elder, and a few other ubiquitous species grew along water courses throughout the plains.

Plenty of other plant life existed. The Plains Indians made use of a wide variety of fruits, nuts, and berries. In the north they collected wild currant, gooseberry, serviceberry, and high-brush cranberry. Farther south Indian people collected buffalo berry, chokecherry, grapes, and wild plum. In the southeast they picked nuts of the hickory, black walnut, pecan, and hazelnut trees. They made use of persimmon. They dug herbaceous flowering plants, such as groundnut. Throughout the plains they ate fresh or dried for winter use the starchy roots of the tipsin, or Indian turnip, which contains more protein than the potato and as much vitamin C as most citrus fruits. Dogbane, nettle, certain species of milkweed, and the inner bark of the slippery elm they stripped for cordage in the manufacture of rope and for sewing. They cut and traded wood of the Osage orange (bois d'arc), native to the southern plains of Texas and Oklahoma, for making bows. They boiled the sap of the box elder to produce sugar. In short, the Plains Indians used innumerable plants for foods, dye, fiber, and other benefits.[20]

They made medicinal applications of plants as well. For example, using roots of the American licorice plant, Cheyennes made a tea to treat diarrhea and upset stomach. From the purplecone flower (black susan, comb flower, hedge hog) Poncas and Omahas made an eyewash, and Lakotas used the root and green fruit as a painkiller for toothache, stomachache, and pain in the bowels. Pawnees burned the huge root of the bush morning glory (wild potato vine, bush moon flower) as a smoke treatment for nervousness and bad dreams. Blackfeet used the leaves of dried mint to treat heart ailments and chest pains, and Kiowas chewed the fresh leaves or drank a mint tea for stomach troubles. Otos used ragweed as a remedy for nausea, and Cheyennes drank a tea from its leaves to treat bowel cramps, bloody stools, and colds. Indeed, Indian people on the plains used plaintain, spurge, milkweed, sunflowers, white prairie clover, and numerous other species as medicine for a wide variety of illnesses.[21]

Nevertheless, grasses dominated to such an extent that the Great Plains have been called an "ocean of grass." The dips and swells of the land appeared as motionless waves, and the grass, when it was high, rippled before the ceaseless winds. The plains had the monotony of the ocean, too, for the view from each rise seemed exactly like the one before it.

Here lived an exceptional variety of wildlife. Along the winding arms of timber that extended up river valleys westward into the grasslands hid woodland game and fur-bearing animals. An anonymous Omaha informant indicated that "when I was a youth, . . . I could see the trails of many kinds of animals" in the woodlands.[22] Beaver and raccoons were perhaps most abundant, but otters, martens, mink, and numerous other small furbearers that also provided food scurried through the trees and shrubs.

Fur-bearing mammals always proved useful to Indian people, but after about 1820, when they took on major economic importance in trade with whites, their numbers declined rapidly. Later, as white settlers penetrated the valleys, cutting the trees for homes and fuel and reshaping the environment, they all but disappeared. Before the coming of whites, badgers, black bears, cougars, and bobcats inhabited the timbered areas, as did skunks, opossums, porcupines (whose quills were used for clothing decorations), and other animals whose habitat was not limited to the plains and prairies. The wooded valleys, juxtaposed against the grassy uplands, also attracted red fox, especially in the north; gray fox, especially in the south; brown bears; and such major food animals as elk and white-tailed deer. A few bighorn sheep occupied the mountain uplands. In times of scarcity Plains Indians might take any of these species for food.

Fish, turtles, and shellfish inhabited the rivers. Although among the hunting groups widespread taboos on the eating of fish existed, the Arikaras and their horticultural neighbors fashioned hooks and weirs to catch large channel catfish and, less frequently, gar pike in the Missouri River. Other streams also held catfish as well as bullheads and buffalo fish, and in small arroyos of many rivers people found and used sunfish and related species. Rivers on the northwestern plains and in Canada held bass, trout, and similar game fish. Turtles, symbols of long life, existed along all major rivers, and Indian people ate the dark red meat of the larger varieties. Native people manufactured a number of items, such as ornaments, spoons, and paint receptacles, from shellfish, and the shells became an important trade item.

Bird life was abundant and varied. The Plains Indians took some for food, some for feathers, and some for bones, which they made into ornaments and tools. Blue and bobwhite quail occupied wooded valleys. Long-billed curlews nested in damp, grassy creeks and ponds. Along eastern margins of the Great Plains wild turkeys, which preferred to stay close to wooded areas, could be found in large numbers from Texas to South Dakota. Few Indian people made use of the tasty bird for food, however, because folklore held that those who ate such birds would become cowardly and run from their enemies just as the turkey fled from its pursuers.[23]

Prairie chickens, grouse, sage hens, and cowbirds preferred the grasslands. The cowbirds, or "buffalo birds," remained close to the muzzles of grazing bison to capture insects frightened up from the grass. Meadowlarks, killdeer, ravens, magpies, and many other species, including an occasional falcon, inhabited the plains, and everywhere hawks and owls could be found. For its feathers, Indian people sought particularly the great horned owl.

Of all the varied bird life, few were more important to the Plains Indians than the bald and golden eagles. From the skies the majestic birds patrolled the prairies and uplands with eyes keen enough to see every movement on the ground. The eagles typified dash and courage needed for success in war, and the Plains Indians considered eagles as sacred representatives of the spirit beings. They prayed to eagles and used their feathers and bodies in ceremonies, in decorations, and in symbolic references to successful raids, hunts, and wars. Some Indian peoples employed eagle bone whistles in ritualistic dances and such important ceremonies as the Sun Dance. The golden eagle, more numerous on the plains, they called the "war eagle." The bald eagle, more numerous in the foothills and mountains, they prized for its distinctive white-tipped feathers.

The most characteristic plains animals ranged the grassy uplands, and they retained many common features. Shy but sociable, they preferred the open country. They got by on little water and possessed extraordinary vitality and enormous stamina. Most, but not all, were grass eaters and fast afoot.[24] Such animals included prairie dogs (relatives of squirrels who lived in underground colonies), coyotes (carnivores that resembled dogs and ate prairie dogs and rodents), and jackrabbits. A voracious grass eater who sometimes foraged on Indian garden vegetables, the jackrabbit, or hare, was a pest. But Indian people made ropes of its hair, ate its flesh, and used its soft skins for robes. Another little animal was the sandy yellow-gray furred kit fox. A close relative of the red fox, it roamed western deserts as well as the plains. Although it weighed only four to six pounds, the kit fox gave its name to several Indian warrior societies.

Far larger and more dangerous was the plains grizzly bear. It haunted the northern regions from western Kansas to Saskatchewan and Alberta, feeding chiefly on insects, roots, and grass. In the late summer it entered chockecherry and wild plum thickets to enjoy the ripening fruit. Although perhaps the only carnivore strong enough to kill a full-grown bison, grizzlies preferred to sniff out a decaying carcass. Indian people respected the grizzly as much for its spiritual influence as for its physical strength.

More dangerous to bison was the gray or timber wolf. A tireless, rangy animal, the large gray wolf roamed throughout the plains. Wolves hunted in packs, and because most bison were too strong or too wary to be singled out as easy prey, wolves watched for an unprotected calf or an aged or weak straggler. When they found a lone bison, they attacked the flanks, hoping to bite through the tendon of a hind leg and thereby make the animal helpless. They also hunted sick or injured elk, deer, and pronghorns, and they ate smaller animals as well. Plains people admired the wolf for its prowess, cunning, and perseverance in the hunt. Because it symbolized skill in war, scouts wore its skin while on a raid, and many leaders, such as Sharitorish (White Wolf) of the Pawnees, took its name.

Three larger game animals, also native to the western plains, included the mule deer, pronghorn, and bison. The mule deer, or blacktail deer as Indian people called it, ate grass during the spring but lived on buds, leaves, and twigs of shrubs the rest of the time. It inhabited the plains from Canada to Texas. A beautiful animal that had large, furry ears similar to those of a mule, the mule deer was gray-brown in color and about three to four feet tall with spreading antlers.

The pronghorn inhabited the open plains. Perhaps the fastest of all North American mammals, it could for a short distance sprint at a rate of sixty miles per hour. Sometimes called "the phantom of the prairies," it relied on its speed and a keen sense of vision to escape its principal enemies—wolves and coyotes. Graceful, sociable, and curious, the pronghorn was not a true antelope, had no close relatives anywhere, and had changed little from its ancient ancestor of a million or more years ago. Because it seldom exceeded 120 pounds, Plains Indians did not pursue it for food with sustained energy, but they used its distinctive horns to manufacture bows.

For their major food supply, the Plains Indians relied on the North American bison, or buffalo, a majestic animal that embodied the special character of the plains grasslands. Perhaps no animal anywhere has had such an impact on a people as the bison had on the western Indians. A veritable commissary, it provided not only food but also a startling array of material items. Indian people used the entire animal, from hoofs to horns and from viscera to hides. In addition, they perceived the animal as a sacred being to whom they prayed and offered sacrements. Their tribal hunts featured prehunt ceremonies and, after a successful harvest, posthunt thanksgivings. They named social organizations after it. Holy men sought its powers to help them perform their rituals. Indian people painted bison skulls and used them in such characteristic ceremonies as the Sun Dance and vision quest. They revered, studied, and imitated the bison, all the while weaving legends and folktales that maintained a close relationship between man and beast. A Kiowa woman named Old Lady Horse said: "Everything the Kiowas had came from the buffalo. . . . The buffalo was the life of the Kiowas."25

The bison was the largest North American land mammal. A mature bull stood over six feet tall and weighed sixteen hundred to two thousand pounds. The female rarely weighed over nine hundred pounds. Long, coarse hair of brownish-black covered the head, neck, and distinctive hump; the rest of the animal was brown. The black horns, similiar to those of domestic cattle, spread as much as thirty-five inches at their widest point. Tough, hardy, and relatively fast, bison could run at about thirty miles per hour for many miles over rough or level ground. They fed on grass but ate a few other small plants as well as twigs of willows and low shrubs.

Great herds of bison once roamed over North America from the Appalachian Mountains on the east to the Rockies on the west, and they extended from Mexico northward into Alberta, Saskatchewan, and Manitoba. The largest concentration occurred on the central Great Plains between the South Platte and Arkansas rivers. Although in some localities on the plains herds moved seasonally between warm and cold weather ranges, no regular migrations took them south each winter. Through the freezing months northern herds, kept warm by their thick winter coats, continued to roam wind-tossed uplands, rooting in shallow snow to graze. If necessary, they could feed in snow up to four feet deep by swinging their huge shaggy heads to push aside drifts and clear a path to the cured grass. At frozen waterholes they broke the ice with hoofs or muzzles, and when no water could be reached they ate snow. They faced winter storms on the uplands and waited them out, but in severe blizzards, they moved to protected bottomlands. An icy crust on the grass or snow, of course, complicated winter feeding, for it made travel difficult and eating painful, as bison scraped their noses. The southern herds endured less severe winters, but they faced their own problems, including excessive heat and lengthy dry spells that depleted the scarce water sources of their environment.

Nevertheless, bison were numerous, as many European and American accounts testify. Throughout the Great Plains they probably numbered about thirty million. Most estimates place the figure closer to sixty-five million, but such a large count was too high, for the western grasslands even in wet seasons could not sustain such large numbers.[26] Heavy eaters, bison could not stay too long in one place without eating all the grass. When they moved to another range, they sometimes drifted slowly, grazing along the way; sometimes they strung off in a long line, moving steadily, or trotting, for many miles. In their wake remained a depleted feeding ground; fires, reoccurring drought, plagues of locusts, and prairie dogs also turned good pasture into barren waste.[27]

The development of horse nomadism and the appearance of European livestock altered bison grazing patterns and other dynamics of native fauna. Bison instinctively grazed the most abundant areas. After grazing they moved to another area of relative abundance, not returning to the grazed-over area until it again became the most abundant range. But in competition with horses and other domesticated livestock, such grazing habits began to unravel. Concomitantly, the Plains Indians altered their economies from subsistence-for-use to other modes, causing them to kill large numbers of bison for the hide trade. The pressure of increased hunting, which included grass firing, plus growing competition from horses and later cattle, forced bison to graze unrecovered and less productive ranges. Moreover, European animals harbored diseases, such as anthrax, brucellosis, and tuberculosis, that negatively affected the numbers of native species. By the late 1830s disease, habitat destruction, and changing Indian hunting patterns had seriously cut into bison numbers.

The result was a cultural and environmental paradox. Many of the shifting ecological dynamics (bison, grass, horses) that had created the traditional Plains Indian world were the same forces that ultimately contributed to its decline.

Before the acquisition of horses, Plains Indians walked the plains, using dogs to transport their small tipis. They hunted bison on foot, again using their dogs to pack the meat. They used sticks, bones, horns, and stones for tools. Many used only skin bags for cooking and storage, although the semi-sedentary groups used pottery and basketry. Some people planted crops, and people in all groups collected seeds and nuts and dug roots.

Then the Plains Indians became mounted horsemen. Horses attracted new people to the plains, increased mobility, and improved hunting. They allowed all peoples to erect larger tipis, acquire more personal possessions, travel farther, and live more comfortably. They transformed worldviews, changed social structures, and altered value concepts. They became an important new symbol of wealth and trade. Although they may not have revolutionized ways of life, clearly, horses created richer, more dynamic cultures that brought the Plains Indian societies to full flower sometime after the middle of the eighteenth century.

The unique Plains Indian societies that followed lasted just over a century. They extended roughly from 1750 to 1890. Constantly in a state of change and transformation, they were colorful, dynamic societies that in most cases began shortly after their people's first arrival on the Great Plains.

2 : FIRST ARRIVALS

Ancestors of the first humans to occupy the Great Plains came to America from Asia. They were hunters whose lifestyles reflected a dependence on big game. The people used the animals' flesh for food, the hides for clothing and tentlike dwellings, and the bones for tools and weapons. In small bands the Asian hunters followed herds of mammoths, woolly rhinoceros, caribou, reindeer, musk ox, long-horned bison, and other large animals into the verdant range of Beringia, a one-thousand-mile-wide stretch of land—about the distance from New York to Kansas City—in the Bering Strait. Beringia emerged during glacial periods when water collected in ice and thus lowered the sea level some three hundred feet.[1]

Probably unaware that they had crossed to another continent, the migrants entered North America at different periods over a long span of time. They came during the last, or Wisconsin, glacial period (seventy thousand to ten thousand years ago), which occurred at the end of the lengthy Pleistocene geological epoch (one million to ten thousand years ago).

Some archaeologists suggest that the Asian arrival began about twenty-five thousand years ago and ended about ten thousand years ago, when melting ice closed off the Bering land bridge (Beringia). In recent years, however, rapid and sometimes dramatic changes in archaeological evidence have made it difficult to date the first arrivals with precision, and, in fact, many scholars now argue for a date closer to fourteen thousand years ago.[2]

As time passed, perhaps some hunting groups discovered a few periodically ice-free valleys opening to the south. Other groups moving east located a substantial ice-free corridor extending southward along the eastern slope of the Rocky Mountains. They pushed through the valleys and corridors to beyond the southern points of the glaciers, roughly the present-day northern border of the United States, and from there elsewhere over the Americas.[3]

The process was probably a gradual one, taking hundreds or perhaps thousands of years, but eventually, humans spread southward from Alaska to Cape Horn at the extreme tip of South America, a point they reached by at least nine thousand years ago. Anthropologist Paul S. Martin, however, argues for a sudden and rapid appearance of humans, one that took people from Alaska to the tip of South America in only one thousand years.[4]

Paleo-Indian peoples, as archaeologists call most of the early arrivals, lived below the glacial ice during a time when the environment differed from the modern one. The people enjoyed a generally uniform climate, regulated by the powerful influences of the huge glaciers: temperatures stayed mild, with abundant rainfall over much of the continent and no seasonal extremes. On the Great Plains they hunted savannahs of tall, coarse grass with scattered trees and entered thick forests interspersed with many lakes, swamps, marshy grass-lined sloughs, and beaver meadows. Over this wet, fertile land they hunted on foot, using wooden and bone clubs and long spears. They sought a variety of large fauna dominated by mammoths and mastodons but including now extinct species of horse, camel, long-horned bison, giant sloth, and other large game, plus pronghorns, deer, elk, and probably many small animals that survive today.[5]

As time passed Paleo-Indian peoples spread across the continent. They adjusted to local conditions, making changes, some almost imperceptible, in their habits, music, religion, and folklore while maintaining an unsophisticated nonmaterial culture. Although in the Pacific Northwest and in southern reaches of the Great Basin notable exceptions occurred, a generally continent-wide cultural homogeneity developed and characterized the Paleo-Indian tradition.[6]

Through succeeding millennia, as generations passed slowly from one to another, Paleo-Indian groups evolved through several cultural patterns. On the Great Plains these included the Clovis (or sometimes Llano) cultural complex, active in North America from about 11,500 years ago or earlier to 10,500 years ago, and the Folsom culture, active from about 10,500 years ago to about 9,500 years ago. Peoples of these hunting cultures lived in scattered camps of thirty to fifty persons from several interrelated families. They maintained small sociopolitical organizations and carried few possessions. Men spent much of their time pursuing large game animals or such smaller ones as coyotes, rabbits, and muskrats; women collected seeds and nuts and dug roots of various plants.

Over time changes occurred. Clovis people, for example, often hunted mammoths, mastodons, bears, elk, deer, and other large game, but Folsom people rarely pursued mammoths or mastodons. Changing weather patterns, and probably heavy pressure from hunting, allowed few of the elephantlike creatures to survive beyond the Clovis period. Instead, Folsom men hunted the now extinct long-horned bison, pronghorns, elk, deer, and smaller game, including ducks, geese, and several species of turtle. In many ways, however, the Folsom culture mirrored the Clovis, as people of both hunting groups migrated in cyclical patterns from one campsite to another. They both used the surround to drive their prey into a swampy bog, where it became mired in the mucky bottom, or into a box canyon. Folsom people, however, may have developed the bison jump-kill technique, in which they drove game over a steep cliff.

About ten thousand years ago the Folsom cultural complex began to give way to several regional cultures often classified under the name of Plano. Difficult to date with confidence, the Plano (or sometimes Plainview) culture remained active from about ten thousand years ago or earlier to about seven thousand years ago. It represented a transition period between Paleo-Indian peoples and subsequent cultural traditions.

Plano peoples were big-game hunters who sought deer, elk, pronghorns, and other game, including bison, but they took small animals as well. They did not hunt mammoths or mastodons, as the huge animals by this time had disappeared. The techniques they used in hunting suggest that they had worked out more complex sociopolitical organizations than their Clovis and Folsom ancestors. They employed the jump-kill method for hunting but also built corrals into which they drove their prey. Moreover, they developed a process for preserving meat by drying small strips of it in the sun, mixing it with animal fat and berries, and packing the product in skin bags. They also depended more and more on seed collecting and root digging, thus demonstrating the development of a varied diet on the Great Plains.

About ten thousand years ago—about the time the Folsom complex started to give way—the great glacial ice cap began to fade. With its retreat not only did the Pleistocene epoch end, but also the weather shifted; the nearly constant mild climate, which had helped to maintain a nearly homogeneous Paleo-Indian tradition, disappeared. Modern weather patterns, such as an arid Great Basin and the desert Southwest, emerged, producing enormous ecological changes. On the Great Plains, for example, over a two-thousand-year period after the end of the Pleistocene, a postglacial vegetation cover of perennial grasses replaced what had been deciduous woodland; trees now occur only in scarp lands, hilly localities, and stream valleys. Major alterations, indeed, the shifting weather patterns caused swamps, bogs, and marshes to dry up, many Pleistocene animals—in one of the planet's greatest die-offs—to disappear, and humans to modify their subsistence habits.

The remarkable transformations ushered in the Archaic tradition. It extended on a general basis from about eight thousand (or more) years ago to about twenty-eight hundred years ago. A wide variety of culture areas, each determined by its natural environment, or ecozone, characterized the Archaic tradition. In the early period perhaps the difference between Paleo-Indians and Archaic peoples rested on the availability of game. Because they were no longer able to obtain large amounts of meat from a giant mammoth or long-horned bison kill, Archaic peoples probably turned to more frequent hunting of smaller animals, to more frequent food collecting, and then to the cultivation of some of the plants they used. They also developed more efficient methods for food storage.[7]

Nonetheless, most Archaic peoples of North America were hunters and food collectors who, in face of increasing human populations during the period, produced a richer, technologically more advanced and versatile lifestyle than Paleo-Indian peoples. Some, such as Poverty Point peoples in the lower Mississippi River Valley, may have been horticulturalists, but whether hunters or farmers, they developed a degree of complexity in their socio-political organizations unknown to their ancestors. Perhaps local leaders or patriarchs dominated clan groups or small nomadic bands. They led a more settled, stable life than their ancestors, however, one based upon the seasonal collecting of plant foods available in their particular ecosystems. Although universal, continent-wide characteristics existed, Archaic traditions showed many regional specializations.[8]

On the Great Plains, Archaic peoples remained few and scattered. Changing climatic patterns at the end of the Pleistocene, as noted above, turned the coarse vegetation cover from woodland, marsh, and prairie to semidesert grassland, thereby forcing large game animals—those that had survived overhunting—to drift to other regions toward the east or north where heavier precipitation occurred. Probably many Archaic people followed, not returning to the plains in significant numbers until after forty-five hundred years ago, when temperatures cooled and rainfall patterns increased again.

Although not heavily populated, the plains contained clusters of Archaic people throughout its length and breadth. Archaic plains people used cutting, scraping, and chopping tools, but their weapon points showed much less skill in flint working than those of Paleo-Indian hunters. They collected in season several types of fruits, seeds, nuts, berries, and edible roots and leaves, as plant sources rather than game became the main foodstuff. They continued to hunt a variety of large and small animals, including the modern bison, which during the Archaic period came out of Mexico, multiplied, and spread over most of North America. They also took fish and birds, but deer represented the major prey.

Over time Archaic traditions slowly gave way to more sophisticated life patterns. People took to using tobacco, for example, and spending more time on handicrafts. Toward the east they developed a fascination for the dead, at least as suggested by the huge burial mounds that appeared. Social organizations became more complex, and nonmaterial culture traits grew in importance. Although many features of the Archaic tradition continued in use for several more centuries, particularly on the Great Plains and in the Great Basin, life over much of the American continent underwent a gradual adaptation to other subsistence modes.

The new modes of life placed greater emphasis on horticulture and communal living. In the American Southwest, from about 2,800 years ago or earlier to about A.D. 1200, a desert culture emerged, one characterized by irrigated horticulture, hunting of small game, gathering of nuts and nutritious seeds, and a close adaptation to the harsh desert environment.

At least three distinct cultural communities, each having evolved from various Archaic traditions of the desert, appeared: Hohokam, Mogollon, and Anasazi. Two of them, the Mogollon and Anasazi, influenced Archaic traditions on the Great Plains. The Mogollons were a horticultural and collecting people whose culture was centered at Casas Grandes in northern Mexico but spread through the mountains of southeastern Arizona, southern New Mexico, and far western Texas. The Anasazis (often called the Basket Makers or the Cliff Dwellers of Mesa Verde) lived in the "four corners" region, where Arizona, New Mexico, Utah, and Colorado come together. Both flourished independently, reaching a peak of development in the eleventh and twelfth centuries.

Each of the major southwestern cultures changed its subsistence economy to horticulture. Although hunting and food collecting persisted as secondary enterprises, the people lived in settled villages where they raised corn, beans, squash (the "three sisters"), and cotton. They kept dogs and used turkeys as a source of food and feathers for personal adornment. They made pottery and developed the craft to high levels of sophistication, in both design and technique. They also learned to weave textiles from cotton and animal fibers.

During the apex of their development, the Mogollon and Anasazi peoples possessed large populations and complex social organizations. They traded baskets, blankets, and pottery to people far beyond their territory. Along regularly used, overland routes traders carried goods to the Pacific and Gulf coasts, the Great Plains, and elsewhere in exchange for marine shells, animal skins, and other items. The settled life, surplus goods, and community existence promoted significant advances in nonmaterial culture. Religion, dance, and music became well developed, for example, and the artistic creativity and folklore of the people assumed new and important roles in their lives.[9]

East of the Mississippi River a Woodland tradition emerged. Characterized by a close adaptation to the environment, this culture continued in most respects the older Archaic traditions; but Woodland people made some social refinements and added such material culture improvements as limited horticulture, mound building, conical pottery, and the bow and arrow. The Woodland tradition, which exerted a strong influence on people of the Great

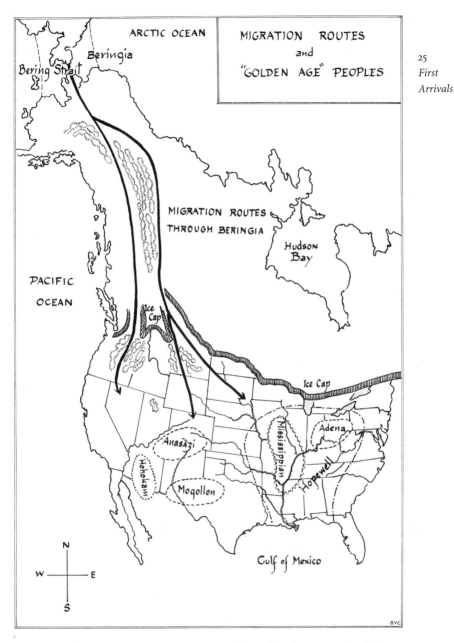

MIGRATION ROUTES
and
"GOLDEN AGE" PEOPLES

Plains, continued for the most part its stable cultural patterns until Europeans arrived about A.D. 1500.

Within the general Woodland pattern, however, at least three distinct cultural communities appeared: the Adena, Hopewell, and Mississippian traditions. All three were "mound builders" who practiced horticulture, gathered seeds and nuts, hunted, and lived in settled villages. The Adena tradition, which centered in the upper Ohio River Valley but radiated out to other parts of the East, flourished from about 2800 to 2200 years ago, but it had little influence on the plains.

The Hopewell tradition, which covered wide areas east of the Mississippi River and extended westward onto the plains, flourished from 2200 years ago to A.D. 500. The Hopewell people followed many of the same customs as the Adenas, but with more vigor and elaboration. Like the Adenas, they engaged in extensive mound building and held a deep concern for death and afterlife. They adopted horticulture as their principal subsistence mode and enjoyed a richer technology than the Adena people.

The Mississippian tradition, in the lower Mississippi River and its tributaries, extended from about A.D. 500 to A.D. 1200. The Mississippian people maintained the mysterious death cult and mound-building practices of their two predecessors, but with some changes. Some burial mounds existed, but most of the mounds of this tradition were large solid earthen pyramids without burial chambers. Perhaps influenced by Central American cultures, the Mississippian people constructed the truncated pyramids, or platform mounds, in groups around a large central court, thus providing high places on which they built ceremonial temples where priests conducted elaborate rituals. Masters of horticulture, the Mississippians concentrated on corn (actually a late arrival to the Mississippi Valley), beans, and squash for a livelihood, but they also cultivated sunflowers, pumpkins, amaranth, and other crops. Hunting and gathering remained important to their economy. They also fashioned artistic ceremonial pieces of a variety of materials, excellent globular pottery, and numerous personal ornaments, including human and animal figures.

With far-reaching trade relations, Mississippian people enjoyed a high standard of living. In their scattered communities they maintained a complex, well-integrated, well-organized society that developed structures to deal with the sophisticated engineering and horticultural systems they established. Around their temple centers, towns appeared. The largest, Cahokia, located near present-day St. Louis, about A.D. 1000 covered five and one-half square miles and held a population estimated between ten thousand and thirty-eight thousand people. Cahokia controlled or influenced the entire Mississippi River basin and much of the area to the southeast.[10]

On the Great Plains, people maintained basic Archaic hunting-collecting traditions that had begun with the retreat of glacial ice. To these subsistence patterns, however, they added material and nonmaterial cultural designs of the more populous groups on their borders. Thus, a few small horticultural-collecting communities showing Mogollon or Anasazi influence appeared in river valleys of the southwestern plains. Bordering the southeastern plains a series of sedentary, village-dwelling people of Mississippian influence constructed their platform-mound ceremonial centers and made their globular pottery in northeast Texas, Louisiana, and Arkansas, with various manifestations farther west in southeastern Oklahoma.

Of greater importance, perhaps, was the impact of general Woodland and Hopewell traditions. Woodland features spread onto the eastern plains over a wide area from Manitoba and southeastern Saskatchewan southward to Oklahoma. Conical pottery and other Woodland manifestations, including horticulture, have been found. Hopewell mound-building influences, dating on the plains from about A.D. 10 to about A.D. 500 or afterward, likewise extended from Manitoba southward along the eastern edge, but in watered-down versions they enjoyed particular ascendency on the eastern prairies of Kansas and Nebraska.[11]

By A.D. 1200 such traditions as the Mississippian in the East and the Anasazis in the Southwest had entered a period of decline, perhaps for a variety of reasons relating to recurring war, endemic disease, sustained drought, unstable food sources, or faltering sociopolitical organizations. The period, characterized by the division of American Indian groups into hundreds of different communities, or peoples, pursuing a variety of lifeways, social and religious customs, political organizations, and subsistence economies, extended from about A.D. 1200 or before to the arrival of Europeans. Many older sociopolitical groups broke down, and new ones appeared. Modern Pueblo people of the Rio Grande, for example, emerged from the dispersed Anasazis and Mogollons, and some groups in the upper and others in the lower Mississippi River basin may have descended from the Mississippians.

The Great Plains now became an active place. Globular pottery–making, semihorticultural plains people of an unmistakable Mississippian influence spread over much of the eastern prairies before extending their settled communities far up the rivers and onto the plains. The Missouri, Platte, Loup, Dismal, Republican, Arkansas, Red, and Canadian river valleys received many new people, but other valleys attracted substantial settlement as well.

Although most are not conspicuous in character, archaeological sites dating from the period number into the hundreds. On the southwestern plains they display some Pueblo influences, particularly the apartment-styled houses of adobe and stone. In the southeastern regions and extending northward through central Texas, Oklahoma, Kansas, and into Nebraska they reveal a significant Mississippian influence, especially in pottery and craft skills. Farther north in Nebraska, the Dakotas, and the eastern plains of Canada, some aspects of old, eastern Woodland cultures remained but with strong Hopewell or Mississippian traits, particularly in the pottery designs and the burial mounds.[12]

In the upper Mississippi River Valley and its tributaries, an Oneota culture, which may have developed in the eleventh century in Wisconsin, spread after 1200 as Mississippi-related groups disappeared. Red pipestone, or catlinite, is one of the characteristics of the Oneota culture; its people made pipe bowls of the material and traded them over long distances. Oneota people cultivated corn and other crops as well as tobacco, and they hunted bison. Oneota may have been ancestral Oto, Iowa, and Missouri peoples of the prairie-plains, and western Oneota perhaps were ancestral to historic Siouan-speaking communities in the same area.[13]

On the central plains one of the many important cultures archaeologists discovered was that of the upper Republican. Distributed widely along the Loup and Republican rivers in western Kansas and Nebraska, the upper Republican tradition dates roughly from 1200 to 1400. Semihorticultural, pottery-making plains people (perhaps ancestral Pawnees) inhabited the sites. Their houses, sometimes erected over pits, were substantial earth-covered dwellings with a square or rectangular pattern containing long, covered entrance passages; four center posts supported the roof. They based their economy on the cultivation of corn, beans, squash, and sunflowers and supplemented it by hunting deer, pronghorns, bison, and small game with the bow and arrow. The people kept dogs; made an abundance of globular pottery; used tools of bone, stone, wood, and horn; and fashioned beads, pendants, and personal adornments from shells.[14]

On the northern plains, occupants of the middle Missouri River valley, possibly descendants of the Cahokia complex who dispersed up the Missouri with Cahokia's breakup, were village farmers who built permanent houses that date from before 1200. They erected large rectangular houses in and over pits; the structures contained long rows of posts supporting hip roofs of grass, twigs, and sod. The people sometimes enclosed their scattered villages with log palisades surrounded by ditches reminiscent of fortified Mississippian communities. The inhabitants cultivated new strains of corn and other domesticated plants from the southeast, but supplemented their crop economy with trading, fishing, and hunting of deer, elk, bison, and small game. They dug cache pits, manufactured quantities of globular pottery, and fashioned tools and weapons of bone, stone, wood, and horn. From freshwater clam shells they made personal adornments of various kinds. They also crafted bone whistles, shell and bone effigies (often carved in the form of birds), and other ornaments.[15]

After A.D. 1400, changes came. Major alterations, indeed, they helped to produce the modern Plains Indians. First, strong groups of Athapaskan-speaking people, dominated by Apaches, migrated south from a northern homeland sometime after 1200 and advanced, with devastating results, through the Great Plains. Although some groups moved southward through the Great Basin west of the Rocky Mountains, most Apaches after 1400 struck along the eastern front. They overran much of the western high plains, with some of them later taking up semipermanent residence, adopting horticulture, and raiding plains villagers.[16]

Second, after 1470 a series of three prolonged droughts, spanning a combined total of forty years, hit the western plains. The climatic changes, producing successive crop failures, forced plains villagers to abandon their homes and disperse. Many once flourishing villages disappeared. In the middle Missouri and upper Republican river valleys, the scattered villagers drew together into tightly packed settlements, causing cultural differences to fade and broader, more uniform cultural characteristics to emerge.[17]

Third, Europeans arrived. On the southern plains Spaniards appeared first. Alvar Núñez Cabeza de Vaca, who in the 1530s skirted the region through Texas and northern Mexico, and Francisco Vásquez de Coronado, who in 1541 reached ancestors of modern Wichitas near the Great Bend of the Arkansas River in central Kansas, led the way. The French came first to the northern plains. Unknown voyageurs and coureurs de bois arrived in the mid seventeenth century. Following them came three agents of Daniel Greysolon, sieur Du Luth. In 1679 the three Frenchmen explored westward from Mille Lacs in east-central Minnesota until they reached a point twenty days from a great lake whose water was not fit to drink, meaning, presumably, the Great Salt Lake of Utah.[18]

These dramatic changes—the Apache invasion, the climatic shift, and the arrival of Europeans—combined with enormous pressures involving trade and war with native people of the eastern forests, produced the Plains Indians. Rarely sudden, the transformations developed over many decades. They also produced a blending of divergent cultures. Through much of the central and northern plains, for example, there appeared tendencies toward circular houses placed close together, toward far-flung trade, toward horticulture limited to river flood plains, and toward annual bison hunts. A blending of certain nonmaterial aspects also occurred.

Such blending and transformation brought the modern village peoples to the plains. Among the first to arrive were three divisions (Chaui, Kitkahahki, and Pitahawirata) of the Caddoan-speaking Pawnees who, after coming from forest lands of the lower Red River in Texas in the thirteenth century, moved in slow stages up the Platte River to the western plains, bringing older Mississippian farming traditions and hardy new strains of corn with them. The Apache invasion from the north caused them to pull back to compact villages on tributaries of the lower Platte and other rivers in central Nebraska, where they reunited with the Skidi Pawnees. The Skidis may have migrated from Texas to the Ohio Valley, where perhaps they became associated with the Siouan-speaking Omahas before heading west. Once on the plains they left their recent companions, continued up the Platte River, and reassociated with their Caddoan-speaking cousins.[19]

The Siouan-speaking Mandans and Hidatsas and the Caddoan-speaking Arikaras were also early arrivals. Siouan speakers may once have lived in southeastern parts of the continent. Migration northward divided the people, splitting them into various groups, many of whom settled along the Ohio Valley. Later migrations took some toward the east, some to the upper Mississippi, and scattered some toward the plains. After crossing the Mississippi River from the Ohio Valley in the late fourteenth century, the Mandans moved by slow stages to the middle Missouri River Valley and by the mid-1400s had established their riverine farming villages in the Dakotas. The Hidatsas, after leaving the Ohio Valley in the fifteenth century, headed north toward the Canada-Minnesota border country and established homes in Manitoba before pushing southwestward to settle along the Missouri above the Mandans. The Arikaras, who had split from the Pawnees, took up residence along the Missouri below the Mandans. The three tribal groups formed a large, almost identical hunting-farming culture on the rich alluvial floodplains of the middle Missouri River.[20]

The Caddoan-speaking Wichitas and related peoples of a Mississippian tradition also arrived on the plains at an early date. Leaving the Texas forests during the fourteenth century, they pushed north and west to the Arkansas River in central Kansas, establishing a way of life that in most respects mirrored that of the Pawnees. The Wichitas became a hunting and farming people who lived in fixed villages of circular grass houses and adopted several of the characteristic plains traits.[21]

Later-arriving sedentary people remained on the edge of the plains. The Siouan-speaking Iowas, Otos, and Missouris (who spoke the Chiwere dialect), driven by population pressures and other threats to their homes, entered southern Minnesota and northeastern Iowa before approaching the plains in the seventeenth century. Driven by growing Iroquois attacks to their Ohio Valley homes, the Siouan-speaking (Dhegiha dialect) Omahas, Poncas, Kansas, Osages, and Quapaws in the early seventeenth century joined the other groups on the western prairies. Again, possibly, with the breakup of Cahokia its descendants moved up the Missouri River, which would explain the patrilineal organization of the Dhegiha speakers.[22]

On the western high plains, nomadic, big game–hunting cultures emerged. They developed with the arrival of Europeans, whose presence intensified forces, already in motion, that crowded many peoples toward the plains. Among the first on the plains were the Kiowan- or Tanoan-speaking

(Tiwa) Kiowas, who cannot be traced on the basis of historical documents outside the region. Before inhabiting the central and southern plains, they may have lived in the upper Missouri and Yellowstone river country, but they show an intriguing relationship to Tanoan Pueblos of New Mexico.[23]

About the same time the Athapaskan-speaking Apaches arrived. They occupied much of the western high plains just before and during the first European contacts. The "Querecho" and "Vaquero" peoples mentioned by Spanish chroniclers were ancestral to modern Apaches (probably Lipans). As early as the 1540s, various Apache groups held the plains from Wyoming and Nebraska through eastern Colorado and western Kansas to Texas.[24] Foot nomads and armed only with stone-tipped weapons, they variously traded with or harassed early settlements of Pawnees and Wichitas from Nebraska to Oklahoma. They struck Pueblo villages in New Mexico (both Tanoan and Keresan, and sometimes Zuni), and some Apache groups spread their raiding into Arizona. Once mounted on horses obtained from Spanish herds, they widened their attacks into Texas and deep into the central plateau of northern New Spain. Few native peoples, except perhaps for the Jumanos in southwestern Texas, could counter them. In the late seventeenth century Apache raiders struck at targets over a wide area and worried little about retaliation.[25]

The Apache hegemony did not last. From the northwestern deserts and mountains the Shoshonean-speaking Comanches pushed into the bison-rich southern plains. Perhaps forced out of ancestral homelands about the upper Missouri River by the Gros Ventres and Blackfeet with guns, the Comanches and their linguistic kinsmen, the Utes and Shoshonis, moved into the Western Plateau. Some continued a southerly trek through the Great Basin. By at least 1700 the Comanches, now separated from the Shoshonis and fighting the Utes, mounted on horses, and attracted by enormous bison herds, had invaded Apache land. Over the next two decades they rolled through eastern Colorado and western Kansas, fighting the Wichita-related allies of the French to their east, Spanish and Pueblo allies in New Mexico, and the Apaches to the south. Only the Apaches proved formidable foes, but after several decades they withdrew, leaving most of the southern plains to the Comanches. In the 1740s the Comanches entered into a long-lasting alliance with the Wichitas, and after 1790 they worked out an accommodation with the Kiowas, their northern neighbors, and the Kiowa Apaches, who maintained a close relationship with the Kiowas.[26]

The other Apache divisions scattered, many to Arizona. The Mescaleros and Jicarillas, however, drifted into the mountains and deserts of New Mexico but stayed close enough to the plains to hunt bison in seasonal migrations. Although retaining many of their plains lifeways, they adopted something of a nonplains, Puebloan society. The Lipans rode south and established traditional Apache *rancherias* (here meaning small villages) along both sides of the Rio Grande, where they "remained a southern plains" people.[27]

Comanche raids, Apache pressure, and the disrupting activity of the Spanish presence, coupled with European-borne endemic diseases, scattered the Tonkawan people of central Texas. Reduced in population during the seventeenth and eighteenth centuries, the surviving remnants united to become by 1800 the small Tonkawa group, a relatively well organized and cohesive unit that hunted the Edwards Plateau and the upper South Texas Plains. Because of new pressures, their numbers continued to decline through the nineteenth century.

In the far north other pressures brought nomadic peoples to the plains. Such eastern, forest-dwelling groups as the Hurons, having obtained guns from the French, terrorized their western neighbors, forcing them out of their homelands. In turn some of them, particularly the Ojibwas, Crees, and Assiniboins, equipped with guns from French traders who came to the Lake Superior region after 1650, raided people beyond the western Great Lakes. As they pushed westward beyond Lake Winnipeg, the Crees and Assiniboins drove the Blackfeet, Gros Ventres, and Arapahos from their homes in the lower valley of the Red River and farther north. The Ojibwas attacked the Dakotas, driving them westward, and they in turn squeezed the Cheyennes, who had already given way to pressures from groups below the Great Lakes.

The Algonquian-speaking Blackfeet were among the first of the northern nomadic groups to enter the plains. Indeed, some Blackfeet people may have been using the Canadian plains from a date centuries before eastern influences forced them permanently west. Under pressure from the Crees in the seventeenth century, other Blackfeet groups moved onto the plains of Saskatchewan and quickly abandoned their forest ways to adopt the plains culture. Harassed now by Shoshoni bands who had horses and other goods (but not guns) acquired from the Spanish, the Blackfeet suffered. Sometime about 1750, however, the Blackfeet, having secured muskets from French traders, broke the Shoshoni assaults. Then, from the Saskatchewan River basin, Blackfeet war parties attacked and scattered their southern enemies, stealing their horses, usurping their land, and driving them into the Great Basin area. In 1800 the Blackfeet confederation claimed a broad area just east of the Rocky Mountains extending from the North Saskatchewan River southward to present Yellowstone National Park. It dominated the far northwestern plains.[28]

The Sarsis, attracted by the wealthy and horse-mounted Blackfeet, left the Canadian Rockies. Splitting from the Beaver people, the Athapaskanspeaking Sarsis moved southeastward onto the plains of Alberta, acquired horses sometime after 1750, and converted to a nomadic, bison-hunting plains culture. The Sarsis, a numerically small group, maintained a close association with their powerful neighbors.

The Algonquian-speaking Gros Ventres and Arapahos, like their Blackfeet kinsmen, were also early inhabitants of the northern plains. Pressured by Cree and Assiniboin people, who were exchanging furs for guns and other European items with English traders at Hudson Bay and with the French from Lake Superior, the Arapahos and Gros Ventres separated, ventured onto the Canadian plains, and dropped their forest ways. Their conversion to the plains culture was early, swift, and, after the acquisition of horses, complete. The Gros Ventres remained close to the Blackfeet, hunting the grasslands astride the present-day U.S.–Canada border. The Arapahos, who may have been with the Cheyennes in the eastern Dakotas, after 1775 associated with the Cheyennes in the Black Hills region.

The Algonquian-speaking Cheyennes in 1673 lived on the east bank of the Mississippi. About twenty years later their villages ranged along the upper Red River in Minnesota. Under pressure from the Dakotas, they migrated westward to the Sheyenne River in North Dakota. Here they continued their sedentary farming ways, living in scattered communities but with a central village that contained seventy circular earth lodges. After an Ojibwa raiding party about 1770 destroyed their homes, they moved again, heading southwestward toward the Black Hills. As they moved, they gave up many of their horticultural practices to concentrate on the hunt, and they joined the Suhtaios (or Half Cheyennes), a small, bison-hunting people already on the plains. The Cheyennes entered the Black Hills, but shortly afterward the Lakotas ousted them from the beautiful mountain country.

By 1806, when members of the Lewis and Clark expedition located some of them near the Black Hills, the Cheyennes had split into two groups. A northern group concentrated in the rolling grasslands west of the Black Hills. A southern group in 1806 ranged along the South Platte River near the Rockies, but by 1820 it had reached the Arkansas River in eastern Colorado; it remained in the area between the Arkansas and South Platte rivers. The Cheyennes, who in the late eighteenth century allied with the Arapahos, only slowly gave up their settled eastern ways, but in the nineteenth century they became the epitome of mounted, bison-hunting Plains Indians.

The Siouan-speaking Crows also took slowly to plains nomadism. An offshoot of the Missouri River Hidatsas, the Crows migrated westward beyond the Black Hills, where for a time they continued to farm along river bottoms in eastern Montana. After they acquired horses through trade and theft from the Shoshonis, the Crows gave up most horticulture. Maintaining close ties with their former kin, they traded meat and hides to the Hidatsas for such crop foods as beans, squash, and corn.

The Siouan-speaking Oceti Sakowin (Dakotas and Lakotas) approached the plains from Minnesota. Organized in Seven Council Fires (Mdewakantonwan, Wachpekute, Wachpetonwan, Sisitonwan, Yankton, Yanktonai, and Lakota), they lived a very long time in the upper Mississippi River country, from Green Bay westward to the Red River, before the Ojibwas arrived. The gun-toting Ojibwas in the late seventeenth century advanced westward along the northern waters of Lake Superior, and in the eighteenth century with French weapons and possibly French assistance, they successfully challenged the Oceti Sakowin west and south of the great blue lake. The Lakotas pushed west, crossing the Missouri River sometime after 1750. They drove the Cheyennes out of the Black Hills about 1775 and shortly afterward became typical nomadic Plains Indians who hunted the region north of the Platte and west of the Missouri.

The Yanktons and Yanktonais followed the Lakotas as far as the Missouri River but remained semisedentary hunter-farmers in the eastern Dakotas. The four other tribal groups, collectively called the Santee (Isanti), fought off the Ojibwa raids, remained in southwestern Minnesota, and, after the French pulled out about 1763, struck back at the Ojibwas in the north. Thereafter they shared the country, Ojibwas in the north, Santees in the south.

The Siouan-speaking Assiniboins (perhaps the only group who can properly be call "Nakota") were an offshoot of the Yanktonais. After the split, which may have occurred as early as 1550, the Assiniboins moved north and later became enemies of all Siouan-speakers, including their kin. From Lake Superior to Lake of the Woods in southwestern Ontario and northward from there toward Hudson Bay, they inhabited a wooded and well-watered area, becoming intimately connected with the Algonquian-speaking Crees of the same Ontario forests. Like many northern woodland people, the Assiniboins and Crees in the 1660s gathered wild rice, hunted, and moved about in hand-somely made, sleek-lined birch-bark canoes. With the arrival of French and English traders, the Assiniboins and Crees turned trappers to supply furs, as well as dried meat, to the European intruders. Armed with French guns, they forced the Blackfeet and Arapahos westward. The Plains Cree split from their eastern cousins and with the Assiniboins pushed onto the western prairies. Both groups were in Saskatchewan in 1730, and by 1775 they had abandoned most of their eastern lifeways and acquired horses to become mounted bison hunters.

Thus, by 1750 or so the horse-mounted, bison-hunting Plains Indian culture had begun. In many ways it was a recent development, for the plains had been dominated by riverine gardeners and foot nomads for centuries before the 1750s. Once mounted on horseback, however, both the eastern village peoples and the western high plains hunters saw their life patterns change abruptly, reverting to a big game–hunting culture dominated in the early years by the newly arrived Apaches and Kiowas.

Quickly afterward, traditional Plains Indian societies emerged, and on the Great Plains they prospered. Adjusting to meet new conditions and pressures and adapting their lifeways to match their changing needs, the people collectively created what has been called "a flamboyant culture," a set of very practical, multifaceted, and active societies.

3 : HORSE AND BISON CULTURE

By the 1750s the Plains Indians, a mix of more than thirty different peoples, had established themselves on the western prairies and Great Plains. After a long period of white contact, borrowed traits, disease pandemics, shifting alliances, and new circumstances, they had developed societies that showed a large degree of homogeneity. Although their societies had sprung from varying cultures and different geographical settings, their rise to prominence created a dramatic and unique era. Quickly and voluntarily they transformed their lifeways into "a flamboyant culture whose vigor was for a time unequaled."[1]

Horses and firearms were the catalyst. For some groups firearms represented a major expelling force driving them to the plains. Cree and Ojibwa people, for example, possessed guns in about the mid seventeenth century and used them to force Blackfeet and Lakota groups westward, where both peoples quickly adopted plains nomadism. The Blackfeet, in turn getting firearms from Cree and European traders, used them early to drive the Shoshonis, Flatheads, and Nez Percés from the Bow River country of Alberta southward to the Sweetgrass Hills and beyond. The Arapahos, Cheyennes, and Gros Ventres, pushed westward by gun-toting enemies, likewise shifted, although more slowly than the Lakotas, to plains nomadism.

For some groups the desire for horses represented a major compelling force drawing them to the plains. In their quest for horses, for example, the Comanches separated from the Shoshonis and headed south to remain near the Spanish herds in New Mexico, Texas, and elsewhere—although the enormous bison herds also attracted them.[2]

Although it is difficult to determine when various Indian groups acquired the animals, some Apache bands owned horses by 1630, and perhaps earlier. Not long afterward a few other groups had them. After the great Pueblo Revolt of 1680, when Indian people drove Spanish settlers temporarily out of New Mexico and the Spanish left behind their livestock, horses spread northward. The Wichitas, Pawnees, Missouris, Kiowas, and Comanches possessed them before 1700. The Shoshonis, Nez Percés, eastern Utes, and Kutenais got horses not long afterward. The Cheyennes, Arapahos, Kansas, Crows, Blackfeet, Lakotas, and Sarsis (the northernmost tribe) rode them before 1750. The Assiniboins and Plains Cree used them before 1770.[3]

Horses produced dramatic changes. On the southern plains, for example, the Kiowas, after the arrival of horses, shifted to a social hierarchy based on the acquisition of horses, and the idea of property took on a dramatic new meaning. New social classes appeared, which in turn produced long-term shifts in the composition and role of men's societies. On the northern plains before the arrival of horses, the Crows, farming in eastern Montana, were connected on cultural and political levels to the Hidatsas. But the presence of horses changed the relationship as the Crows abandoned permanent dwellings and shifted to an economy based on horse-mounted, bison-hunting nomadism.[4]

Many people accomplished the transition quickly, if not always without upheaval. Because they saw in it a loss of status, Cheyenne women, for example, may have resisted the development of a hunting culture among their people. As gardeners who owned the fields, women controlled production and by extension the larger economy, a role they lost in the transition to a horse and bison culture in which men dominated production.

Even among some Great Basin and western peoples, horses brought changes. They allowed the Jicarillas and Mescaleros to remain near the plains, where they hunted bison and maintained their marginal plains lifestyles. They made it possible for the Kutenais and Nez Percés to enjoy long, periodic, but easy trips to the bison country, from where they adopted such plains traits as the Sun Dance and the use of tipis. Moreover, the Nez Percés, among the few American Indians to protect breeding mares, developed the distinctively spotted and often celebrated Appaloosa horse. The eastern and northern Shoshonis, heavily influenced by the plains culture after obtaining horses, adopted feathered war bonnets, decorated with porcupine quills, accepted the plains bison complex, and after 1800 took over many other features of the Plains Indians.[5]

In a relatively short time the Plains Indians passed from terrified amazement at the sight of a horse to complete equestrian mastery of the animal, and, in fact, some Indian people came to deny that there had existed a time without horses. Their horsemanship elicited admiration from all who observed it.

By the time that Americans came into regular contact with Plains Indians, the horse fit perfectly with plains lifeways. It enhanced the ability of nomadic peoples to congregate in large numbers in the summer months for communal bison hunts and tribal ceremonies and disperse in winter months to protect themselves and provide adequate grazing for their horse herds. To a large extent the nomadic peoples adapted their cultures to the horse, and among such groups as the Comanches, Kiowas, and Lakotas, the significance of the animal is difficult to overemphasize. Others have suggested that, because they so thoroughly incorporated the horse into their life patterns, some groups might be more clearly understood not as bison hunters but as pastoralists who moved about the plains with their horse herds.[6]

In using horses, for example, the Plains Indians came to pay close attention to grassland availability. Horses, like bison, consumed large amounts of grass for sustenance. Because the grazing requirements of their mounts led Indian people to seek camps that would provide adequate forage for their large herds, good horse pasture became as vital as good hunting territory. Although other factors (such as bison grazing patterns, spiritual needs, and cosmological views) were involved in the dynamics of social organization, many people, in order to ensure adequate forage for their ponies, separated into smaller (family, clan, or band) hunting units for much of the year, especially in winter when grass was scarce. They organized into larger (band or tribal) units in early summer when grass, lush and plentiful, could support the intense grazing of large numbers of horses.

Plains Indians as individuals owned horses. (Such ownership was unusual when compared with other herding groups who treat herds as communal—usually clan—property.) Some people marked their own horses by a slit in the ear, and all people took pride in their best animals. They kept their favorite ones close to the tipis, and the Mandans corralled them inside their lodges. Boys watched the herds as they grazed away from camp. Men raced the fastest ones against other horses, gambling on the outcome with sometimes very high stakes involved. They normally did not shod the hoofs, but they sometimes toughened them in various ways. Some Indian people practiced gelding, allowing only the best stallions to breed mares and castrating others when they reached two years old. Still, problems existed. Because of hard riding by their owners, pregnant mares often aborted or struggled to foal.

The result was a constant quest for horses. Acquisition of the animals became a central factor in intertribal conflicts. In their disputes with enemy groups, the Plains Cree found that horse stealing and counterstealing became more significant than struggles over territory or problems associated with trade. Closely tied to horse stealing was the prestige, the thrill, the excitement in the risk involved. The bolder, more daring the raid, the greater was the honor to be gained.[7]

Horses counted for something. They represented wealth and stature; individuals and groups came to be judged by their horse herds. Assiniboin men, for example, considered superb warriors when they pressed onto the plains, became famous about 1800 for their horse stealing. In 1830, however, after prolonged fighting with the Lakotas and Blackfeet, many people believed that the Assiniboins had become poor and weak, for they were no longer able to acquire wealth in the form of horses. Having only two horses and one gun per lodge, they found themselves unable to launch successful horse-stealing raids, and the high esteem with which other peoples once regarded the Assiniboins fell.[8]

Clearly, the possession of horses glorified the Plains Indians and lifted them to positions of eminence they could not have attained as dismounted hunters. While it may not have encouraged the evolution of new plains traits, the horse broadened and intensified those already in place to such an extent that a veritable revolution occurred, producing profound economic, social, and intellectual changes.[9] The adaptation of the travois (a drag) to the horse, for example, brought about a new ease of transport. With a travois a horse could drag a load four or five times heavier than it could carry on its back, resulting in the adoption of larger tipis with lodge poles ranging up to thirty feet high. In addition, the new ease of transport resulted in a new wealth of possessions that could be carried along as the band moved from place to place.

The Plains Indians, accordingly, developed new social and material cultures. With horses they could take more bison and animal skins to exchange with traders for blankets, beads, knives, hatches, kettles, guns, and vermillion color with which to paint their bodies. With hunting easier and faster, the men had more time for warfare and to devote to decorating their weapons, tipis, and clothes. Moreover, horses became a significant element in gift giving—important in the Plains Indians' concepts of status and rank. Horse ownership became a symbol of a man's skill and bravery, for he had to acquire the horses by raiding the enemy or by capturing them in the wild.

In short, the horse became the most important vehicle of transportation, medium of exchange, and regulator of economic values and social status. It came to exercise considerable influence over the minds of the people, altering world views, religious practices, subsistence patterns, and even the traditional nature and ideology of warfare.[10]

As significant as the horse was to the Plains Indians, the bison was more important. The entire life of the plains people revolved around it. "To us," said First Boy, an Assiniboin, "the buffalo was more than an animal. It was the stuff of life." He indicated that "organizations were named for it, and medicine men relied on [its] powers. . . . Its name was given to children . . . [and] no animal gave so much to the people."[11]

Probably no animal anywhere affected any people to the degree that bison affected people of the plains. Indeed, Tom McHugh writes that "the Plains Indian culture *was* the buffalo culture."[12] Plains people manufactured many artifacts from the hides, horns, and hoofs of the animal, subsisted on its flesh, wove legends about the herds, and accepted the bison as a spiritual force of their Great Plains world.

Until the late 1830s, bison and the Plains Indians lived in relative harmony (but not perfect balance), with Indian people taking what bison they needed and, as McHugh notes, "gearing their rhythms and rituals—their mode of life—to the ways of the roving herds."[13] As described by First Boy and others, for much of the year bison cows, calves, and yearlings formed a small herd led by a mature female. Most bulls grazed apart. In early summer an abundance of fresh grass drew the small herds together, with bison sometimes gathering in incredible numbers. During the rutting season in late summer the bulls and cows came together. By the middle of September the herds had separated again, and they began to graze their way back to protective canyons and river valleys, where they sought relief from harsh winter weather.[14]

The Plains Indians, at least the nomadic peoples, patterned their movements on the ways of the bison. Several hunting bands or the entire ethnic group came together in early summer for large communal hunts and tribal ceremonies when bison likewise congregated in large herds. In the fall the people again broke into small hunting bands to follow the separate, smaller herds and to winter with their horses in protected areas. Over time, but especially after about 1840, constricted grazing lands and declining herds altered bison-Indian dynamics.

Before then, the Plains Indians employed several methods to hunt bison. Some were ancient techniques used before the arrival of horses. Others they developed after they became mounted. The foot surround, in which a long line of people encircled a herd and then moved in for the kill, remained one of the oldest procedures. Best held on a still day, when the animals were less likely to scent the hunters, the surround gradually tightened. As they closed on the bison, the participants yelled, tossed robes in the air, and shot arrows at their prey until they had slain all the animals. Sometimes they took more animals then they could use, but folklore among some people held that the bison must be slaughtered to the last animal or escaping bison would warn other herds to avoid the area.[15]

Plains people supplemented the surround by grass firing. During the dry season, selected hunters might set fire to patches of grass around a grazing herd. As the burning circle squeezed the prey into an ever diminishing area, the hunters moved in to kill the terrified bison. Grass firing proved an effective surround method of hunting, most popular on the prairies of Minnesota and Iowa, where the Santees, Iowas, and others practiced it. But it occurred on the plains as well, and sometimes the fires turned into roaring infernos that burned for days and weeks or longer.

A related hunting method was impounding, or *pis kin*, meaning "deep blood kettle" in the Blackfeet (Algonquian) language. When impounding bison, the people drove a herd into the wide end of a funnel formed by two lines of camouflaged hunters. As the animals approached, the hunters, with sometimes women and children participating, one by one came from hiding to frighten the bison through the narrowing trap into a stout enclosure of logs and brush at the spout, sometimes two or more feet below the funnel. Once they had the bison impounded, they might butcher the entire herd, perhaps netting as many as three hundred to six hundred animals.[16]

The Plains Indians also drove bison over cliffs or a steep cut-bank along a river. Using means similar to those in impounding, they directed the bison toward the kill site. Pressed over the edge by animals immediately behind them, bison slammed to the bottom, where many died or became disabled, and the hunters slaughtered their badly bruised prey. If the drop-off was slight, they constructed a corral at the location. This ancient method had survived from the favorite bison-hunting forms of the precontact people. After the acquisition of horses, mounted hunters often drove the bison toward the precipice.[17]

Horses also turned bison hunting into something of a sport. Mounted on a good horse, one that knew how to keep out of the range of the bison's horns, a hunter with a lance or a bow and arrows pursued his running game. Guiding the horse only with his knees, he approached the bison from the rear and side and dispatched the animal with a powerful thrust of the lance aimed at the heart, the horse knowing to turn aside in response to the new pressure of the thrust. If the hunter used a bow and arrow, the horse swerved and turned as soon as it heard the twang of the bow. Hunting in such a manner took skill and courage, but the killing of his first bison became a proud moment in the life of every young Plains Indian. Bison running slowly increased to become the predominant hunting technique on the plains.[18]

Weather permitting, hunting in winter proved a fairly simple task. In the north the men used snowshoes to run over the soft snow drifts. With their huge weight, bison frequently became exhausted or mired down in snow drifts. The men, with little danger to themselves, could approach such an entrapped or tired animal and dispatch it with arrows or a lance. Black Elk remembered when as a youth on horseback he pursued bison into a snow-filled gulch: "There we were all together—four bison, my horse and I all floundering and kicking, but I managed to crawl out a little way" and killed the animals.[19] Men in the Plains Cree tribe liked to drive bison onto a frozen lake or river, where the animals skidded and lurched about in a helpless manner, some breaking legs in a fall on the slippery ice. The hunters quickly killed their easy prey.[20]

In warm seasons the Plains Indians on occasion killed bison while the animals swam rivers and remained defenseless. The younger men swam alongside the bison or crawled on top of the swimming animal and then used a knife to cut the throat. A dangerous method, it served as sport more than as an effort to procure meat and hides for sustenance.

Sometimes people alone or in groups of two or three individuals hunted bison. In such an instance the hunters wrapped themselves in the hide of a wolf or a bison and crawled within shooting distance of the unsuspecting animals. If they took care to approach the game toward the wind, the hunters with bows and arrows might kill several animals before the herd moved away.[21]

The typical hunts, however, remained collective efforts held in the summer and fall. Major tribal affairs, they included, both before and after the hunt, elaborate ceremonies that represented a complex fusion of practical habit and religious ritual. During the hunt, eastern village people abandoned their settlements for the open plains, where they pitched their tipis in a circle as they searched for game. To call bison to them, some people employed various devices with magical properties. Others, such as the Mandans, believed that in a time of scarcity a special bison dance would bring herds near the village. In a few tribes people played the hoop game to lure bison.[22] When the bison came in range and other preparations had been completed, the people moved out, having predetermined to use one of the collective methods: surrounding, driving off a cliff, impounding, grass firing, or bison running.

At the time of the hunt the entire camp buzzed with excitement. The village crier, or herald, rode around the circle of tipis, dressed in all his finery, to announce the presence of game. The camp "police" (marshals), galloping back and forth, assigned each man his proper place in the hunt and warned mothers to watch their children, especially their high-spirited boys.

If the herd grazed many miles away, a grand procession occurred. Women dismantled tipis, packed travois, and with other band members fell into marching order. Far ahead, scouts kept an eye on the bison. A few miles behind, the main column with its flanks protected by warriors moved out. Depending on the tribe, first came the pipe bearers, or advisers, or shirt wearers, or sacred buffalo-stick holders, or other important persons—dressed in their finest feathered, fringed, and beaded costumes—whose magic medicine objects held the key to a successful hunt. Behind the pipe bearers rode tribal leaders dressed in all their splendor. Finally, in a helter-skelter assemblage came a jumble of women and children, men too old or ill for the hunt, and others with their dog and horse travois, all watched over by one of the warrior societies serving in its capacity as marshals, or "police."

Clearly, it was a joyous and excited group that rushed overland toward the bison. Then, as soon as the band reached the herd, the hunt—which would last about thirty minutes—began, with each hunter using arrows or a lance of his own design and color pattern so that he could tell which animals he had slain.

The people, men or women, quickly butchered the slain animals. They heaped the travois with meat to haul to a temporary campsite, where women prepared the meat for eating or preserving and stretched the hides on wooden frames for scraping and tanning. Such a camp was a busy, active, and exciting place. As evening approached, most bands prepared for an elaborate ritual of dancing, singing, and eating designed to give thanks to their spirit beings and to consecrate the spoils of the hunt. In the days that followed, the people, with perhaps the men enjoying a good smoke, related tales of the successful hunt.[23]

If the hunting camp was in territory claimed by others, particularly enemies, the people moved out as quickly as possible. Although such a camp was active, the people remained apprehensive and watchful. Boys guarded the horse herds and scouts rode out to protect the camp. Women packed the meat and dismantled the tipis, and everyone prepared to hurry away to a safer range.

With Plains Indians ranging widely over the plains, intertribal contact increased after the 1750s. The contacts created channels for the diffusion of ceremonial practices, beliefs, and social and economic features of their plains cultures. As the power and resources of certain peoples rose while those of others fell, the Plains Indians made new alliances, banding together for defensive purposes or to expand hunting ranges.[24]

Indeed, the acquisition of new hunting ranges became an essential aspect of intertribal relations; it caused conflict of all kinds, including warfare. Although the taking of new lands became a part of plains warfare, prolonged wars and standing armies—at least until the mid–nineteenth century—remained wholly absent. They were not needed, for major tribal forces rarely met. Rather, personal revenge, individual honor and glory, and the desire for horses established a pattern of sporadic warfare that was characterized by raids and counterraids involving only a few warriors. Although a condition of peace predominated among allied tribes, every group had enemies with whom warfare became nearly continuous, including its raids, counterraids, and constant surprises. When they were fought, battles were individual affairs, where each warrior fought for individual glory, honor, and prestige.[25]

Nonetheless, large tribal forces fought to expand their range of territory, secure access to the bison herds, and perhaps ensure security through aggression. Not long after their arrival on the plains, for example, the Lakotas drove the Cheyennes from the Black Hills, and more than half a century later a force of one thousand Lakota warriors routed a large band of Pawnees under Sky Chief hunting bison along the Platte River; some 150 men, women, and children died in the attack. Between these dramatic encounters, the Lakotas on occasion and for a variety of reasons fought other offensive wars.[26]

Defensive warfare, on the other hand, was a matter of continual concern. Many villages on the plains became armed camps. Enemies existed on all sides of every plains tribe, and on horseback they could travel long distances with speed and relative comfort unencumbered by extra baggage needed while on foot in prehorse days. With male members of every band seeking to gain honor, bolster wealth, or obtain revenge, there were, except in winter, few times when the Plains Indians lived in security. For the Lakotas, who were expanding through others' ranges, few periods of peace existed and no nights passed without the danger of a possible attack upon them. The men slept with weapons beside them, guarded the horse herds, and watched over the women and children.[27]

Warfare changed over the years. As with most institutions on the plains, it was not frozen in time but rather evolved in response to other developments, both historical and environmental. When they first entered the area, plains people tended to fight on foot and in tribal units, with large numbers of warriors on either side facing one another at some distance. They might shout insults at one another and shoot arrows across the distance dividing them. If one line of fighters attacked, a general melee might follow. With horses, however, young men soon found that they could strike out in small groups and cover a lot of ground to hit an enemy camp, not to conquer it necessarily, but to steal its horses or otherwise gain glory. Black Chief, a Skidi Pawnee who had lost the respect of his people, once went alone to a Crow village some two hundred miles away. He quietly killed two men, a woman, and a child and took their scalps before stealing a horse and fleeing back to his home. The scalps and his stories soon restored his honor. Although plains warfare did not respect sex or age, a concept of limited war developed, one that stressed such ideas as fighting in close contact or touching the enemy, stealing his horses or capturing his people, and taking his scalp or disgracing his soul.[28]

Characteristic warfare, therefore, involved the incessant marauding of small groups. Participants designed war parties of this kind for either killing the enemy (revenge) or stealing his horses. The spread of firearms, however, made the former so hazardous that some people, such as the Plains Cree, abandoned revenge raids. The latter, as horses increased in number, became more prominent. In a general sense, then, warfare among the Plains Indians often evolved into horse stealing—highly individualistic, but systematically organized and skillfully executed. Treachery, stealth, and wariness, with boldness in an advantage but readiness to flee if necessary, characterized plains warfare.[29]

Ritual and ceremony also characterized it. Because fighting had religious ties, a warrior sought aid form his spirit helper and went through a number of rituals both before and after a raid. He dressed and painted himself according to a prescibed formula that may have been revealed to him by his guardian spirit or animal helper. In addition, a warrior, if he did not believe his personal power (medicine) was in working order, did not go on a raid or participate in fighting. Warriors respected their war medicines—their personal amulets, charms, and talismans. The idea became serious business. When he neglected the messages of his medicine, for example, and in 1867 charged an enemy position, the admired Cheyenne war leader Roman Nose (Woquini; Sautie, the Bat) was among the first to die.

Anyone could organize a raiding party. Those warriors with a record of successful raids had little trouble finding volunteers, but the leader of a party that had not returned safely might have difficulty finding others to join him on subsequent raids. The Plains Indians believed that to return without the loss of a man was vital, and their concept of fighting contained little in the way of deliberately accepting losses for strategic ends. Their education and training, writes a contemporary observer, "their social laws and condition of physical existence, demand a certain order of strategy; and the great vital principle of this is to do the greatest possible amount of damage to the enemy with the least possible loss."[30]

Wooden Leg, a Cheyenne warrior, talked about strategy and fighting. He noted that "there were frequent gatherings of warrior societies . . . where chiefs exchanged ideas about methods of combat." He reported that when "a general war was contemplated, [the] chiefs agreed upon the plans." Once the fighting began, however, "it was a case of every man for himself. There was then no ordered groupings, no systematic movements in concert, no compulsory goings and comings." The warriors now went their own way, and "everyone looked out for himself only, or each helped a friend."[31]

Successful war parties returned to a joyous welcome. The band held victory dances and other celebrations to honor the heroes. "We rode into our village singing of victory," remembered Plenty Coups, a Crow warrior returning from his first successful raid. "Our chiefs . . . came out to meet us, singing Praise Songs. My heart rejoiced. . . . I shall never forget . . . how happy I felt." The warriors gloried in describing their fruitful efforts, and they gave thanks to their guardian spirits for their safe return.[32]

Men who returned from an unsuccessful raid entered the camp under cover of darkness and as secretly as possible. Even worse was a raid that ended in tragedy, with one or more of the participants killed. News of such a raid produced intense wailing, general lamentation, and loss of respect for its leader.

Tragic results did not discourage raiding, as the rewards of success were enormous. For the band or tribe, success helped to ensure the economy. It meant that by securing the region in which large numbers of bison grazed, the community could sustain its wealth. At a time when bison proved vital for both food and trade, the situation became important to both semisedentary and nomadic groups.[33]

For the individual, capturing horses meant wealth and influence. Successful warfare brought prestige, honor, and leadership, for men with enviable war honors advised headmen on tribal matters and gained influence among the political leaders. Moreover, war honors led to chieftancy. Successful warriors became tribal heroes, and the pattern of heroics became so institutionalized in some communities that individual well-being and group self-interest became subordinate to the idea that war was an end in itself—the great "purpose of life."[34] Washakie remembered that "as a young man I delighted in war. When my tribe was at peace, I would wander off sometimes alone in search of an enemy. . . . I killed a great many Indians."[35]

Others, including some women, spoke of a similar fondness. "If I live to see you a man, and to go off on the warpath," a Pawnee woman told her son Lone Chief, "I would not cry if I were to hear that you had been killed in battle. That is what makes a man: to fight and to be strong." An old Piegan headman, Saukamappe, who was actually Cree, noted that "we were fond of war" and "even our women flattered us to war and nothing was thought of but scalps for singing and dancing."[36]

Warriors often acted with exuberance and flair. They were somebody, and they wanted to call attention to their showmanship in ways that witnesses would remember. Roman Nose, the Cheyenne war leader, for example, in front of a thousand warriors in 1865 rode along a line of federal troops. The soldiers shot repeatedly at him as he passed before them, hitting his horse and knocking it to the ground, but Roman Nose survived unscathed. No one who saw it likely forgot the event. Moreover, because war was a path to status, as we have seen, warriors, to denote their successful exploits, put feathers in their hair or in horned war bonnets and depicted their accomplishments on bison hides.

There emerged a general pattern for recognizing war honors: counting coup. The coup, or blow (to strike the enemy), represented an individual exploit made in contact with the enemy and was formally awarded at a ceremony after a successful raid. To take a coup represented in essence the taking of an enemy's spirit. Originally a man received a coup for striking an enemy's body with his hand, his bow, his lance, a special stick, or other paraphernalia, but later the plains people granted coups for other acts of bravery and daring. On the same enemy the Comanches authorized two men to count coup, the first toucher taking precedence. The Cheyennes allowed three men to collect a coup, and the Arapahos, Assiniboins, and Crows permitted four men to score in descending order of merit.

Among the Lakotas four men might count coup. As described by Royal B. Hassrick, the first man to score earned "the right to wear a golden eagle feather upright at the [back] of his head." The second could "wear an eagle feather tilted to the left." The third wore his "eagle feather horizontal," and the fourth wore "a buzzard feather hung vertically." The Lakotas granted coups for the touching of a man, woman, or child. They granted credit "for touching, not killing," an enemy, "except in hand-to-hand combat." Hassrick indicates that "it was the daring required of close contact for which the honor was given. Thus an individual might mortally wound a man with an arrow yet gain no coup because four of his fellow [Lakotas] literally beat him to the touch."[37]

By the early 1840s major changes had come to plains warfare. Not only had the bow and shield become smaller as people adapted them to horse-mounted fighting, but also improved firearms had made fighting far more deadly than in the past. As bison diminished in numbers, the various plains people, hunting fewer animals over a restricted range of territory, crowded in on one another. With game scarcer, people of some tribes, who had once geared their raiding to the rhythms and movements of the bison, broke up into small thieving and marauding bands. New intertribal agreements and alliances emerged. The Comanches, Kiowas, Cheyennes, and Arapahos, after holding a grand council in 1840 below Bent's Fort on the Arkansas River, became less hostile toward one another and encouraged their young men to seek peace or to raid elsewhere. In response, Buffalo Hump, a Comanche war leader of high intelligence, led raids deep into Mexico. Other people, such as the Pawnees, Lipans, and Crows, found themselves isolated and subject to attack by several enemies.

Moreover, the presence of whites also changed the patterns of warfare. Traders provided guns and ammunition, items that facilitated war. Missionaries struggled to establish peace through Christian teachings, and people of the plains, if they believed that a missionary's medicine proved stronger than their own, might put aside fighting, raiding, and war. The Plains Indians also fought against whites, particularly after the 1850s when whites in increasing numbers pushed onto the Great Plains.

The changing nature of plains warfare established a dynamic of war, revenge, and peace. Rival groups suspended hostilities while they traded at Wichita camps on the southern plains or Mandan and Hidatsa villages in the north. Enemies might enjoy a smoke together in a trader's lodge and recount to one another their exploits. While his picture was painted, the dignified Blackfeet leader Buffalo Bull's Back Fat sat for hours visiting with enemy warriors of the Crow, Assiniboin, Cree, and Ojibwa tribes. They laid all day around the sides of the room, wrote George Catlin, "reciting to each other the battles they have fought, and pointing to scalp-locks, worn as proof of their victories and attached to the seams of their shirts and leggings."[38]

Not everyone admired warfare. Pretty Shield, a Crow woman, claimed that "we women did not like war." She noted that "always there was some man missing, and always some woman was having to go and live with her relatives, because women are not hunters." She complained that warfare resulted in too many orphans. "When we women lost our men," she said, "we lost our own, and our children's, living."[39]

Warfare produced ethnic mixing. Women captured in a raid became wives of men in another tribe and gave birth to mixed-blood children. The famous Crow leader Rotten Belly, with a large force of warriors in 1832, after badly shooting up a large Piegan village, captured over two hundred women and children. The Piegan captives, through coercion or adoption, soon became part of Rotten Belly's Crow people. Not only did the captured women and children become a source of additional numerical strength, but also the women brought with them their own folktales, myths, and religious concepts. The captured youths raised and adopted into the Crow tribe further added to the ethnic mixing.[40]

Such ethnic mixing produced many prominent leaders. Saukamappee, a Piegan headman, was originally a Cree who as a young man had joined the Piegans. The great Shoshoni headman, Washakie, recognized by many Indian people of his day as a masterful military leader, spent the first four years of his life in the Flathead village of his father. When twenty years old, he transferred allegiance to the Bannocks for a time before settling with his mother's people. Woman Chief of the Crows, one of many women who became successful warriors, was a Gros Ventre girl whom the Crows had captured and raised in their society. She led several successful raids against the Blackfeet before her former people, the Gros Ventres, killed her.

Results of such activities produced intertribal marriages and joint participation in economic efforts, social activities, and religious ceremonies. Often members of otherwise hostile tribes fraternized while trading with horticultural peoples or at jobbing centers among the Mandan, Hidatsa, Arikara, and Wichita villages. At other times, especially after raids when prisoners had been taken, captives transmitted information about practices and activities of their own groups. If they escaped to their own people, the former captives took back with them information about activities of their captors.

Out of these developments grew a commonality of plains traits that had not existed earlier. After the 1750s Indians of the plains began to follow generally common patterns of life. Although minor distinctions remained, their dress and habits became similar, their tools and weapons universal. Their spiritual and intellectual views differed very little. Many of them adopted the Sun Dance, pursued bison on horseback, and placed greater value than in earlier times on material objects. As warfare intensified, war leaders gained ascendency over civil leaders in tribal political control and in social rank and status. Symbols of successful military exploits became major marks of individual distinction.

The emerging Plains Indian societies were colorful and attractive. Plenty Coups, an elderly Crow leader, recalling memories of the era, said: "The weather was cold [as we began our trip], but in those days in all kinds of weather men had good times. Cold days were the same to us as warm ones, and we were nearly always happy." Upon returning home, "our hearts sang with the thought of visiting friends we had not seen in a long time. It was good to live in those days."[41] Black Elk, a Lakota holy man, wrote: "We were happy in our own country and we were seldom hungry, for then the two-legged and the four-leggeds lived together like relatives, and there was plenty for them and for us."[42] Noting this circumstance, Richard Irving Dodge, who lived among them, wrote that the Plains Indians were, "habitually and universally, the happiest people I ever saw. They thoroughly enjoy the present . . . [and] make no worry over the possibilities of the future."[43]

The horse and bison culture did not exist when Europeans first explored the region. Quickly afterward, the adoption of horses and the reliance on bison, the great ritualism and the Sun Dance, the military emphasis and the feathered warbonnets all produced cultural change in which some people from the Great Basin and some from the eastern forests—two thousand miles apart—emerged on the plains and in a few generations became nearly identical.[44]

Many institutions on the plains, however, were neither fixed nor firm. Seemingly in a state of constant flux, the institutions lacked rigid structure, and given the short time that people had to adapt to major new elements on the plains, the situation is not suprising. Moreover, whether or not practices and institutions would have stabilized is a moot question. Just over a century later, the Plains Indians were living on reservations, and many of their traditional ways changed again—or for a time endured—beneath a dominate white culture before reemerging again in the twentieth century.[45]

The reservation system, coupled with the loss of bison and destruction by disease, altered the Plains Indians' system of status, wealth, and rank, changing radically their traditional life patterns. Although large parts of their ancestral cultures remained, the end of a nomadic hunting way of life encouraged profound changes in their societies and cultures. Reflecting these circumstances, a Hidatsa woman, Waheenee (Buffalo Bird Woman), said that "the buffaloes and the black-tail deer are gone and our Indian ways are almost gone." Pretty Shield, a Crow woman, said that "ours was a different world before the buffalo went away." Plenty Coups concluded: "When the buffalo went away we became a changed people."[46]

On their reservations the Plains Indians adapted to a settled life, one significantly removed from their horse-mounted, bison-hunting traditions. Before then, the Plains Indians, although varying from plains to prairies, north to south, and one ethnic group to another, developed societies with a high degree of cultural similarity—evident in their economy and material culture.

4 : ECONOMY AND MATERIAL CULTURE

uropean influences profoundly modified the economies and material cultures of the Plains Indians. On the northern plains the influences began in a limited way with the earliest French traders. On the central and southern plains they began with the first Spanish explorers. The white influences increased in the eighteenth century, and after the beginning of the nineteenth century there emerged on the Great Plains dynamic but variegated societies whose economies represented unique blendings of traditional Indian subsistence forms with European trade goods.

As adaptive societies, the Plains Indians developed material cultures that combined ancient items of bone, stone, shell, horn, and wood with modern products of iron, wool cloth, and European manufacture. The economies of the nomadic peoples, although in some ways a reversion to an Archaic-age subsistence mode, became rich and attractive, with material possessions characterized by ease of transport, lightness of weight, and durability of use. Bison hides supplied basic raw materials. Indian people supplemented them with many useful and ornamental European products through regular trade—with white agents on occasion but more often through various Indian middlemen.

The economic systems of the village groups, except that they reflected a semisedentary, horticultural life, did not differ markedly from the neighboring nomads. The horticultural people manufactured pottery, possessed heavy wooden mortars and pestles, and for cultivating crops used such items as bison shoulder-blade hoes, antler rakes, and wooden digging sticks. Like their nomadic counterparts, the semisedentary people used many items of European manufacture, including firearms, metal utensils, farming equipment, textiles, and luxury goods. Many of them became middlemen in the far-flung trade relationships that developed with the arrival of whites.

The idea of production for its own sake did not exist among the Plains Indians; nor did the concept of property accumulation as a positive good, at least in the early period. Thus, freed from long hours in the pursuit of material wealth (except horses), men enjoyed plenty of leisurely activities—far more than their white counterparts. With bison usually plentiful, a good hunter in a few hours could collect enough meat to feed his family for weeks. Women, who likewise experienced a less taxing life than their white counterparts, built the tipis, tanned the hides, worked the fields, and took responsibility for camp chores. They also owned the lodges and the fruits of their labor. It was not a static system, however, and significant changes occurred.

Again, horses and firearms were the catalyst. The horses, Spanish breeds of mixed ancestry, appeared tough, relatively small, and often "pinto" in coloration, and they possessed extraordinary stamina. The firearms were muzzle-loading, smooth-bore weapons that in the early years enjoyed a popularity among American Indians far out of proportion to their effectiveness. In the mid–nineteenth century, however, Indian warriors acquired modern rifles, many of them superior to the federal army's equipment.

Because Indian people in the early contact period often equated them in trade values, horses and firearms spread with relative ease from one tribal group to another. Broadly speaking, guns arrived on the plains from rival French and British traders in the Northeast, and as early as 1720 the Pawnees and Otos used French muskets against Spanish soldiers in western Nebraska. In 1759 the Taovayas (Pawnee Picts) of the Wichita confederation used guns and a plentiful supply of ammunition against Spanish troops along the Red River. Although the bow and arrow remained the principal weapon among Plains Indians, horticultural tribesmen through much of the eighteenth century traded firearms westward to the nomadic groups.[1]

Horses made a greater impact. Spreading from Spanish settlements in the Southwest, they eased the burden of transportation, revolutionized bison hunting, and led the Plains Indians into a pattern of horse raids, counter-raids, and sporadic plains warfare. They helped to make possible the plains culture. Once hunters who trudged the plains on foot or horticulturists who planted crops in muddy river bottoms, the Plains Indians soon became masters of horsemanship and used the majestic animals to establish a unique and flamboyant equestrian life.[2]

Horses altered economic concepts, established great differences in wealth and correlative prestige, and, in what once had been an egalitarian society, created socioeconomic classes based on wealth, particularly horses. Village paupers, those people with only one or two horses, had to walk when the camp moved. People of wealth owned many horses, with individual herds sometimes numbering one hundred or more head. A man with horses could buy ceremonial privileges or enhance his social position by giving them away. A young man in love, through a male family member who conducted negotiations with the prospective bride's family, might offer several horses to the father of a beautiful and virtuous girl he wanted to marry. As time passed, then, accumulation of horses (property wealth), rather than the sharing of property, began to define one's social position.[3]

Property wealth, measured in numbers of horses, assumed signficance in that a wealthy man must be a successful hunter or warrior. Wealth validated bravery, for through successful hunting and raiding a man obtained new wealth in the form of horses and goods. It also became tied to status in that one might improve one's social position by an unselfish sense of sharing, even to the extent of giving away personal possessions. Moreover, because socioeconomic values emphasized generosity (or *wacantognaka* to the Lakotas, one of their four principal virtures), the more horses one gave away, the higher one rose in the status system. Reciprocity characterized exchange among plains peoples, however, and thus gifts might create reciprocal obligations to the recipient.[4]

Horses and firearms for some prairie-plains peoples intensified their roles as traders and middlemen. Even before they saw their first Europeans, such people without realizing it became part of the European imperial trade systems. Caught up in the rival trade through Indian counterparts to the east, the horticulturalists killed animals whose hides and furs they could exchange for horses, guns, liquor, and other items of European manufacture. From other Indian groups or from white traders, Indian people on the plains learned quickly the European rules of trade.[5]

Partly as a result, the economic base of various semisedentary groups shifted from a subsistence mode to one designed to secure goods for exchange in the European trade. The Osages, for instance, although not abandoning the horticultural base of their economy, devoted more and more time to hunting and raiding to secure trade goods. By the end of the eighteenth century, they had become a seminomadic people who spent only enough time in their riverine villages to plant and harvest crops and transact business with white traders.[6]

Many other village groups also intensified their hunting practices without abandoning horticulture. The Pawnees, Poncas, and Omahas, for example, retained their horticulture and village life, but at certain times of the year entire village populations left their homes and fields, moved onto the plains, and hunted bison. They looked less like sedentary horticulturists and more like full-time bison hunters.[7]

All across the Great Plains, intertribal trading for horses, firearms, ammunition, and other European goods increased. On the southern plains the Wichita villages and on the northern plains the Arikara, Hidatsa, and Mandan villages became busy jobbing centers for far-reaching trade. Nomadic bands regularly came in to exchange bison hides, beaver furs, eagle feathers, bear claws, elk teeth, horses, and other items, including Indian slaves, for guns, ammunition, metal tools, textiles, tobacco, corn and beans, and sundry other goods.[8]

The trade fairs were colorful and spectacular events. Hundreds, or on rare occasions in the early years perhaps thousands, of nomadic people might arrive at once and pitch their tipis adjacent to the earth or grass lodges of the village people. Dressed in all their finery, people smoked the pipe of friendship and turned the affair into an elaborate ceremonial. Bargaining became lively, for to obtain a fair trade they sought an even exchange, which among all the plains tribal groups was based on reciprocity. Lucrative to both sides, the trade clearly influenced material values, social customs, and spiritual activities, producing changes of all kinds.

Although the Plains Indians reacted differently to the arrival of European goods, the effects everywhere became significant. Many people accepted such new foods and stimulants as bread, sugar, coffee, and liquor. They adopted metal utensils in place of pottery and skin cooking bags, "strike-a-lights" in place of the fire drill, cloth in place of skins for clothing, metal knives in place of flint ones, and iron arrow points in place of chipped-stone weapons. Tiny European-made glass beads replaced porcupine quills as the favored element in decoration of clothes and moccasins. New luxuries and gaudy fineries appeared, and a good portion of the precontact culture faded. A hybrid and compelling material culture emerged.[9]

While recognizing the superiority of metal tools, utensils, and weapons, the Plains Indians did not abandon all their familiar implements of bone, stone, horn, and wood. The bow and arrow remained the preferred weapon. Men often used knives for hand-to-hand combat, and the lance continued to be used long after the appearance of firearms. War clubs with stone heads—some spherical, some pointed at both ends, and some ax-shaped—held in place by shrunken rawhide and attached to a wooden handle remained common well after white contact. Men continued to smooth arrow shafts between two grooved stones. Even as they acquired iron implements, they still fashioned some arrow points and knives of bone, stone, and horn. Until recent years women preferred to pound chokecherries and other berries on a flat stone with a grooved-stone hammer. Skin dressers used several tools of bone, horn, and antler, and bone awls served to punch holes for sewing. Nonetheless, in their dynamic material cultures ancient implements tended to give way to modern ones, and thus sometimes scholars are hard pressed to identify all the precontact tools, utensils, and implements.

Food sources remain easier to identify. Sustenance was based on bison meat and a few assorted horticultural crops, including corn, sunflowers, beans, pumpkins, and squash. But the Plains Indians also used a dozen kinds of wild fruits and berries, dug roots, and collected nuts. They ate elk, deer, pronghorns, black bears, rabbits, water fowl, game birds, and a variety of wild vegetables. Some people consumed turkeys, frogs, snakes, dogs, horse flesh, land tortoises, turtles, and other animals. Some ate fish, but others, such as the Blackfeet, Comanches, and Crows, regarded fish as taboo. Except perhaps for symbolic or ceremonial purposes, none ate human flesh. The Santees gathered wild rice in Minnesota, and the Pawnees and a few others harvested wild rice in the sandhills of Nebraska. Many people ate fresh thistle stalks, milkweed buds, and rose hips. Southern people sliced the fruit of the prickly pear cactus and added it to bison soups and stews.[10] In short, food was usually plentiful—at least until the 1840s. When it became scarce, mainly in February and March, the Plains Indians, of course, accepted all food sources for nourishment.

The horticultural peoples also relied on their garden plots. Each from one to five acres in size, rectangular in outline, and separated by an uncultivated area about four feet wide, the fields belonged to the women who worked them. Younger children assisted, and when seasonal activities required many workers, young men might aid the women. Among the Mandans and most other horticulturists women owned the product of the garden plots, and they saw to its family and household distribution. The Plains Indians did not know about rotating crops and lacked fertilizers, but they allowed fields to lie fallow and often burned brush and trees on them. The burning destroyed weed seeds, and the resulting ash had some effectiveness as a fertilizer.[11]

Corn provided the staple vegetable fare, and it dominated the fields. Although farming was hard work and labor intensive, women often enjoyed their time in the fields. Waheenee, a Hidatsa woman, remembered that "as I [hoed] the corn I [sang] to it."[12] Hidatsa women planted at least nine varieties of corn; Santee women could produce up to twenty bushels per acre in a good season. The women grew sunflowers around the edges of the corn plots. Hidatsa women planted their five varieties of beans in hills between rows of corn, but on occasion they used separate plots. They planted squash and pumpkins separately because the plants spread and did not thrive when shaded. In the early days, before long bison hunts took them away from their villages for extended periods, women and children hoed the fields, constructed sunshades for young corn, and kept watch over the crops to prevent damage from birds, stray horses, deer, rabbits, and other animals. Many people, such as the Mandans and Pawnees, associated their horticultural activities with ceremonials designed to secure spiritual assistance in the growing of crops.[13]

The men hunted. They sought elk, deer, bears, pronghorns, and smaller mammals—all important in the diet, but bison provided the basic source of meat. Individuals could hunt at any time, but major tribal hunts, conducted in the summer and fall, secured large amounts of meat that women dried, cached, or otherwise preserved for later use.

During a tribal hunt, the butchering site became a busy place. After killing a bison the hunter and his family gathered about the slain animal, opened its veins, and drank the warm blood. As they sorted and cut carcasses, all the people shouted, quarreled, and laughed with neighbors. While they worked, writes Tom McHugh, "most participants snacked on raw morsels taken still warm from the slain buffalo, including livers, kidneys, tongues, eyes, testicles, belly fat, parts of the stomach, gristle from snouts, marrow from leg bones, and the hoofs of tiny unborn calves."[14] They took raw brains and bone marrow, stirred them together using a section of the ribs as a bowl, and ate them.

Culinary tastes varied. Although a few people abstained from it, most people of the plains consumed vitamin- and mineral-rich bison viscera. They ate raw kidneys, tallow around the kidney, loin tallow, and the paunch. Some took curdled milk from the stomach of a suckling fawn or bison calf. Many people, especially children, considered the fresh liver, which they sprinkled with bile from the gall bladder, a culinary delicacy. Herman Lehmann, who lived among the Plains Indians, refers to Comanche people as eating the raw heart. Not only did it taste good, but also the bison heart symbolized the animal's strength and bravery.[15]

Food preparation was the responsibility of women. They cooked food by boiling it in a skin container, roasting it on a spit, broiling it on coals, or baking it underground. In semisedentary groups they used earthenware pots for boiling. In nomadic groups they dug a small hole, lined it with a skin bag, filled the bag with water, and dropped in red-hot rocks. After European contact women acquired brass kettles and iron pots for the task and could place them directly on the fire.

The women dried those foods not prepared for eating right away. They made jerky by cutting meat into thin strips across the grain and placing it on racks to dry in the sun. They sliced squash and strung it on a long pole to dry. They left some corn on the cobs, but they placed shelled corn on skins to dry and then stored it in skin bags.

Women preserved some meat as pemmican. To produce it they took sun-dried slices of meat and pounded them fine with a maul and mixed the resulting product with melted fat, bone marrow, suet, and dry paste from wild berries, cherries, or plums that had been crushed, pits and all. For flavor they might add walnuts, pecans, or other nuts, and they stored the mixture in skin bags, in large intestines, or in paunches. They sometimes used melted tallow to make the container air tight. Pemmican would keep for years. Warriors carried it while on a raid, and children ate it as a snack. But more often women saved it for winter use, and on the northern plains it became an important item of trade with whites.[16]

Until the early 1840s the Plains Indians found relatively abundant food supplies. But changing subsistence patterns, growing trade in bison hides, and declining animal populations compromised their ability to maintain adequate food sources. The plains people themselves were not without fault. They preferred to hunt two- to five-year-old bison cows, thus removing large numbers of breeding females. Their large horse herds negatively affected the ability of the plains grasslands to support large numbers of animals, and they spread disease to bison.[17]

Growth in the bison-hide trade placed additional pressure on bison as a food source. To compensate, such people as the Comanches extended their raiding deep into Texas and increased their forays into Mexico. Nomadic peoples traded with, or raided, horticultural peoples for some foods and turned to whites whose trading houses appeared on the plains for others.

Trade with whites produced enormous changes. New foods, tools, weapons, utensils, and equipment represent obvious alterations in plains material possessions. But more subtle, perhaps more basic, changes occurred too. For example, men once hunted on a subsistence-for-use basis. As they began to hunt for a commercial trade with whites, they spent more time away from their villages, and correspondingly the number of game animals in the vicinity of the villages declined, which in turn caused men to travel farther and to be away longer. Sometimes they were gone for weeks or months at a time.

Women, in response, took ever greater responsibility for camp life and daily decision making. With the men gone, women also took on many of their partners' chores. When the men returned, usually with hides to process and meat to preserve, the women had to work harder preparing the extra skins for trade, a difficult and time-consuming task in which men did not participate.

Partly as a result of the men being gone for long stretches, some Indian groups moved their villages. On the northern plains and in the Canadian parklands in the late seventeenth and early eighteenth centuries, they set up semipermanent camps closer to European trading posts and government forts. The posts provided some protection for women and children while the men were away, and the new locations gave villagers, as the hunters returned, the advantage of proximity vis-à-vis competing tribal groups. In addition, women married white traders. The marriages created Indian-white alliances, intercultural bonds, and social and economic benefits, and from the traders' viewpoint, of course, the women provided such necessities as moccasins, snowshoes, firewood, and food.

On the southern plains, Spanish officials encouraged Indian people to settle at missions. The system may have succeeded along the upper Rio Grande in New Mexico, but such Plains Indians as the Tonkawas and Lipan Apaches in Texas seldom stayed at mission sites. French traders, however, pushed up the Red, Arkansas, and Missouri rivers from very early in the eighteenth century. They carried European goods to villages that became important trade centers, and subsequently developments similar to those on the northern plains took place; that is, interracial marriage, intercultural bonding, and trade advantages between whites and Plains Indians occurred.

To carry the hides, the trade items, and themselves, the Plains Indians had several means of transportation. In winter some northern groups used dog sleds. The Métis of Canada, while on their long treks to the plains for bison, used two-wheeled carts. The Santees did not abandon canoes until the nineteenth century. The Missouri River people, particularly the Arikaras, Hidatsas, and Mandans, used the bull boat, or coracle, a circular, basin-shaped tub of bent willow frame covered with green bison hides. When it dried, the rawhide formed a drum-tight covering, and the boat with a driftwood drag for stability served as transportation on the river. Most groups trained dogs to transport small items, and all of them used horses to carry goods and equipment.[18]

Equipment for riding horses the Plains Indians copied from Europeans. All people adopted bridles or hackamores, a bridle with a loop capable of being tightened around the nose or lower jaw, and most used saddles. The saddle had a wood or elkhorn frame that Indian people shaped and glued together, and over it they tightly stretched a green bison hide. Later they got saddles from whites. The Blackfeet and Crows used the horse crupper, a leather loop passing under a horse's tail and buckled to the saddle. When they used them, Indian people made stirrups of wood wrapped with rawhide.

While they themselves rode horses or walked, the Plains Indians used a travois to transport their tipis, meat, firewood, household utensils, and other personal possessions. The travois, an A- or sometimes X-shaped drag, consisted of two long poles that converged at or near the tips for attachment to the shoulders of dogs and horses. The butt ends dragged along the ground, but midway along the poles the women fixed a frame of leather thongs and wood and tied the load to it. A travois belonged to the woman who made it. A simple but ingenious method of transportation, it worked better on the rolling plains than wheeled carts.[19]

A dog travois, of course, was much smaller than one for horses. Although a sixty-pound load was normal, some dogs could drag a travois with perhaps one hundred pounds of firewood on it or an eighty-pound green bison hide. Sometimes women packed food or household utensils on a dog's back; such a load seldom weighed over forty pounds.[20]

Dogs were numerous. A few served as pets, and by warning of intruders they guarded camps. Both the community at large and individuals, men as well as women, owned them. Among the Assiniboins a family might own as many as twelve dogs, but six or seven per family was more common. Each Hidatsa family kept from four to twenty of the animals. With each family owning several dogs, camps became filled with animals scurrying about the village and running amid the tipis or lodges, fighting with each other, and playing with the children. In some tribes the animals played a part in sacrificial rites, with relatives destroying the favorite dog of its deceased owner.[21]

The lodges around which the dogs ran also varied in style. Most horticultural people erected circular earth lodges or, as in the case of the Wichitas in the south where winters seemed less severe, domelike, grass-covered dwellings. While they differed somewhat in appearance, exterior design, and construction techniques, most earth lodges, using four to eight wooden posts as the central frame, were large, confortable, and durable, lasting seven to ten or more years and accommodating from one to several families. The Arikara, Mandan, and Pawnee people erected their houses over pits about two feet deep and shoveled the excavated dirt around the building. Some semisubterranean Pawnee lodges extended fifty feet in diameter. Mandan lodges reached eighty feet in circumference, but communal structures became much larger.[22]

Wichita grass houses were not so large. The people built them on the ground with a conical skeleton of stout poles bent toward the center. Over this they placed, like shingles, grass and straw held in place by slender wooden rods attached to the framework. They placed the houses close to one another in tightly packed villages.[23]

The Osages, and to a lesser extent the Missouris, erected houses of an oval or oblong design. As described by an Osage historian, the people used upright poles interlaced with horizontal rods to build a domelike structure covered with mats, bark, and skins. The houses ranged up to thirty, or sometimes one hundred, feet in length. About fifteen to twenty feet wide and ten feet high, the larger houses held more than one family.[24]

Interior lodge forms, although not identical, became somewhat standard. Along the middle Missouri River, for example, the people reserved in their houses special places for storage of food, firewood, and ceremonial equipment. They curtained off beds along the wall but provided sleeping accommodation for elders near the fire and located cooking gear at the center of the lodge under the smoke hole. Inside near the door the Mandans often maintained a small corral for their favorite horses. The general design of earth lodges dates back to precontact periods.

The tipi, the home of nomadic peoples, changed after white contact. With the adoption of horse transportation, it increased in size and elaboration.

When on their seasonal bison hunts, most horticultural groups and such western mountain people as the Mescaleros, Jicarillas, Nez Percés, Utes, and eastern Shoshonis also adopted horse-transported tipis.[25] Occupied by a single family, the tipi was a conical skin tent, round at the base, and tilted slightly forward with the door facing the rising sun. About twelve to sixteen feet in diameter at the base, it was light, portable, and quickly erected.

Women, who owned them, constructed tipis with ten to twelve or more tanned and tightly sewed bison hides stretched over a pole foundation. They used poles of any straight, light timber, peeled and sharpened at the butt end, and ranging from ten to forty feet long, but averaging about twenty-five feet. In a general sense women who lived in areas of high wind velocity used a three-pole foundation for the tipi; those in more protected areas—near mountains or wooded river valleys—used a four-pole foundation, with additional poles placed about thirty inches apart. Thus, Arikara, Blackfeet, Comanche, Crow, Hidatsa, Mandan, Omaha, and Sarsi women used a four-pole foundation. Arapaho, Assiniboin, Cheyenne, Gros Ventre, Kiowa, Kiowa Apache, Pawnee, Ponca, and Lakota women preferred a three-pole foundation, which gave the projecting tops of the poles a spiral appearance.

Depending upon their width and height, tipis were of different design. Crow women used very long poles, projecting them high above the skin cover as a funnel. Some women, such as the Cheyennes, liked a wide tipi base in proportion to the height; others, such as the Arapahos, preferred a narrow base in proportion to the height. Although the Crows preferred elegant, unpainted tipis, the Lakotas embellished theirs with both realistic and geometrical designs. Blackfeet tipis contained pictographs of animals and birds, both real and mythological, and the people often placed a Maltese cross on the west side of the top to symbolize the morning star. The Kiowas also richly embellished their "murals in the round." The designs, acquired in dreams and visions, remained full of spiritual significance.

Interior tipi patterns became fairly standard. With the door facing east, the women placed beds on the south and north sides against the wall. They made beds of poles and rawhide with bison robes for covering in winter, but sometimes they set beds on the ground. Below the pole and rawhide beds they stored food, utensils, and personal items in skin bags. On the west side facing the door they maintained a place of honor, and just east of center under the smoke hole they built a fire. From about four or five feet up the wall women hung an inside lining to the ground, thus providing insulated protection from winter cold. For ventilation in the summer they took down the lining and often rolled the tipi sides up several inches.[26]

The household inventory included a number of items. Eastern village peoples used many pottery containers. Most plains families had wooden bowls, ladles, and spoons, but such items remained rare in the southern regions where the Tonkawas and Comanches made only the simplest of wooden bowls. The Plains Indians also made spoons, ladles, and dishes from bison and mountain sheep horns. Later they acquired from whites a wide variety of metal utensils, iron pots, and machine-made knives.

Rawhide bags were numerous. All adults used paint and saddle bags. To hold dressings, tools, and sewing equipment, women used a variety of rectangular bags. They also kept various kinds of soft bags designed to hold household items, including bags for clothing and utensils. Men owned long, slender smoking bags and "strike-a-light" pouches. Both men and women painted their bags, and women decorated them with porcupine quills and beads and fringed them in various ways. The colorful bags became beautiful but useful works of art.

The parfleche was the most common bag. A person using the parfleche, a large section of rawhide with flaps, laid it flat on the ground and placed items for storage on the central portion. Then the user turned up the four flaps and laced them together. Usually people stuffed the parfleche with dried foods and, when traveling, strapped it to a horse's side.

The Plains Indians made tools from green wood, bones, stones, and horn. They made bone and flint knives, stone drills, stone and antler scrapers, and stone mauls. They put handles on most of their tools. When attaching a handle to a stone maul, for example, they tightly wrapped green wood and rawhide around a grooved stone and dipped the tool in a pot of glue. After the wood and hide shrunk and the glue dried, they owned a solid and serviceable implement. European trade introduced metal tools, including knives, scrapers, awls, drills, and axes.

Major weapons included the bow and arrow, of course, plus the lance, knife, war club, and shield. Firearms became important after white contact. The Plains Indians made war clubs in much the same way that they made stone mauls, but the handle might be longer and the stone smaller than a household maul. They often decorated the war clubs with feathers and various personal fetishes. They made the lance from a stout pole tipped with a flint or metal point, and they decorated it. The shields, constructed of bison bull shoulder hides, they made circular in shape, light of weight, and fixed with a strap to attach to an arm. Owners regally and symbolically decorated their shields, and perhaps a shaman or holy man blessed them. Although effective only when struck at an angle, the shield became a sacred possession treated with great care. Most warriors carried one while on a raid or with a war party.[27]

The bow and arrow remained an indispensible item for bison hunting and, as we have seen, an important weapon in warfare. The Plains Indians made bows of wood or horns of the pronghorn. The preferred wood was Osage orange, also called bois d'arc. When Osage orange could not be obtained, they used ash, elm, cedar, willow, mulberry, or any number of other varieties. They cut, sliced, fitted, and glued the wood or horn to the proper length, ranging from about three to four feet. Then, to strengthen it, northern craftsmen among the Blackfeet, Cheyennes, Crows, Lakotas, Hidatsas, and Plains Cree backed and wound the bow with long sinew taken from either side of a bison's backbone. Men in southeastern sections of the plains did not use sinew-backed bows.[28] Men manufactured bow strings from a variety of materials. Although they made most from the long bison sinew, they sometimes crafted bow strings of rawhide strips, twisted vegetable fibers, or bear intestines. Some southern craftsmen employed squirrel hide for strings.

Good arrows were not easy to make. Because a crooked arrow or one with improperly placed guide feathers proved worthless, the men took great care in making arrows. They used wood of the gooseberry, juneberry, chokecherry, ash, birch, cane, dogwood, currant, willow, and wild cherry saplings. Lakota men preferred gooseberry, with cherry and juneberry as second choices; Blackfeet men used shoots of the serviceberry, a straight, very heavy, and tough wood; Comanche men preferred young dogwood, with mature ash as a secondary choice. The men cut the shafts to the desired length and shape, tied them in a bunch, and to season them hung them near a fire for about ten days.

Then, in a tedious process the arrow makers straightened the shafts. Over a period of several days, they used their teeth, grease, fire, and a special arrow straightener—a bone or horn with a hole slightly larger than the shaft through which they passed the arrow back and forth—to make the arrow perfectly round. They scraped it to proper size and taper. Most of the better arrows they grooved from the end of the feathers to the head of the arrow point. Next, they polished and painted the shaft. Finally, they attached the feathers—owl, turkey, or buzzard feathers preferred—with glue and fixed the point, which after white contact increasingly became metal.[29] In fact, after the 1850s many men could not remember using stone points.

Weapon making was one of many craft arts. Skilled in several common but diversified handicrafts, the people used wood, stone, bone, horn, leather, and other materials. Their taxidermy became highly developed, as did their hide dressing, quill embroidery, and bead work. They designed each work to intensify their spirituality, to play a utilitarian role in life, and to be mobile and durable.

Artwork was symbolic, religious, colorful, and dynamic. The Plains Indians painted, sculpted, carved, sewed, wove, pottered, and otherwise engaged in several art forms, displaying both skill and sensitivity in the use of textures and colors, lines and lilt. Using pure vegetable and earth colors, for example, they painted on hides, wood, horses, and themselves. They skillfully executed their painting and maintained a broad range of creations; women often painted in geometrical form, men often realistically. Like most everything else in their material culture, their art forms were influenced by exposure to white materials. Their artistic styles, therefore, were not static but rather in a continual state of change.[30]

Dress styles also offered variety to basic designs. Climate, older customs, and degree of European contact influenced plains styles. Routine, workaday attire remained simple and unadorned, but for festive occasions the Plains Indians kept fancy dress garb. As white contact increased in the early nineteenth century, plains people increasingly adopted clothes and blankets made of cotton and wool cloth.

In summer regular attire for men consisted of only a breechclout, leggings, and moccasins. The breechclout extended about four to six feet long and one foot wide; a hair or rawhide belt held it in place. Before 1810 men of the northern plains may not have worn a breechclout, but perhaps reflecting European influences, by the 1830s all of them had adopted the practice. Most of the southern tribesmen wore two-piece moccasins with buckskin uppers sewed to a stiff sole of tanned bison hide. Many of the northern people, including the Assiniboins, Blackfeet, Crows, Lakotas, Gros Ventres, Omahas, Pawnees, Plains Cree, and Shoshonis, wore a one-piece, or soft-sole, moccasin. The buckskin leggings, attached to the belt, were close fitting and extended from the foot to the thigh. Some people, such as the Comanches, liked long fringes on the leggings, which were sometimes ornamented with beads, bits of metal, shells, or other items.[31] Increasing white contact encouraged the Plains Indians to adopt European-made items, such as metal bells, to their dress.

In winter regular attire for men stressed warmth. It included bison robes, knee-length boots of bison hide with the hair inside, and shirts made from skins of deer, pronghorns, or mountain sheep. Most northern people wore mittens and fur caps of beaver during the coldest days. However, except for ceremonial occasions, Crow men even in winter did not wear shirts.

Fancy dress was colorful and richly detailed. The Plains Indians used elaborate war bonnets, bison caps, and various headdresses as part of ceremonial regalia. They decorated the ceremonial war shirt. The Comanches fringed it around the collar and sleeves with buckskin strings often extending twelve or more inches in length. They ornamented the shirt, which extended below the top of the leggings, with beads, metal, and sometimes enemy scalps. George Catlin described the Mandan leader Mato Topi (Four Bears) who came to be painted in fancy regalia by the artist: "No tragedian," he wrote, "ever trod the stage, nor gladiator ever entered the Roman Forum, with more grace and manly dignity than did Mah-to-toh-pa enter the wigwam." His dress, "which was a very splendid one," Catlin noted, "was complete in all its parts, and consisted of a shirt or tunic, leggings, moccasins, head-dress, necklace, shield, bow and quiver, lance, tobacco-sack, and pipe; robe, belt, and knife; medicine-bag, tomahawk and war-club."[32] He wore a soft and supple ceremonial robe with brilliant colors.

Women's dress patterns also changed. On the southern plains women wore a poncho and a short wrap-around skirt during the early period, a style not unlike that used by women in Mexico. Later they adopted dress designs that more nearly resembled styles worn by Anglo women.

Personal adornment varied. The Plains Indians wore necklaces, earrings, gorgets, and a variety of other articles, some indicative of status. Tonkawa men wore ornaments in their hair, earrings, and necklaces of shell, bone, and feathers. Lipan warriors pierced the left ear with from six to eight holes, the right with one or more. On dress occasions they wore earrings in all the perforations. Women also used earrings. Nearly all men plucked out their beards and eyebrows, laboriously spending many spare moments at the task. Body and face paint, with red pigments being perhaps the most usual, were common. Tonkawa men lavishly painted themselves and their horses yellow, red, green, and black. According to a contemporary observer, Tonkawa women painted "black stripes on their mouth, nose, back, and breast. On the breast the stripes were painted in concentric circles from the nipple to the base of each breast."[33] Being personal possessions, individual facial designs held significance, and others did not copy them without permission.[34]

Although not common, tattooing was far from rare. The Tonkawas, Wichitas, southern Siouans, Hidatsas, Crows, Comanches, Plains Cree, and Lakotas used tattoos, with the Tonkawas and Wichitas carrying the practice to high levels. Tonkawa males heavily tattooed their bodies; Wichita men and women tattooed both their faces and bodies. By having his pubescent daughter tattooed, an Omaha man might enjoy prestige for both himself and his child; the man's family placed a tattoo in the center of the young woman's forehead and another on her chest. The Osages tattooed both sexes, but only after a warrior gained the privilege by a deed of valor. Tattooing by the Plains Cree included only the space between the lips and chin for women, but for men it covered the arms and chest.[35]

Hair styles displayed considerable differences. Many Plains Indians believed that their hair related to their soul, and accordingly most of them treated and groomed it with special care. For both men and women a favorite style had them parting their hair in the middle and letting it flow along both sides of their head. But for men styles varied and changed over time by imitation of European or other alien fashions. In early days Crow men divided their hair in two parts and let it fall loosely down the back and sides of the face. Sometimes it extended to the ground. Later they adopted braids. Some of the Crows adopted a high pompadour effect. In early days Kiowa warriors cut their hair short on the right side to show off their various ear ornaments. The hair on the left they grew long, tying or wrapping it to hold it in place. Lipan men cut their hair on the left side even with the top of the ear, but they allowed the hair on the right side to grow long, sometimes almost reaching the ground. However, they folded up and tied the long hair in such a way that it seldom fell below the shoulders. Tonkawa men parted their hair and wore two braids, but Blackfeet men preferred three braids. Most people of the plains grew their hair to the greatest length possible, letting it fall over their shoulders.[36]

For men at least two distinctive hair practices existed. In one, some Pawnees, Lakotas, Otos, Missouris, and others adopted the practice of closely shaving their hair on either side of their head, leaving only a central ridge of hair standing. To the ridge some men added a headdress called a roach, made of deer tail hair, porcupine hair, and horse hair. Later various societies of other tribes adopted the roaching of hair as a ceremonial badge. In another distinctive practice, young men from a number of groups trained a forelock of hair on the crown. Omaha men separated the forelock and kept it distinct and braided; they tied emblems of war honors to it. Lakota men lengthened it by attaching to it a small string of beads.[37]

In a common female style, women let the hair grow long, parted it in the middle from the forehead to the nape of the neck, and painted the parting line red. They plaited it in two braids, or, allowing it to hang free, secured it with a head band. Lakotas, as well as other plains women, sometimes artifically lengthened the braids by intertwining extra strands of human or horse hair. Some women decorated the braids by adding colored textiles or by wrapping them with mink or otter skin. Some women, of course, cut their hair short, particularly when in mourning for a dead relative.[38]

From hair designs and personal adornments to horses and firearms, white influences touched the Plains Indian world. Indeed, horses helped to create it, and not long afterwards Indian people of the plains became dependent upon white traders for weapons, clothing, and cooking utensils. European material items made life on the plains easier, but by the 1830s they had become so intrusive that even fancy-dress regalia contained machine-made items.

Clearly, the economies and material cultures of the Plains Indians were variegated and full of growth. They combined older items of bone, stone, wood, and horn with European trade goods. Although they shortened the hours spent at cooking or sewing or chopping, the manufactured products made the plains people increasingly dependent upon metal utensils, blankets, firearms, tobacco, liquor, and other foreign trade items. The nomadic people once placed emphasis upon bison hides for the manufacture of many of the significant pieces in a person's material inventory, but as white contact increased they turned more and more to processing bison hides to trade for the manufactured goods that they needed and the luxuries that they craved. For many horticultural groups the procurement of bison hides and beaver skins for trade came to dominate the economy, changing the villagers, though not completely, from sedentary farmers to seminomads who spent long periods in pursuit of game animals.

In their rich and dynamic material cultures, the Plains Indians displayed a buoyant optimism about life. Although essentially conservative peoples, they readily adapted strange, new items to their economies, enriching their lives and easing their daily routines. Recent and evolving, their societies continued to adapt and to change in response to new circumstances and borrowed traits. The Plains Indians displayed much of the same optimism and evolutionary status in their social organization.

5 : SOCIAL ORGANIZATION

The Plains Indians possessed varied societies and social organizations. Marriage conventions, kinship structures, nonkinship sodalities, social customs, and sociopolitical units differed slightly from tribe to tribe. In addition, meaningful contrasts sometimes existed between the largely clan-organized semisedentary horticultural peoples and the mainly band-organized nomadic hunting groups.

The diverse sociopolitical organizations grew from a combination of precontact experiences, adaptation to the plains, and adjustment to the arrival of European-based institutions. The horticultural village dwellers, in the area long before white contact, developed relatively complex politics and tended toward social stratification with marked prestige differences among tribal members. The nomadic peoples possessed more egalitarian societies. Complex sociopolitical controls arose among them only in summer, when, with populations experiencing higher densities, tighter restraints became necessary. For most of the year their small scattered populations required fewer social and political controls.

During most of the year, several nomadic families lived together as a band—a confederation of local hunting families. They remained near enough geographically so that they could unite for defensive purposes and meet for social and ceremonial occasions. Although bands represented social, economic, and political units, band membership was fluid; people in one band likely had relatives in other bands. Not only could a family shift band affiliation, but also when band size became too large, a series of families broke away to form a new one. The members also created new bands when conflicts and factions reached such a proportion that fragmentation of the original group proved the only solution. Thus, band structure and names changed, sometimes often.

When the band united with other bands during the summer, the combined group became a functioning tribe. Tribal meetings, ceremonies, and communal bison hunts took place, thus renewing tribal identity. At times other than that of the summer encampment, nomadic peoples maintained their tribal identity through common language, traditions, histories, and nonkinship sodalities. Among the Blackfeet, Lipans, and Comanches, however, and to a lesser extent the Lakotas and Crows (plus the village-dwelling Pawnees), the tribal name represented as much a sociological designation as an organized group. For such peoples the major divisions, subgroups, villages, or moieties formed the largest sociopolitical unit.

Moieties, or halves, represented a sociopolitical organization in which a group split into two complementary units with separate systems of headmen and councils. The Crows possessed such dual organization, with one branch called the River (or Downstream) people and one the Mountain (or Upstream) people, but they lacked true moieties; in fact Dale Old Horn, a Crow scholar, argues for a third division—the Kicked in the Bellies. The Tonkawas and many of the semisedentary peoples, including the Iowas, Osages, Omahas, Poncas, and others, also split into two groups, each composed of a number of hereditary clans. Sometimes moiety peoples when playing games split according to moieties, when stopping while on a hunt camped in moiety clusters, or when engaging in tribal ceremonies sat in moiety arrangements. In some village groups one must marry outside his moiety, in others moieties had nothing to do with marriage.[1]

Social and political organization for semisedentary Siouan-speaking groups centered in villages and/or in clans—affiliated lineages descended from a common ancestor. Clan names might be traced back for generations, and heredity determined clan membership, which cut across village boundaries. Clan representatives, dominated by headmen from prominent lineages, made up councils that governed both the villages and the confederation of allied towns that comprised the tribe, or ethnic community.[2]

The clans, which also served as important economic units, did not have equal status. Some clans held responsibility for distinctive ceremonial or other tribal functions. Among the Omahas, for example, one clan kept the peace pipes, one took charge of sacred tents, and a certain subclan became the only group whose members could wear down in their hair. Each of the thirteen Mandan clans held responsibility for one variety of corn. In some village groups clans owned property, garden plots, lodges, and ritual bundles.[3]

Because most clans were quite large, not all families of a particular clan lived or traveled together. Although they might not know personally each member of their clan, people accepted such obligations as protecting a fellow clansman in battle or sharing the moral responsibility of another member's wrongdoings. Most of the Caddoan-speaking groups did not have clans but maintained bands and/or villages of related and unrelated lineages. Among these groups, families might own certain names, songs, and ceremonies they had received in dreams or visions.

Some village peoples, such as the Wichitas, Mandans, and Hidatsas, possessed matrilineal clans, and descent passed through females. Where women controlled production in the fields, matrilineal systems were common and expected. Others, such as the Omahas and their Dhegiha-speaking relatives along the lower Missouri, maintained patrilineal clans, and descent passed through males. Patrilineal systems, rather unexpected where women controlled production, may have developed with increased warfare, when men became important as defenders of the village. If, however, they had descended from patrilineal chiefdoms of Mississippian times (possibly Cahokia), such groups as the Omahas may have entered the plains with a patrilineal system already present.

Among the full-time bison hunters, where men controlled the herds and the hunt, loosely affiliated patrilineal descent systems existed, but with a difference. With a few exceptions, such as the Crows, Tonkawas, and Gros Ventres, the nomadic hunters were without clans.[4] Clans gave (and required) stability, but with their lives organized in large communities during the summer and small band-like groups in the winter, the nomadic peoples needed to be highly flexible. Bands split and reformed, and families went their own way, living for a time with the mother's relatives and then for a time with the father's relatives. As a result the full-time bison hunters adopted a bilateral system in which they traced descent through both sexes. Indeed, most Indian people of the plains became basically bilateral, and families of both parents took active roles in their children's lives.

Social organization never remained static, however. The experience of the Crows illustrates how people adapted to new circumstances on the plains. Crow kinship terms reflected typical matrilineal descent, but in behavior the Crows became typically bilateral; in response, their clan organization weakened. In the precontact period they had been horticultural village dwellers who associated with the clan-organized Hidatsas. With the acquisition of horses they struck out onto the open plains, where they became nomadic bison hunters and adopted a bilateral descent system, necessary perhaps to survive the northern winters.

Further indicating the dynamic nature of the Plains Indians, sociopolitical arrangements near the end of the period of their ascendency shifted slightly toward something akin to chiefdoms. Most societies organized as chiefdoms, such as the Chinook, Salish, Nootka, and other peoples of the Northwest Coast, maintained complex social and political structures in which rank became important. The chief served as the central authority figure, and, although he may have held little real political power, he represented the social and economic head of the community, particularly for the distribution of surplus food stuffs. Likewise, on the plains rank became important and toward the end of the era headmen, or "chiefs," came to have greater authority.

An explanation is needed. Before the appearance of Europeans, most people on the plains had basically subsistence-for-use economies. Everyone of the same sex and age did about the same work, and no ranking positions existed for aspiring individuals to seek. Not everyone was equal, but people of the same sex and age enjoyed roughly the same standing in society. After European contact, however, many tribal groups became commercially oriented, and the egalitarian nature of their societies changed. Among the Wichitas, for example, a modified class system based on wealth appeared, and a few families became wealthy and influential as a result of their trade advantages with the French from the east and Comanches from the west.[5] The Kiowas also shifted to a social hierarchy, one based on the acquisition of horses. They developed full-blown social classes related to their age-graded societies.

No true chiefdoms occurred, for band and tribal groups both remained basically democratic. In developments similar to chiefdom societies, however, wealth and rank on the plains became more important, ceremonies and social organizations became more intricate, and voluntary associations, such as nonkin sodalities, became more complex. Over time, wealth in horses and other goods allowed some families to gain more prominence than others and to control access to political office.

White traders, government agents, and later army officials aided the process. They preferred to deal with one individual as the group's principal spokesperson, a leader who thus received special recognition and respect. In time, certain of the more charismatic spokespersons might earn greater attention as prominent community leaders. Village, band, or tribal representatives who went to Washington, D.C., to visit the President (the "Great Chief") gained additional recognition for themselves, and they brought back medals, canes, and other symbols of their importance and position.

Such leaders came to be respected figure heads, or "chiefs." As time passed, loyalty to such a chief, especially a highly charismatic one, bound the group together, and the people participated in his activities. The respectability of the band or village now depended upon the celebrity of the chief, and thus the chief expected and got help and support from his followers. Sitting Bull and Crazy Horse of the Lakotas, Quanah of the Comanches, Black Kettle of the Cheyennes, and Washakie of the Shoshonis were such charismatic leaders who in the mid nineteenth century and afterward emerged as influencial chiefs identified closely with their band or tribal group.[6]

Clearly, then, although they belonged to a communal, family-oriented people, the Plains Indians were independent members of basically democratic societies. Plains Indian sociopolitical units had little formal structure, and political organization should perhaps be considered in terms of loosely associated confederacies bound together by a common language, tradition, and history.

Such tribal groups as the Lakotas, Comanches, and Blackfeet had several divisions or subgroups; others, such as the Tonkawas and many of the horticultural peoples, possessed only two independent subdivisions, or moieties.

Most smaller divisions—hunting bands among the nomads and farming villages among the horticulturalists—were autonomous under their own leaders: headmen and others who, having obtained their office by popular recognition, had only vague powers. They made most of the key decisions by mutual agreement, and if other people disagreed with the decision, the military societies might enforce them. Although a farming village roughly corresponded to a hunting band as an independent sociopolitical unit, many semisedentary peoples divided into villages, clans, moieties, and other units, but not bands (except when hunting bison).

On those occasions, usually in the summer, when several bands, or the entire ethnic group, came together, the Plains Indians celebrated. Everyone participated in games, gambling, and races on foot or horseback. They sought out old friends, gossiped, laughed, and told stories, and young people might seek marriage partners. Communal activities occurred as well, including tribal hunts, public festivals, spiritual ceremonies, and diplomatic councils.

Thus, social organization among Great Plains people became diverse. Such factors as population decline among the Mandans altered it, causing Robert H. Lowie to conclude that the Plains Indians presented an extraordinary diversity of social and political organization where "matrilineal and patrilineal descent, . . . tribal subdivisions approximating, but not quite attaining clan status, and completely loose band organizations are all found."[7]

Political leadership and authority also remained diverse, but a general pattern of egalitarianism prevailed. Headmen and other leaders (or chiefs) ruled only to the degree that they could get people to follow them. They could never speak for the whole group. No autocratic rulers existed, and in postcontact times, although the people assumed that headmen's sons—if they possessed the desired characteristics—would also become headmen, few hereditary leaders prevailed.[8]

Headmen usually came from respected families. "Your father was a chief, but you must not think of that," a Pawnee mother instructed her son. "Because he was a chief it does not follow that you will be one." She indicated to him that "it is not the man who stays in the lodge that becomes great; it is the man who works, who sweats, who is always tired from going on the warpath."[9]

Headmen obtained the position in a variety of ways, the most common of which came through successful warfare. A headman, however, could be a person of mature and respected judgment who had never distinguished himself as a warrior. He could be a man noted for his generosity or a man whose past actions stood above reproach and who fulfilled tribal ideals of male behavior. An informant from the Hunkpapa division of the Lakotas said that "chiefs were always poor men" because property distribution by gift giving became a prevalent way of maintaining the position. Although supported in his position by public acceptance, some groups removed, or "set aside" for a period of time, as chief (or headman) a person who grossly offended or broke a band or tribal custom or law or who did not maintain the varied obligations of his position, including even temper, sound judgment, concern for the welfare of the group, and generosity to the poor.[10]

Because they accepted as a basic principle the separation of civil and military leadership, most plains groups maintained two kinds of leaders: civil and war. Civil leaders were often past the age of active participation in warfare. When asked how they obtained the position, Comanche informants said they "just got that way."[11] Of course, prestige, honor, good deeds, success in the hunt, and other factors elevated a man to civil leader, or chief. His major responsibilities were holding the band or village together and protecting his people from attack. When he failed in those duties, he lost followers and prestige. The civil leader epitomized the ideals of wisdom, order, generosity, and peace.

War leaders came from among vigorous and popular younger men. Selected individually for each war or raiding party, they had no further function when the war or raid was complete. Thus, they held little responsibility except in time of war or during a raid, when their rule became nearly absolute. During hostilities they formulated the general tactics, designated the scouts, decided the camping places, ordered the expedition to turn back, made a truce with the enemy, or in other ways directed the fight. Many groups, however, recognized one individual as the principal war leader. He gained the position by leading successful war parties, by collecting war honors, and by gaining tribal respect for his military wisdom and leadership. War leaders epitomized the Plains Indian ideals of bravery, courage, strength, and fortitude.

Sometimes war leaders led the annual bison hunt. More often tribal groups appointed a warrior society, such as the Cheyenne Bow String society or one of the Lakota *akacita* (warrior society), to exercise authority. As tribal "police" (marshalls), usually appointed to the task for a year, they directed the hunt, demanded careful obedience to instructions, restrained misbehaving individuals, and meted out harsh punishment to anyone who might spoil the hunt by frightening the herd away or by not cooperating in the communal effort. During the hunt, the only period of peace when major decisions remained absolute, all groups functioned under a single authority.

Civil leaders governed through a loose council, dominated by a headman, who served as a sort of chairman, or by a principal leader. Although rarely getting formal recognition for his position, the headman often enjoyed genuine attention given to his advice and general subordination to his influence. Other leaders functioned in an advisory capacity.

The council acted as a unit, going about its business with deliberation. Its unanimous decisions, which reflected public opinion, were neither arbitrary nor authoritarian, for the council had only its prestige and influence to back its decisions. It governed by persuasion and its members' natural gifts of leadership, wisdom, and intelligence. People often regarded decisions of the council as final, but to ensure acceptance council members sought support from the military societies. Each such society maintained several leaders, also known as headmen, who sometimes represented their groups when serious tribal matters came under discussion among council members. Decisions about external affairs—intertribal wars or peace—proved most effective when council members obtained the concurrence of the military societies.

Council members among the Comanches conducted their meetings in a formal and courteous manner, maintaining a high degree of parliamentary decorum. After all of them had assembled, they sat in silence for a few moments while they smoked the council pipe, passing it according to tribal custom from one member to another clockwise around the circle. Then one of the older men arose to introduce the subject at issue. A brief silence followed as the councilors considered the remarks before a second speaker began. The council, starting with older men, gave each member an opportunity to speak, but often only a small minority of them spoke, and some limited their utterances to a few words to indicate their assent.[12]

The council considered each question with care. If the issue was a difficult one, it took considerable time to reach a decision, as it wanted a consensus. But no matter how vociferous the debate or how sharply opinion differed, no man interrupted the speaker, who was entitled to be heard with respect and dignity. At a difficult Comanche meeting in 1843, after everyone else had spoken, the headman Pahayuco, whose turn had come, remained silent. No one moved or spoke for four hours while he pondered the matter.[13]

Tribal councils considered many issues. They acted to promote the general welfare and protect the common interests of their people. They treated such problems as undertaking war, making peace, seeking alliances, settling intertribal conflicts, and selecting the time and place for the annual Sun Dance or bison hunt. But with little formal organization, tribal councils rarely assembled. The Comanches, for example, had no tribal council, and the entire confederation came together only once—in 1874 when it held a Sun Dance. Among the Cheyennes, where it held considerable respect, the tribal council—the Council of 44, which contained four leaders from each band and four headmen selected at large—met only once a year.

The band and village councils, accordingly, served more often. In populous groups, such as the Oglala and Brule Lakotas, or in confederacies, such as the Blackfeet and Comanches, they took over many functions that smaller groups, such as the Kiowas and Cheyennes, reserved for tribal meetings. They deliberated on such questions as those of moving camp, disposition of spoils belonging to the group, internal conflicts of significant proportions, and the regulation of trade with outsiders. With few exceptions, therefore, self-governing villages and bands represented the supreme political unit.

Leadership and authority also extended to shamans, or "medicine men" as white people called them, the holy men of the band and village groups. Shamans, who could be men or postmenopausal women, were healers, priests, and slight-of-hand magicians. Among the Comanches shamans also practiced witchcraft and sorcery. Highly successful in experiencing visions (a personal communication through a trance or dream with the spirit world), shamans gained reputations as having exceptional abilities for dealing with the spirits. Among some groups, however, such as the Lakotas, a distinction existed between shamans who served mainly as healers ("medicine men") and shamans who communicated with the spirits. Master shamans surrounded themselves with apprentices and trained them in the art and mysteries of healing, magical tricks, and vision seeking.

People of lofty intelligence with strong and persuasive personalities, shamans held considerable influence. Sitting Bull, the great Hunkpapa *Wichasha Wakan* (or holy man), in addition to serving as civil and war leader, for example, used his enormous prestige and the position of his office to dominate tribal affairs.[14] Although their functions stood largely outside of politics, shamans, as admired individuals with mysterious powers, might use their skills to foretell the future, cast love spells, find lost objects, ensure a successful hunt, or bring about good weather. Individuals, small war parties, and on occasion the entire band all sought aid or guidance from shamans.[15] They became important and respected leaders—at least until a vision about some crucial matter failed, whereupon they might be ridiculed and threatened for their failure.

Similar to shamans were members of a priestlike group. Shamans, some have suggested, acquired their positions through visions and learned their craft through individual experience. Priests, by contrast, underwent long and detailed preparation to convince the people of their powers. Moreover, because they used the drama of dance, music, song, masks, and prayer, priests received training that required coordination with others, especially in the complex matters of tribal ritual. During the long apprenticeship, they memorized all the details, sacred songs, and ritual procedures of the various tribal ceremonies. Only well-trained individuals, for instance, could supervise such elaborate festivals as the Pawnee Morning Star ceremony, the

Cheyenne Arrow Renewal ceremony, the Lakota Sun Dance, or the Mandan Okipa ceremony.[16]

In some communities the shamans and priests might be the same individuals. However, priests were more common in larger societies, usually horticultural, while shamans existed in hunting bands. The Pawnees had a formalized and hereditary priesthood in which the position passed through the maternal line. In the nomadic groups shamans became active among bands in the winter, while priests conducted the Sun Dance and other complex rituals in the summer.[17]

In the absence of written law, leaders exercised social control through established customs, public opinion, and respected taboos. The plains people relied on recollections of similar cases and the precedent such cases established. In addition, clear legal concepts and strong moral codes existed. Among the Cheyennes, for example, people considered the murder of a fellow tribesman a major transgression, requiring the tribe to clean its Sacred Arrows and causing the murderer's band to move its camp from the unholy place. The Cheyennes denied the guilty person participation in tribal activities for up to ten years. Crow and Lakota people, however, considered murder a private affair and encouraged the accused's family to offer payment to the victim's family.[18]

Public opinion helped to regulate social norms. Sensitive to gossip that might affect their social standing, Plains Indians avoided unpopular activity. Among the Blackfeet a thief, or anyone who made himself or herself a major nuisance, faced biting ridicule and scornful laughter. Such a person might leave the camp or village in self-exile. In some communities a person held up to general ridicule would burn with shame and embarrassment. Joking relatives, called *iwatkusua* among the Crows, were cousins or in some groups brothers- and sisters-in-law who ridiculed and teased one another's poor taste, laziness, ineptitude, or other faults. The purpose was to improve one's social behavior.[19]

Tribal taboos also played a role in social control. They kept and enforced proper behavior, established custom and procedure, and in some cases played a role in punishment. Band and tribal leaders, as well as parents, used taboos to establish and maintain moral codes, ethical standards, political control, and social organization.

Nonkinship sodalities formed a significant part of plains social organization. Most remained voluntary associations in which both men and women participated, but some nonvoluntary age-graded societies existed. They fulfilled a variety of needs and served various purposes. They crossed family, clan, band, and village affiliations, provided tribal unity, and promoted intratribal harmony and good feeling. Because the nomadic peoples broke into small units each winter, however, formal activity in their fraternal organizations occurred only in the summer months, when some of the clubs maintained their own lodges, where members could eat, lounge, sleep, dance, and enjoy themselves in relaxed association with other members.[20]

Nonkin sodalities included military associations, guild and craft groups, feast and dance societies, and dream clubs. Men maintained more such groups than women. Women, who formed auxiliary units to many male organizations, had their own clubs. Among the Kiowas there occurred an association known as Old Women to whom warriors went to seek council and prayers both before and after their raids against an enemy. The Pawnees maintained an association of single women and widows who wore shabby dress and tortured prisoners. The horticultural groups of the upper Missouri had several female societies, many of which carried out important tribal ceremonies; Mandan Goose Society members, for example, performed special rituals to encourage the corn to grow. In many plains groups the female clubs existed as guildlike associations of skilled quill and beadworkers; Cheyenne women, for instance, could join a society of tipi decorators.[21] In some communities women joined military societies with their husbands.

Nonkinship sodalities for men also varied. Old men's lodges, military fraternities, and dream societies existed. Old men's lodges, called "headmen's" societies among the Lakotas, comprised men past the age of active warfare (about forty years) who had distinguished themselves in the past. The Oglalas maintained at least four such groups. They crystallized public opinion and may have had an impact on community morals and values.

Military fraternities were numerous. The Hidatsas, at least before smallpox reduced their population, had ten of them. The Mandans counted eight and the Cheyennes claimed six, the most famous of which became the Crazy Dogs of the Northern Cheyennes and the Dog Soldiers of the Southern Cheyennes. The Dog Soldiers, who formed their own distinct band, developed at a date later than most of the others. The Plains Cree, on the other hand, maintained only one military society per band, and all age-eligible men belonged. The Comanches had no special military groups.

Members of military societies shared common battle experiences and their own secrets, dress, regalia, and ceremonies. They defended the community and policed tribal hunts, village encampments, camp moves, and certain tribal ceremonies, such as the Sun Dance. Some military societies selected beautiful young women as fraternal sweethearts or mascots.[22]

Several tribal communities made important distinctions between military fraternities. For the Oglalas, one can distinguish between the *akicita* war societies and other soldier groups. All were military fraternities, but more mature men composed the *akicitas,* and from among the *akicitas* the people chose their annual camp marshalls, or police. The Braves, for example, an *akicita* group, became the strongest of the Oglala soldier societies, and it served more often than others as the camp marshalls. Its organization included two leaders, two warbonnet wearers, four lance bearers, several other officers, and perhaps thirty or forty additional members. Its leaders vowed never to turn in fighting. In battle the bonnet wearers fastened themselves to the ground with a small stake and a sash and, once in the position, remained there until the war party drove the enemy away or until another member of the society released them. The Stong Hearts of the Hunkpapas became a similar group, and the Yanktons, Yanktonais, and Santees all had variant forms of the Braves and the Strong Hearts.[23]

Similar fraternities existed among the Arikaras, Assiniboins, Cheyennes, Crows, Kiowas, and Pawnees. To a lesser degree the Sarsis, some Shoshonis, and the southern Siouan-speaking groups formed such associations, although among the latter peoples societies of strictly sacred order eclipsed them. Among the Plains Cree each band held only one dominant soldier society.[24]

Perhaps the most characteristic of the plains military fraternities was the Kiowas' *Kaitsenko* (Red Dogs, or Society of the Ten Bravest). Aristocratic and exclusive, members of the *Kaitsenko* society pledged to fight every battle through to victory. As such, their society mirrored the Braves and the Strong Hearts of the Lakotas. Of the ten members, three wore sashes of red cloth, six wore red elkskin sashes, and the leader wore a broad black elkskin sash that trailed from his neck to the ground. In a fight to the end, the leader pinned himself in position with a ceremonial arrow through his sash and remained at his spot until victory or, if the cause was lost, until a fellow member of the society freed him. Satank (Sitting Bear), an old but courageous *Kaitsenko* leader, while enroute to a Texas prison in 1871, determined to die rather than face a life in confinement. Although bound in a wagon and under protective watch, he escaped from handcuffs, stabbed a guard, screamed his war cry, seized a carbine and ammunition, and worked feverishly to load the gun as soldiers emptied their rifles into him.[25]

Some military fraternities were age graded, and thus membership could not be voluntary. The Arapahos, Blackfeet, Gros Ventres, Hidatsas, Kiowas, and Mandans had age-group organizations. Such fraternities tended to be more elaborate and more structured than comparable groups among peoples without age-group determination. Members of each society remained very close to the same age, and the societies ranked in successive order based on ages of their members.

Among the Mandan societies, for example, the Buffalo Bulls, composed of older males, was the highest. One gained membership in the society through invitation, and a man needed to prove his abilities through good deeds and good character. In addition, he had to have been a member of each age-graded fraternity leading to the Buffalo Bull group at the top. Aspirants purchased membership in each society from a current member, who then bought his way into the next higher group. Membership in each successive society became more expensive than the previous, and only a few men reached the top. After repeated smallpox epidemics, the Mandan system broke down.[26]

Dream societies represented yet another type of men's organizations. Although they shared many of the qualities of the military fraternities, their functions extended beyond fighting. Dreams and visions determined membership. The Lakotas, for example, had societies of deer dreamers, bear dreamers, buffalo dreamers, and elk dreamers, with membership restricted to those men who had experienced the same animal in their dreams. The Elk Dreamers society conducted ceremonies relating to matters of love and sexuality. Among the Crows, and to a lesser extent among Blackfeet and Sarsi peoples, tobacco dreamers formed a society devoted to rituals associated with the cultivation of the tribe's sacred tobacco plant.

Perhaps the most dramatic dream societies were the Cheyenne *hohnuhk'e* and the Lakota *heyoka* organizations. These were groups of sacred clowns known as contraries, men and, very rarely, women who did the reverse of what was accepted as normal. They shivered from cold on a hot summer day, rode their horses while facing the tail, held their bows in a reverse position, and otherwise acted in a clowning manner that delighted the people and provided comic relief.[27] "One of their most spectacular feats," according to an eyewitness, had them putting their "arms in boiling water . . . [and] complaining that it is cold," an ordeal they performed by smearing their arms with chewed leaves of the mallow plant.[28] Contraries, called Crazy Dogs among the Arapahos and Crows, were also brave warriors who fought with uncommon valor and even recklessness, sometimes lived alone and away from the camp, wore ragged clothes, and took up their responsibilities after a dream involving thunder and lightning. Members of the community regarded them with awe and admiration; valued their service; and praised their fighting skills, their public entertainment, and their difficult role in society.

Dream societies and other sodalities changed, sometimes dramatically, in response to high mortality rates from repeated disease epidemics. In fact, disease epidemics nearly destroyed some Indian groups. The Mandans almost completely disappeared. The Blackfeet also suffered. More than half of the Piegan population died in a smallpox epidemic in 1781. In an 1837 epidemic two thirds of the six thousand Blackfeet people died, including large numbers of Bloods, Piegans, and Small Robes. Smallpox epidemics among Blackfeet people occurred in the years 1781, 1837–38, 1849–50, and 1869–70. Scarlet fever in 1837 and measles in 1864–65 also reduced the Blackfeet population.[29]

The 1869 smallpox plague resulted in disaster. Perhaps a Piegan who had stolen an infected blanket from a Missouri riverboat unknowingly brought the disease to his people. Through the long winter of 1869–70 the Siksikas, Bloods, Piegans, and Sarsis abandoned tipis, with whole families dying in blizzards. Proud young men killed themselves to escape the swelling, the foul odor, the delirium, and the disfigurement caused by the disease. Older men, rather than watch their families suffer through the degrading effects of the pox, sometimes murdered their wives and children before killing themselves. At times the delirium seized whole villages, with warriors running into icy rivers or making suicidal attacks on enemy bands or forts of area fur traders. When the epidemic subsided in the spring of 1870, the Piegans counted over one thousand dead, the Siksikas and Bloods more than six hundred each. Among those dead, of course, were many important leaders, headmen, and wise councilors.

A cholera epidemic in 1849, carried along the Oregon Trail by California-bound gold seekers, caused the death of an estimated twelve hundred Pawnees. Fearful of the dreaded disease, the Pawnees fled in all directions, refusing to bury their dead. A government surveyor, coming up the Platte River in June of the same year, reported dead and dying people in most of the Lakota villages of the valley. The Comanches, who contracted the disease from gold seekers en route to California through Texas, suffered greater death from cholera than from smallpox, a disease that struck them in 1816, 1839–40, and 1861–62.[30]

Alcohol also affected Indian lives. In the nineteenth century the use of spirituous liquors—rum and whiskey the most common—produced a whole series social ills, but it did not result in social breakdown. For the Plains Indians, consumption of alcohol was usually a social affair connected to trade or diplomacy—a preliminary to bargaining—rather than a solitary event, and the participants often continued until the supply disappeared. People of the plains attached little stigma to excessive drinking or to acts committed while intoxicated.[31] Not all Indian people drank, of course, and some groups, such as the Crows, Comanches, and Pawnees, were once known to have abstained from alcohol.[32]

Over the years white traders came to produce a cheap, rotgut whiskey. They obtained it from distilleries in St. Louis and then mixed it with various ingredients. Some traders used red ink for color, some doctored it with molasses to make it resemble rum, and some added bitters or cheap, all-purpose painkillers and patent medicines. One of many special mixtures contained water and raw alcohol at three parts to one, chewing tobacco, ginger, and tea leaves for color. No wonder alcohol sometimes resulted in shock, poisoning, or serious illness.[33]

The high death rates from European diseases resulted in profound changes in family relationships, tribal life, and contact with other peoples. Family and band units suffered, particularly in such cooperative economic endeavors as hunting, trading, and farming. Their ability to compete successfully with other groups declined. In addition, the balance of power among tribal communities shifted, resulting in a realignment of tribal boundaries and allegiances. The loss of manpower in terms of warriors reduced the ability of some groups, such as the Assiniboins, Pawnees, and Poncas, to defend themselves, their villages, and their crops. Over time many semisedentary peoples turned to whites for protection against the growing power of such groups as the Lakotas on the northern plains and the Comanches on the southern plains. Sometimes intertribal trading systems broke down. Moreover, with family relationships (the key to collective tribal life) broken, traditional patterns in the division of labor were disrupted, further transforming societies on the plains.[34]

Clearly, the Plains Indians for all their significant homogeneity displayed various degrees of cultural plurality. Many of their customs were old, dating from a time before they reached the plains. Many others, however, developed on the plains and after white contact. Like people everywhere, the Plains Indians enjoyed constantly evolving rather than static societies that changed over time, as is demonstrated in their social conventions and the great circle of human life.

6 : SOCIETY AND
SOCIAL CONVENTIONS

The Plains Indians, although their societies and social organizations varied from plains to prairies, north to south, and one ethnic group to another, exhibited, as we have seen, significant homogeneity in lifestyles. Many exceptions existed, of course, and changes occurred, for Indian societies on the plains lived in a state of constant flux.

A Plains Indian male usually became a joyous warrior in battle, a devoted parent at home, and a reliable provider in the hunt. War, often characterized by horse stealing and small, quick raids, was the principal occupation of the men; they conducted it for economic gain, for expanding tribal territory, and for personal honor and glory. In camp men attended council meetings, fashioned arrows, and prepared knives and bows for future use. They enjoyed a good smoke and around the fire related tales of a successful hunt or raid.

In tribal society women were equal participants with men. They took charge of the tipi, prepared the meals, worked the fields, and fashioned the clothing. They possessed excellent hide-dressing skills and made fine bead and porcupine-quill embroidery. Cheyenne people admired women for such qualities as responsibility, modesty in demeanor and attitude, skill in creating community, and steadfastness in maintaining tribal ideals and values. A Cheyenne woman, for example, advised her niece about courtship: "It is silly to exchange too many glances and smiles.... [Your suitor] will think you are too easy and immoral.... You must never consent to marry your suitor the first time he asks."[1]

Women held considerable influence. On occasion they sat on tribal councils, and sometimes they determined which men rose to power. With men frequently away to hunt or raid, women often dominated camp life and daily decision making. Some women, such as Pretty Shield of the Crows and Sanapia of the Comanches, became healers, and some of them, such as Woman Chief of the Crows and Running Eagle of the Blackfeet, became warriors. Moreover, women handled with greater self-confidence than men the changes that occurred within their evolving plains cultures. Around the campfire, women related tales of child raising, herb gathering, and bead working, and they enjoyed many rights that their husbands had to respect.[2]

Adults welcomed the arrival of children, especially male children, treated them well, and gave them much attention. Children seldom received physical punishment.[3] In explaining what a young man's father had once said about discipline for children, Lone Wolf, a Blackfeet, quoted him as saying "among [our] people, children were never punished by striking them. . . . kind words and good examples were much better."[4]

Play and education of young people were combined. As a significant gender division of labor existed, boys learned to be hunters and warriors by engaging in make-believe bison hunts and sham battles. As the boys grew older, the games grew progressively rough. "Some boys got badly hurt," said Iron Shell, a Lakota, "but afterwards we would talk and laugh about it. Very seldom did any fellows get angry."[5]

But if, as happened among the Crows and Blackfeet, a father had a strong and close relationship with a favorite daughter, the girl could go with him on hunting trips or on a raid. She might thus become proficient in male activities, and clearly a few women became noted warriors and leaders.

Most girls, however, played with dolls, kept house, and learned the skills of cooking and sewing. They played kickball, seeing how many times they could kick a ball of pronghorn hair covered with leather without letting it fall to the ground, and other games that were exciting but less dangerous than those of boys. As they grew older they remained closer to their own lodges and ventured out only when in company of others.

Children also received instruction in tribal histories, myths, legends, and values. Such instruction occurred at different times but often around an evening campfire; with children listening, an adult would describe an important clan, band, or tribal tradition. The next evening a young person might be expected to repeat the oral lesson.

Proud, mystical, and spontaneous, the Plains Indians were tall people (Comanches and Tonkawas excepted), with six-footers common in the north, long-legged, well-built, and muscular. Touch the Clouds, a Lakota, stood nearly seven feet tall, and the Osage people had men of equal height. Robust and usually healthy, plains people were seldom bald or gray and had little facial hair, often plucking out that which they had. They had black or brown eyes, with a slight tendency toward epicanthic fold in children, and black, straight hair. Their skin color was dark brown, with some copper-colored complexions, although the Blackfeet and Mandans were lighter. Facial features varied somewhat: the Blackfeet, Plains Cree, and Assiniboin people, for example, had rounded faces with delicate features; the Lakotas had long faces and prominent noses; the Pawnees had heavy, massive faces;

the Comanches had aquiline noses, thin lips, and brown eyes. Their heads also differed in shape. Some people, such as the Plains Cree, Lakotas, Blackfeet, Cheyennes, Arapahos, and Pawnees, had long, narrow skulls (dolichocephalic). Others, such as the Comanches, Osages, Wichitas, and Kiowas, had short, broad or round skulls (brachycephalic).[6]

Customs associated with birth, growing up, adulthood, and death—the life cycle—demonstrate how in face of constant change Indian societies lived, and enjoyed life, on the Great Plains. Always the basic social unit, the family was both nuclear (father, mother, children) and extended (father, mother, children, grandparents, unmarried aunts, uncles, and other relatives by blood or marriage). Extended families—*tiyospe,* the Lakotas called them—often lived and camped together, providing economic support and social interaction of all kinds.

Most nuclear families were small. Seldom did they contain more than three or four younger unmarried children, including perhaps an adopted child. Because women nursed their children as long as four years and often abstained from sexual relations during the period, children were born three to five years apart. Luther Standing Bear, a Lakota, noted that "not till a child was five or six years of age did the parents allow themselves another offspring." Thus, as he indicated, "Lakota families were not large, four or five children being the rule."[7]

Women in some communities may have used a drug to prevent pregnancy, but contraceptives were unknown to most Plains Indians. Accidental abortion, perhaps from hard, physical labor and constant horseback riding, and a high mortality rate among children also account for small nuclear families, and some women, most often Comanches, practiced birth control and abortion. A pregnant female on the plains could not carry an infant on long treks, nor could she nurse two children; thus, birth spacing became essential. For the horticultural communities data on birth control remains less well known, but women in settled villages probably had less need to spread out childbirth.[8]

The birth of a child was a joyous event. In some groups adults bathed and rubbed the newborn with warm buffalo cow fat. In others they did not bathe the infant but dried it with dry wood or moss. Most people preserved the umbilical cord, placing it in a decorated skin bag shaped like a lizard or turtle—creatures who symbolized long life. Infants wore the bag around their neck, or parents placed it in a tree or fastened it to the cradle board, a decorated affair of wood and hide designed to hold babies and protect them from injury. Small babies spent most of their first year carried on their mother's back, wrapped in a rabbit skin or enfolded within a blanket, and secured in the cradleboard. Dry absorbent plants, such as the down from cattails, and mosses served as diapers.

Soon after the child's birth, a person, usually of the same sex, gave the baby a name. Bestowed at a special feast given by the parents, the infant kept the name until old enough to acquire a new one. The name giver, who might be a father, mother, uncle, aunt, respected warrior, or holy man, derived the name from an episode or a character in the name giver's life. Girls often, but not always, received names that contained the word "woman." Rendered in English the names become Corn Woman or Buffalo Bird Woman, for example, but also Pretty Shield. Boys often received names associated with an animal with a descriptive word or phrase attached. In English the names become White Wolf, Iron Bull, and Sitting Bear. Children might also receive nicknames. Because they believed that names had special power, after serious illness or significant ill fortune in a child's life, people changed the name. A person might also acquire a new name after a significant accomplishment. Blackfeet people changed their names often, sometimes yearly.[9]

The nursing period varied in length. Although it extended up to four or five years, among Plains Cree women and most others on the plains it was not so long. Nowhere did it end before the child reached two years of age.[10]

From the very first days the Plains Indians did not permit their children to cry, for a group hiding from its enemies could be given away by a crying child. To prevent crying, parents satisfied the child's needs or rocked and cuddled the child until his or her desires ceased. A Cheyenne or Lakota mother gently pinched a baby's nostrils to stifle cries, and among some people the parents gently dropped water into the nostrils until the baby quit.

Although children were usually well behaved, boys sometimes became spoiled. Parents seldom punished children and rarely struck them or screamed at them. They did not lack for discipline, guidance, or training, however, and restraints existed. To discipline an ill-behaved child of two or three, parents might dash it with water or frighten it with warnings of the "bogyman," particularly owls or coyotes. In later years the white man became the favorite bogyman; Black Elk, a Lakota, remembered his mother's warnings: "If you are not good the Wasichus [whites] will get you."[11]

Most parents catered to and indulged their children. Elders asked, rather than told, children to do something, and they delivered ponderous lectures on proper behavior, polite etiquette, and ancestral values.[12] For praiseworthy conduct parents often rewarded a child with words of commendation or a delicious tidbit of food. Wise to the ways of building self-importance and confidence, the Plains Indians always boasted of their children's deeds and often held feasts in their honor. "At age of three," writes First Boy, an Assiniboin, "I killed a snow bird with a long stick, and my grandmother gave a big feast on account of it." In honor of his having killed a gray wolf when thirteen, First Boy's family distributed goods to the poor.[13] "The feast and give-away," writes Severt Young Bear, a Lakota, "is one of the family traditions that teaches your child respect and honor."[14]

Young people spent much of their time with grandparents, who typically displayed a great deal of affection for them. Indeed, in many tribal communities, such as the Arapahos, Gros Ventres, Blackfeet, and Lakota, parents gave their young child to an older couple, usually grandparents, to raise. The grandparents not only took care of the children but also prepared and cooked the meals and handled the household chores. Uncles and aunts, especially in clan-organized societies, also doted over the youth, and they accepted part of the responsibility for their training. An uncle or a grandfather, for example, might take a boy on his first hunting trip. An aunt or a grandmother might instruct a girl in beadwork and quilling or in the crucial skill of hide dressing. In any case, childhood remained a happy period, and Plains Indian children seldom spent time alone.

Genuine affection and mutual helpfulness was common among children. An older boy protected and aided his younger siblings, in some groups accepting the same responsibilities toward them as the father. Sisters often took care of their younger brothers. They might make moccasins for their brothers or otherwise aid them. Plenty of rivalry existed too. Sisters sometimes deeply resented the obvious favoritism shown their brothers, and older sisters might pummel their younger brothers. Captive children might also receive harsh treatment from older boys or girls and even from adults; once accepted into the group, however, their relationship improved. Among the Lakotas brother-and-sister relationships between infancy and marriage approached complete avoidance. Boys and girls did not play together after infancy, and brothers and sisters never joked in one another's presence. Even among groups without the elaborate avoidance relationship, social taboos after a boy or girl reached puberty often dictated that brothers and sisters no longer played or chatted together.[15]

At puberty many people encouraged boys to seek a vision. To gain the vision, which he needed to become a man, a boy faced an ordeal of loneliness, hunger, and thirst. Perhaps a relative or a holy man helped him. Taking great care to follow tribal rituals that came full of symbolic meaning, the boy first cleansed himself in a sweat lodge, and then his helper guided him to a lonely and secluded place on top of a hill but near a tree or rock against which the boy could lean when he became weak. Or in some groups the boy entered a "vision pit," a hole dug into the ground.

The boy remained alone in his secluded spot on the hilltop or huddled in the vision pit. With few clothes and without food or water, he waited for his vision to come to him. As the hours and then days passed, he grew faint from hunger and thirst. He slept, dreamed, awoke, and hallucinated until he could hardly distinguish among them, and perhaps then his mind opened to the voices and whispers of the spirits. After three or four long days and nights, when the boy had experienced his dream or vision, the helper brought him back to camp, fed him, and helped him interpret dreams whose meanings might not be clear. Not all peoples encouraged the vision quest at such an early date, and many of them did not consider it a special initiation into manhood.

Crazy Horse (Tasunke Witko), the great Oglala leader, went on his first vision quest when he was twelve years old. He had witnessed the death of Chief Conquering Bear in 1854 when white soldiers fired on Indian people at Conquering Bear's village near Fort Laramie. Deeply moved by the incident, Curly, as he then called himself, left the camp for a lonely spot in the hills. He fasted, and to stay awake he put stones between his toes, walked around, sang songs, and called upon the spirits to visit him. On the third day he fell faint. In his dream he saw lightning on his face and marks of hailstones on his body. A small red-backed hawk flew over his head. Later, as an adult, the lightning and hailstone marks became his symbols and the red-backed hawk his spiritual helper.

Among some peoples, notably the Plains Cree and Lakota, girls at puberty underwent a lonely vigil. During her first menses, elders secluded the girl in a special hut away from camp. They restricted her activities because at this time, they believed, she exuded danger to humans, animals, and sacred objects. The restriction lasted only a few days, but during that time the girl left the hut only at night and in the company of her mother or another older woman, who also provided the girl with food and water. The girl spent her time practicing craftwork and listening to tales of older women who visited her to instruct her on the proper behavior of young women.[16]

After that experience the young woman's father gave her a public ceremony—usually a feast in her honor. The parents gave her new, beautiful clothes and gifts. She paraded around the camp while her elder relatives made speeches about what a fine young woman she had become. The relatives praised her skill in sewing and tanning and in general demonstrated to prospective suitors that she would make an excellent wife. Little Prairie, an Arapaho woman, remembered her own experience in the ceremony as "one of the proudest moments in my young life."

Many opportunities for romance occurred. A girl's first chore each morning was to fetch water, and the path to the stream became a good place to meet a special young man. Or sweethearts could meet as the girl gathered firewood. Among the Cheyennes, girls, often in groups, dug wild turnips and gathered berries. When they returned with their loads, the girls might find their path barred by young men. In such cases Cheyenne youth played the "come and try to take our turnips away" game. Girls laid the turnips on the ground and defended them by pelting the boys with clumps of earth, sticks of dry wood, or buffalo chips. A girl might make it easy for a young man to "count coup" upon a load of turnips, thereby suggesting a friendly relationship. In more serious relationships young men used flutes, or flageolets, to play love songs for the young women they admired.

Well-defined rules and customs applied to courtship and romance. They varied from group to group, but a clear double standard prevailed: elders watched over the behavior of young women, but they rather expected a young man to philander. Feminine chastity, especially among the Cheyennes, was highly prized, for a suitor would not offer many horses to a girl with a reputation of sexual license. A Cheyenne woman warned her niece that when a suitor "comes at night do not let him stay too long, but ask him please to go. If you let him stay till he is ready to go he will think you love him and will surely think less of you. You must always be sure to take great care to tie the hide [chastity belt]."[17]

In choosing husbands, a young woman sought a strong man who was a good hunter and a courageous warrior, someone who would provide hides, horses, and plenty of meat as well as family protection.[18] A young man looked for a modest, virtuous woman who was skilled in tanning and beading. He wanted not only a hard worker but also someone who would be a good wife and mother. Of course, both men and women sought attractive, well-groomed partners, and the Plains Indians, rather vain about their appearance, spent much time caring for their hair, their dress, and their personal cleanliness. A Cheyenne courtship might last four to six years, with the young woman normally having greater power in the choice.

If two families arranged it, a marriage might occur suddenly. Red Feather, a young Assiniboin man, reported that his aunt one day told him: "You are now grown up and should settle down. We have selected a young woman . . . to be your wife. . . . We have already arranged everything so you will be married tomorrow." He noted also that the next day the wedding was announced, his aunt gave a large feast, and both families gave away "many things."[19]

Usually a marriage occurred after the groom's family had compensated the bride's family for her loss, particularly her reproductive loss. Often compensation came in horses, but other gifts or personal services might be acceptable. The practice became common, and the greater the gift, the greater the bride's status. Among some people, such as the Mandans, the families involved exchanged equal gifts. Romance was not lacking, however; lovers found plenty of time for courtship, and on occasion elopements occurred. Men married in their early twenties, women often before they reached sixteen.

Older men who wanted to marry often negotiated through a third person with the prospective bride's family. If his "offer" seemed satisfactory, the parents, suggested First Boy of the Assiniboins, "entreated their daughter to consent to the marriage." He futher noted that "the girl could not be compelled to accept, but the parents always worked on her affection for her relatives and usually, in the end, there was a marriage."[20]

The newly married couple, after perhaps spending a few days alone on the plains, fell in with the natural rhythm of village life. The couple shared various family chores and responsibilities as they went about their daily life. As time passed the husband gained honors by leading successful raids, by counting coup, or by skill in making arrows or other implements. The wife gained honors by her activity with household duties and tanning hides or by winning village craft competitions in quilling and beading. But life on the plains in many ways became a man's world, for the group survived by hunting and raiding—men's responsibilities. Nonetheless a woman's role remained central to tribal success, and her position was one of respect and equality.[21]

After marriage a husband usually brought his wife to live in the band or village in which he grew up, but the practice of patrilocal residence was not universal. The young couple might live, as was common among the Arapahos and Cheyennes, in the band of the wife's parents (matrilocal), or they could live in another band. All married couples among the Cheyenne Dog Soldiers, for example, lived in that band's villages. Matrilocal residence allowed one older woman to be the extended family's matriarch. Exogamous marriage, that is, marriage outside the band or village, was common but not universal. Lakota people sought marriage partners from within the band (or tribal subgroup) or in an adjacent band, but the couple could not be closely related.

Most people practiced the levirate and the sororate marriage conventions. In the levirate, a man married the wife of his deceased brother. In the sororate, a woman married her deceased sister's husband. Because plains people looked upon marriage as a bond primarily between kin groups rather than between individuals, the levirate and sororate systems helped maintain family unity and preserved social stability. They also provided a means by which the brother or sister assumed the obligations of economic participation in family duties and of caring for and rearing the children.

Several plains peoples practiced limited polygyny (multiple wives). Headmen and other prominent leaders, because of demands upon them for entertaining guests, feeding the poor, and processing bison hides, often had polygynous marriages. Some, such as Crow Dog of the Lakotas and Quanah of the Comanches, married four or five women. Polygynous households lived adjacent to each other, or if few children were present, the wives shared the same lodge. In part because women's responsibilities included hide dressing and men with several wives could produce extra furs for trade to acquire goods for gifts, polygyny increased after whites began buying animal skins.

Sometimes the first wife, herself, might suggest that her husband acquire another mate because a warrior, as he rose in prominence, had to provide more gifts and larger feasts. When work associated with such duties became too great for one woman, another wife was needed. If he did not marry his wife's younger sister, the husband might take as a second wife a woman captured in a raid. Many people saw secondary wives as helpers, or "chore wives," to the first wife, who dominated the household.[22]

Sororal polygyny, in which a man had several sisters as wives at the same time, was common. Such an arrangement kept families together, reduced the heavy burdens for the wife of a prominent man who needed to entertain lavishly to retain his status, and provided a workable remedy for the common plains situation of surplus marriageable women. Crooked Neck, a Cheyenne leader, had five wives, all sisters.

Rarely did a woman have more than one husband, but the Comanches to limit population, may have practiced polyandry in their preplains period. In response to greater food sources on the southern plains, however, the Comanches moved to increase their population. With a surplus of marriageable women and a corresponding need to produce hides for trade, the men took additional wives, sometimes from within their band or from another Comanche band, but sometimes from among captured women—including whites.

Nonetheless, most marriages were monogamous. To regulate sexual activity, marriages had to be known to everyone in the community. They were, therefore, public, rather than private and religious, affairs, neither highly formalized nor marked by elaborate ceremony.

Marriages created a series of new bonds with relatives-in-law. Although in most inter-kin behavior warmth and friendliness marked interpersonal relationships, "in-law" taboos existed and special rules of conduct applied. To show reverence and respect, for example, Lakota and Crow men never spoke to their mothers-in-law. An Arapaho wife did not speak to or look at her husband's father, but neither the Pawnees nor Arikaras maintained such elaborate avoidance relationships. The Crows did not allow a man to indulge in vile language in his brother-in-law's presence, but they permitted a man and his sister-in-law license to the extent that they engaged in obscene talk and mild sex play. The Lakotas, one of the most sexually restrained of the plains people, and the Arapahos also practiced such mutual obscenity and sexual teasing. The Comanches, who had very few in-law taboos, approached polyandry, or anticipatory levirate, where brothers lent each other their wives. The Lipans had many in-law taboos.[23]

When high mortality rates associated with European diseases disrupted family relationships (the key to tribal life), marriage customs changed. Some groups shifted from exogamy to endogamy marriage conventions to maintain family structures, and they captured rather than killed enemy women for the same reason. Moreover, such people as the Comanches gave up the older practice of killing a man's wife at his grave.

Although most partners remained lovers and helpmates throughout their lives, either partner could desolve a marriage without much ado. First Boy, an Assiniboin, noted that among his people "marriages were dissolved merely by living apart."[24] In several communities a woman could divorce her husband simply by removing his personal property from the tipi.

A man could divorce his wife for adultery, laziness, slothfulness, or excessive nagging. Among the Lakotas a man for various reasons might publicly humiliate his wife by disgarding her at a dance or other village ceremony. In some communities an adulteress might have the tip of her nose cut off or otherwise be humiliated. "This didn't happen a great deal," said Severt Young Bear. "The old Lakota social system was very strict and there were very few women who broke its rules."[25]

Single adults of either sex were rare. The subsistence-based economy and the sharp gender division of labor demanded joint participation of a man and a woman in the yearly round of activities. "The home," noted Luther Standing Bear (Lakota), "was the center of Lakota society—the place . . . whence flowed the strength of the tribe."[26] Here, in all cases the wife prepared the meals, brought fuel and water, and dressed skins. She usually made the clothing. In the semisedentary communities she cultivated the crops. Among the nomadic peoples she dug roots, collected fruits and nuts, and took charge of the tipi. The husband hunted, made weapons and implements, and provided protection. In the horticultural communities he cleared garden plots for planting and helped erect the lodges. Men usually butchered game, but among some people women also participated in the task.

Nonetheless, some adults lived alone. Most, as we have seen, were male members of warrior or dream societies who sometimes delayed marriage because of the hazardous nature of their occupation. Also, some widows and widowers chose not to remarry.

There were, in addition, homosexuals and *berdaches,* as French traders called them, or transvestite males, some of whom were homosexuals. Ponca people believed that the moon appeared to boys during puberty to offer a bow and a woman's pack strap. If he hesitated when reaching for the bow, the boy got the pack strap, symbolizing a female lifestyle. *Berdaches* adopted a woman's role for life. Normally, they did not fight, but they often went to war to treat injured warriors. Many of them served as matchmakers in arranging marriages. They often became secondary wives of famous men, and many of them gained enviable reputations as craftspersons in skin tanning, clothes

In winter on the northern plains, American Indians hunted buffalo on snowshoes. The hunters could easily approach the animals that struggled to get through the snow, as shown in this drawing from Nelson A. Miles, *Personal Recollections and Observations* (p. 128). *Courtesy Southwest Collection, Texas Tech University.*

The interior of a Mandan earth lodge in 1833. The Swiss artist Carl Bodmer painted the scene when he and Prince Alexander Philip Maximilian stayed among the Mandans. *Courtesy National Anthropological Archives, Smithsonian Institution (neg. 43170 D).*

The Wichitas built a grass lodge with a conical skeleton of stout poles bent toward the center. Over the poles they placed grass and straw held in place by slender wooden rods attached to the framework. The houses stood close to one another in tightly packed villages. *Courtesy Ernest Wallace Papers, Southwest Collection, Texas Tech University.*

This Shoshoni camp, located in the Wind River Mountains, was Chief Washakie's band. The colorful lodges of the Shoshonis pictured here in 1870 are painted tipis. *Smithsonian Institution photo, courtesy Ernest Wallace Papers, Southwest Collection, Texas Tech University.*

Kicking Bear (left), who wanted a return to traditional Lakota lifestyles, is wearing a breechclout with his blanket on the ground. Standing Bear (right), whom some would call a "progressive," is dressed in white-style clothing, including a watch fob and Christian pin. Young Man Afraid of His Horse, who served as an intermediary, wears a combination of white and Lakota clothing. *Courtesy Nebraska State Historical Society.*

INDIAN WEAPONS AND GARMENTS. 1. Bow. 2. Arrows. 3. Sioux Flageolet or Flute. 4. Cheyenne Flute. 5. Cheyenne Rattler. 6. Bow Case and Quiver, made of Panther Skin. 7. Sioux Rattle, made from Ends of Buffalo Toes. 8. Cheyenne Moccasins, Beautifully Embroidered with Beads. 9. Cheyenne Tobacco Pouch. 10. Cheyenne Beaded Cradle. 11. Cheyenne "Squaw Dress." From Miles, *Personal Recollections and Observations,* p. 531. *Courtesy Southwest Collection, Texas Tech University.*

INDIAN WEAPONS. 1. Comanche Tomahawk. 2. Ute Tomahawk Pipe. 3. Bow Case and Quiver of the Bannock Indians. 4–5. Sioux War Clubs. 6–7-8. Sioux Bows and Arrows. 9. Comanche War Shield. 10–11. Sioux War Clubs. 12. Comanche Tomahawk Pipe. 13. Tomahawk Pipe which once belonged to Little Bear, a prominent chief of the Northern Apaches. From Miles, *Personal Recollections and Observations*, p. 185. *Courtesy Southwest Collection, Texas Tech University.*

Many Plains Indians buried their dead in scaffolds four to five feet high or in trees. Sometimes relatives killed the person's favorite horse near the burial site, as depicted in this drawing from Miles, *Personal Recollections and Observations* (p. 158). *Courtesy Southwest Collection, Texas Tech University.*

Carl Bodmer painted this scene of a fight he witnessed in 1833 outside Fort McKenzie in Montana. Blackfeet (mainly Piegans) fought Assiniboins and Cree for trade privileges at the American Fur Company post. *Courtesy National Anthropological Archives, Smithsonian Institution (neg. 43117).*

Red Cloud, of the Oglala Lakotas, was a great warrior who directed the northern plains tribes to victory over white soldiers in the Sioux war of 1866–67. He summarized the Plains Indians' relations with the government: "They made us many promises, more than I can remember, but they never kept but one: they promised to take our land, and they took it." *Courtesy National Anthropological Archives, Smithsonian Institution (neg. 3237-A).*

Sitting Bull (Hunkpapa Lakota) was a charismatic leader who took his followers to Canada after the Sioux war of 1876–77. He returned in 1881 and died in 1890 at his home on the Standing Rock Reservation during a botched attempt by agency police to arrest him. *Courtesy Nebraska State Historical Society.*

Ten Bears, a Comanche chief, was a masterful orator in a society that admired skill and power in public speaking. During negotiations over the 1867 Treaty of Medicine Lodge, his speech brought tears to the eyes of those who listened. *Courtesy National Anthropological Archives, Smithsonian Institution (neg. 1741-A).*

Little Wolf, standing, and Morning Star (Dull Knife), Northern Cheyenne leaders, in 1878 led their people in the "Cheyenne Autumn" flight from Indian Territory back to their northern homeland. *Courtesy National Anthropological Archives, Smithsonian Institution (neg. 270-A).*

Standing Bear, a Ponca chief, refused to submit to the federal government's program to consolidate most Plains Indians in Oklahoma. His 1879 legal battle focused attention on the plight of his people and the government's ill-starred plan and encouraged the government to abandon the program. *Courtesy National Anthropological Archives, Smithsonian Institution (neg. 4176-A).*

Quanah, a Comanche leader, fought to retain Comanche rights to hunting land in western Texas. He practiced the peyote cult but discouraged the Ghost Dance on his reservation. *Smithsonian Institution photo, courtesy Ernest Wallace Papers, Southwest Collection, Texas Tech University.*

Reservation towns in the late nineteenth and early twentieth centuries began to take on the look of most small western communities in America. Here, along the main street of Pine Ridge in 1890–91, soldiers, scouts, and civilians congregate. *Courtesy Nebraska State Historical Society.*

During ration day, sometimes scores of women waited in line to receive rations and supplies. Charles E. Eastman, a Santee physician, described ration day as a time when agency "street and stores were alive with a motley crowd in picturesque garb, for all wore their best on these occasions." *Courtesy Nebraska State Historical Society.*

Joseph Horn Cloud, a Wounded Knee survivor, with the help of friends and relatives, in 1903 placed this monument on the hill at the edge of the mass-grave site at Wounded Knee. People have left gifts in honor of those buried there. *Courtesy Nebraska State Historical Society.*

them gained enviable reputations as craftspersons in skin tanning, clothes making, bead working, tipi building, and other traditionally female tasks.[27]

Because Plains Indian people acted according to their dreams and visions, (usually) little social stigma became attached to *berdaches* or homosexuals. Finds Them and Kills Them (Osh Tisch, or Miakate [Woman] Jim) was a Crow *berdache* or *bote*, as Crows called them, who held prestige and respect and who lived with Iron Bull, a headman of the Crows. Indeed, among the Lakotas some homosexuals *(winkte)* enjoyed a ritual status.[28]

Women *berdaches* also existed. That is, a woman who had thoroughly adopted a male's role in society and occupation might take another woman as a wife. Whether or not such relationships included lesbianism, however, is a matter of much debate. But such a relationship allowed a "warrior woman" to hunt and raid while another attended to the household duties.[29]

Plains Indians participated in a multitude of recreations. They played both large- and small-group games, with gambling, laughing, shouting, and general merriment accompanying all of them. They held races on foot or horseback, wrestled, and competed in archery contests. In nearly all games, as suggested by the active gambling, the spirit of competition flourished. Children participated in all sorts of play activity and sport, much of which mimicked adults.

Plains people had some diversions mainly for men and some mainly for women. Men swapped arrows, buffalo robes, and horses. They played the wheel game, in which the players threw arrows or sticks at a rolling hoop laced with rawhide. They talked and gossiped, as did women. Women played the awl game, in which players, or teams, moved through various positions around a blanket in opposite directions according to points they gained by throwing curved and notched sticks. Both men and women played the button, or hand, game, in which two teams sat facing each other, perhaps across an evening campfire. A player on one of the teams moved the button (a decorated piece of wood) from one hand to the other and passed it, or pretended to pass it, to a teammate. The other team tried to determine which opponent's hand held it, with teams winning or losing points according to the accuracy of the guesser. Many evenings around a fire, as the village or camp settled in for the night, the people sang songs and danced.[30]

In old age the Plains Indians did not fear death. They saw death not as an end but as part of nature's cycle that people passed through to complete the normal round of life. They belived that all people, regardless of merit, went to the same afterworld, where they lived more or less as they had when alive. An elderly person in a hopeless medical condition, when he or she felt death drawing near, disposed of all his property and might retire from the village to a quiet spot to die. Sometimes the band, no longer able to provide for them, abandoned elderly people. Little mourning occurred and only for a short time.

The death of a child or an active adult, however, especially a prominent person, caused intense and prolonged grief. Female relatives testified to their sorrow by wailing, moaning, and howling. Among the Comanches they wore rags, and they gashed themselves across the face, arms, legs, and breast.[31] "I mourn the loss of my only boy," said Comanche headman Pahayuco in 1843. "I must cry and mourn till the green grass grows. I have burnt my lodges [five of them], killed my mules and horses, and scattered ashes on my head."[32] In many tribes the dead person's relatives, men as well as women, cut off their hair and painted themselves mourning colors to show their grief. They might gash themselves and cut off an ear or a finger.[33] When his favorite wife died, One Horn, a Miniconjou leader, rode wildly out from his village. Determined to kill the first living thing he met, he found and wounded a lone bison bull and then with only a knife attacked the enraged animal. Soon both the bison and One Horn died.[34]

Burial followed death rather quickly. Most of the nomadic people used scaffold or tree burial. In such instances relatives placed the corpse in the crotch of a tree or fashioned a three- or four-pole scaffold to which they securely fixed the body to protect it from wolves and other predatory animals. The Plains Cree preferred burial in a five-foot-deep grave, but in winter with the ground frozen, they used the tree or scaffold burial. For Comanches the ideal burial was a shallow grave, over which they piled rocks and logs, or a natural cave, crevice, or deep wash.[35] Wichita people placed the corpse in a grave and covered it with logs and stones to a height of four feet.[36] In many groups relatives bathed the corpse and painted it with vermilion. They bent the deceased person's knees upon the chest, wrapped the body in a fresh buffalo hide, and placed the corpse in the burial place with the head facing the rising sun or facing the heavens and the spirits among the clouds. They might kill the dead person's horses and dogs, and sometimes they buried a few of the deceased person's possessions with the corpse.

Among the Plains Cree, relatives on the fourth night after death held a feast with ceremonial pipe and food offerings to the spirits. They put a braid, cut by a warrior from the deceased's hair, into a sacred bundle with braids of other dead members of the family. While people in some tribal groups avoided returning to the grave, in others, such as the Plains Cree, people upon returning to the burial site would tidy the place. Some Lakota people, after a couple of years, might revisit the burial site, and on occasion an older widow might attach the jaw bone of her dead husband to her clothing.[37]

From birth to death, then, the Plains Indians, despite all their similarities, displayed various degrees of cultural plurality. Many of their customs were old, dating from a time before they reached the plains. Many others, however, developed on the plains and after white contact. As with people everywhere, the Plains Indians enjoyed constantly evolving, rather than static, social conventions. Their belief systems show the same elements of transformation.

7 : CEREMONY AND BELIEF SYSTEMS

The spirituality, worldviews, and cosmological systems of the Plains Indians varied in significant ways. Differences existed between plains and prairie peoples and from north to south. Differences also existed between those peoples who had been on the plains for several generations and those who were more recent arrivals. Once on the plains, however, Indian people readily borrowed traits from one another, and the appearance of whites provided additional elements that the Plains Indians might assimilate into their belief systems.

An important determinant in shaping Plains Indian metaphysics was the Great Plains itself. The huge, open region extended from the Saskatchewan River basin in the north to the Rio Grande in the south and from the western prairies of Minnesota and Iowa on the east to the front range of the Rocky Mountains on the west.

A compelling place, this expansive, wind-swept grassland consisted of an almost level surface that was virtually treeless, semiarid, hot in summer, and cold in winter. The land suggested a high-seas panorama of space and sky and ever changing clouds. In 1850 Thomas Tibbles, a western scout, wrote that "no more beautiful country was ever seen."[1] George Catlin, who toured the plains to record Indian life and customs, noted that it was "a place where the mind could think volumes; but the tongue must be silent that would *speak*, and the hand palsied that would *write*." The plains at sunset, he wrote, "when the green hill-tops are turned into gold—and their long shadows of melancholy are thrown over the valleys are scenes of enchantment."[2]

The Great Plains gave Indian people of the region a feeling of personal freedom and happiness. It had an enchantment, a mysterious quality, that few of them could explain, but they were an inseparable part of it, together with the animals, the winds, and the rocks. "Sometimes at evening I sit, looking out on the big Missouri," reported Buffalo Bird Woman of the Hidatsas. "The sun sets, and dusk steals over the water. In the shadows I seem again to see our Indian village, . . . and in the river's roar I hear . . . the laughter of little children . . . and tears come into my eyes." An anonymous Omaha informant said that "the country was very beautiful." He noted that "in both the woodland and the prairie I could see ... many forms of life, beautiful living creatures which *Wakanda* [the Holy One Above] had placed here."[3]

Indian people of the region did not view the Great Plains as a place to be set apart. Nor did they conceive of the broad, open province as an identifiable entity, for their worldview found little use for geographical definitions and exact boundaries. Rather, they saw the magnificent land as something of a life-giving female—a Mother Earth—who provided them with what they needed, offered them opportunities for a livelihood, and contributed to their happiness. "I love the land and the buffalo," said Ten Bears, a Comanche leader in 1867. "I love to roam over the wide prairie, and when I do it I feel free and happy."[4]

Plains Indian cosmology included the idea of harmony between humans, animals, and the environment. The people accepted the interconnectedness of all phenomena, both visible and invisible, and they regarded all creatures as basically equal. Theirs was a holistic view of the universe. They understood that a conscious life, a soul, existed in animal and plant beings, natural objects, and unknown powers. Everything that could be seen or touched possessed a spirit, and mysterious powers existed in all things, including animals, plants, rocks, and the earth itself. Most people viewed their world as an interconnected series of often unknowable elements. The earth, regarded as a living being (usually a life-giving female), served as the center of this interconnected, undivided, but only sometimes understandable world.

The cosmological system included no concept of private ownership of land (Mother Earth could not be divided), little need to save for the future (food and material wealth were to be shared, not hoarded), and (from a white point of view) a cavalier attitude toward time, which was of minor concern to them. "Hours, minutes, and seconds were such small divisions of time," said Carl Sweezy, an Arapaho, "that we had never thought of them. When the sun rose, when it was high in the sky, and when it set were all the divisions of the day that we had ever found necessary."[5] The people lived in tune with nature and its cycles of life. Nature dictated the time to hunt, the time to plant, the time to pick berries; one of the Lakota words for July, for example, translated into "Moon of the Red Cherries" and one for January translated into "Moon of Frost in Tipis."

Again, however, the Plains Indians were not all alike. They possessed no single epistemology, ontology, or phenomenology. They admired bravery, fortitude, wisdom, and generosity as well as honesty, loyalty, and courtesy. Individual competitiveness was strong, especially among warriors, and the people remained fiercely independent. A creative and inventive people who enjoyed a normal range of intellectual capacity, their education emphasized application and practical experience; it was informal, flexible, and related to the moment. Their measures of wisdom and knowledge were the elderly statesmen and women of their village.

In the Plains Indians' worldview, the family, including the extended family, was paramount. Everything else was never more than second. Elders watched over the young and instructed them by word and by example—the latter a powerful teaching tool. One of a child's earliest lessons touched on ideas about respecting the Holy One Above and about accepting responsibilities. The Plains Indians believed in brotherhood and honesty and sharing.

Spiritual activity, which touched every aspect of their lives, became fundamental to the Plains Indians; sacred and secular life were inseparable. Mystic, but not dogmatic, the people called upon a variety of sacred powers for assistance. They felt a shared attachment to the land and its animals and a reverence for nature. Indeed, their chief aim in life was to become one with the spirit world or, as Calvin Martin has written, "to be saturated with the primordial Power of Nature which seemed to pulsate throughout all creation."[6] Their strong sense of spirituality shaped their minds and influenced their reasoning processes.

Indeed, spiritual activities were a natural component of economic life, social activities, individual actions, child raising, warfare, medicine, and art and decorative designs, and they offered an explanation for extraordinary occurrences. Nearly every activity, both large and small, centered about spirituality. The people transformed simple tasks of daily life into rites, rituals, and prayers, appealing constantly for spiritual assistance by offering sacrifices of food, tobacco, ornaments, a small lock of hair, or even a piece of their own flesh. One could find few, perhaps no, atheists among them.[7]

The spirituality was pervasive. It was both an individual concern and a corporate process. The Plains Indians hallowed their homeland, and the veneration of it was associated with each group's way of life. They honored all of it, including earth and rocks, animals and plants, lightning and thunder, and they believed that disturbing the land would result in cultural disharmony. They believed that all living creatures, both humans and animals, had souls. They further believed that the physical and mystical connections to the land and its creatures were vital not only for the maintenance of their religious practices but also for their very cultural integrity. Thus, for example, Rainy Mountain, a knoll on the southern plains, was holy to the Kiowas, and Bear Butte, located on the northeastern edge of the Black Hills, remained sacred to the Cheyennes and the Lakotas.

Because of the relatively short period of time that most of the people had to adapt to the plains environment, religious institutions lacked firm structure, and the presence of whites required further change. Indeed, contact with whites and European-based diseases sometimes meant extinction of traditional ways as well as sharp declines in population.[8]

Nonetheless, many Plains Indians recognized the existence of a principal spirit being, or Holy One Above. An omniscient, all-powerful force, the Holy One Above was a sky-dwelling creator who imbued sacred power to all elements of life, the first of all addressed in prayer, and the one to whom the first smoke was offered. Although white observers often referred to it as the Great Spirit, the Plains Indians called the creator force by different names. The Cheyennes referred to the primacy of *Maheo* (or *Heamawihio*). For the Lakotas it was *Wakan Tanka,* or the Great Mystery, who was everywhere, his spirit in all things.[9] The Pawnees called their creator spirit *Tirawa,* usually translated as "this expanse." He was to be respected and awed. "You must trust always in *Ti-ra'-wa,*" a Pawnee mother instructed her son. "He made us, and through him we live."[10]

Most Plains Indians saw their sacred world as populated by many forces and spirit beings of a variety of forms with differing degrees of religious power. In several communities, for example, the sky, sun, moon, and earth all remained part of the Holy One Above, but they might also be important spirits by themselves.

Many plains groups did not organize their spiritual world into a highly regularized pantheon of beings, but they often recognized classes of benevolent and malevolent spirits. Among the Lakotas the foremost powers were *Wi,* the sun, and *Skar,* the sky, both looked upon as having male attributes. *Maka,* a female spirit, was the earth. Beneath these highest spirits existed lesser forms, including the Winds or four directions, the Moon, Bear, Thunders, Whirlwind, and a host of others. Additional lesser spirits, which could be animate or inanimate, took many forms. Bodily spirits and ghosts were also *wakan,* or sacred, to the Lakotas.[11]

Through such spiritual characters the Plains Indians perceived reality and grappled with the basic questions of life. Among these was the concept of three parallel worlds: the sky, the earth, and the underworld. Beneath the surface of lakes and rivers existed powerful forces that controlled animals and plants, the underworld spirits. For many groups a horned monster represented the most powerful of the underwater forces. In the sky above the clouds lay the realm of the upper world, dominated by spirits, such as the thunderbird who produced thunder and lighting, that matched those of the underworld. With a perpetual state of war existing between the sky and water forces, the people of the earth constantly sought aid from their patron spirits.

Several elements characterized the Plains Indians' spirituality, including symbolic ritualism, elaborate ceremonies, and renewal activities. Spiritual activity drew heavily on magic and magical practices to cause sacred powers to react in favorable ways, but the Plains Indians made few, if any, distinctions between practices that were spiritual and those that were magical. Indeed, magic in essence was real.[12]

The religious practices often included the use of purifying sweat lodges, special altars, reverential pipe smoking, symbolic body and facial painting, imitation or impersonation of events or spirits, and music and dancing. Ceremonies associated with the movement of the sun and stars also occurred in appropriate seasons. For all Plains Indians, the cardinal points of the compass, the number four, and the circle or hoop were sacred.

The circle symbolized natural harmony. Its shape was a sacred image, the essence of unity and wholeness. The sun and the moon go in a circle above the sky; plants are round like the trunk of a tree; the sacred shield was round. "The Power of the World always works in circles," said Black Elk, "and everything tries to be round." There was "no power in a square." Thus, people in many tribes pitched their round-based tipis in a camp circle and sat in a circle during important ceremonies.[13]

Hundreds of ceremonial sites made of stones placed in circles and sometimes associated with astronomical events, such as the summer solstice, are scattered through the northwestern plains—medicine wheels they are called. Although many date from the precontact period, others, such as the Big Horn Medicine Wheel in the mountains of Wyoming (which dates from about 1700), are more recent. The medicine wheels, especially important to the Northern Arapahos and to a lesser extent the Shoshonis, reflected the reverence that all people of the plains maintained for the circle, a shape that suggested spiritual and political unity and connected people with one another and with the natural world.

The number four also symbolized natural harmony. There were four seasons, four ages in human life (babyhood, childhood, adulthood, and old age), four elements above the earth (the sun, the moon, the stars, and the sky), and many other natural manifestations of the number. The four winds or four directions of the compass represented both natural and metaphysical powers. In effect, because the great creator force (or Holy One Above) created everything in fours, the Plains Indians believed they should do as much as possible in fours.

The purifying sweat bath, often a ceremony in itself and unconnected with preparations for other plains rituals, was important. For a sweat bath one went nearly naked into a tiny, saunalike hut made of hides draped over a willow-branch frame. Inside the person poured cold water onto white-hot rocks, breathed steam, burned sweet grass, smoked a sacred pipe, prayed, and pursued visions. Upon leaving the hut, the person rubbed himself with sage and doused himself with cold water or jumped into a nearby stream before dressing again. Sometimes several people, men and women, crowded into the sweat lodge.

Tobacco also enjoyed something of a ritual status. Because it remained both scarce and strong, the Plains Indians adulterated tobacco with a variety of herbs. The concoction, called Kinnikinnick, included tobacco, dried bark of the red willow, leaves of the bearberry, dried leaves of sumac, cottonwood, or other aromatic herbs, probably including marijuana. They kept Kinnikinnick in small but elaborately decorated pouches.

Although some groups gathered wild species, several of the village peoples raised tobacco, as did such nomads as the Blackfeet, Sarsis, and Crows. The Cheyennes grew tobacco as late as 1802. Among the Mandans, Hidatsas, and Crows, tobacco cultivation became a special task of older men, and considerable ritual surrounded its cultivation, especially among Crows, who planted tobacco as ceremony long after they had given up other horticulture.[14]

Associated with various forms of power, tobacco smoking was often a sacred and ceremonious act. No rite was more widely practiced. A western fur trader noted that pipe smoking served as "the introductory step to all important affairs, and no business can be entered upon with [Indian] people before the ceremony of smoking is over."[15] Among the Comanches smoking in a ceremony represented either a prayer for power on the part of the smoker or an oath, a pledge, a moral commitment. As a formal and sacred act, restrictions and taboos applied to smoking ceremoniously. For the most part smoking remained a men's activity, and many men before smoking offered the pipe to the cardinal directions. Individual taboos existed as well, including taking off one's moccasins before smoking or placing the pipe on a slice of meat or bison tongue.[16]

For casual smoking men used simple pipes, such as tubular pipes made of bone reinforced by rawhide or sinew from the bison. They rarely smoked cigars, but cigarettes, rolled in such materials as inner leaves of corn shucks or leaves of the blackjack oak, were far from rare. Tobacco chewing, at least among the Comanches, did not develop until reservation days. Because it remained in short supply, men saved tobacco for solemn occasions.[17]

For solemn occasions or ceremonial smoking, the people used pipes with bowls. They made the bowls from such soft stone as black steatite and a variety of soapstone called red catlinite, named for the painter George Catlin, who visited the sacred red pipestone quarry in southwestern Minnesota. The Yanktons, who controlled the famous pipestone site, supplied catlinite through trade to most of the northern plains peoples. Many village people used pottery bowls. Later they secured brass, forged-iron, brier, and meerschaum bowls from whites. They made pipestems from ash, willow, or cottonwood.

Calumets were elaborate pipes, seldom intended for actual smoking. The Plains Indians often made calumets in pairs, and many groups used them when making peace treaties. Calumets served the Omahas in certain adoption rites and dances. The Northern Arapahos, Blackfeet, and Lakotas as well as others used pipes in sacred ceremonies. The pipes included a long, carefully carved and decorated stem and a large bowl, which people usually kept separate from one another until they planned to use the pipe, at which time they ceremoniously joined the parts together. The use of elaborate pipes was an ancient tradition, but white contact influenced calumet decoration, as Indian people placed tiny glass beads along the stems and on occasion attached colorful ribbons to the pipes. Pipe designs varied from tribe to tribe.

Spiritual practices and beliefs also varied. Comanche religion, for example, lacked much of the elaborate ritualism associated with other groups. In part the differences may relate to their history. The Comanches came to the southern plains from the Great Basin, bringing its religious traditions with them, while most other people entered the region with spiritual traditions of the eastern woodlands. In many plains tribes shamans and/or priests dominated religious activity; in others they played key roles only in the performance of major rituals and acts of tribal renewal. Some significant differences also existed in the ways in which horticultural and hunting peoples approached religious activities.

Among the eastern village peoples, where individuals were never far removed from local community life, religious activity was public and group oriented. In general, great ritualism characterized the spiritual system of the horticultural groups; it provided tribal identification and gave the tribal culture meaning. But differences existed, and distinctions should be made between Siouan speakers, whose religion had ancient ties with precontact Oneota traditions, and Caddoan speakers, whose religious practices followed precontact Mississippian traditions. Priests, as distinguished from shamans (the spiritual leaders or holy men), became plentiful among the horticultural people, and in some villages they dominated both spiritual activities and temporal affairs.[18]

Pawnee religion, for example, maintained an elaborate and often hereditary priesthood. The priests manipulated the contents of the sacred village bundles, whose powers underlay political organization and formed the basis for the regulation of economic activities and for control of social relations within the village. Pawnee beliefs created a complex mythology. They also underlay a logical religious system in which the spirit beings gave the Pawnees their culture, their sacred bundles, and their knowledge of the bundle rituals. Through the intercession of the priests the bundles promoted health, happiness, and spiritual power (or "medicine," as whites came to call it).[19]

Among the nomadic peoples religious practices reflected adaptation to different seasons on the plains. Having adjusted their rituals and ceremonies to the rhythms and movements of the bison, they held group ceremonies in early summer, when abundant grass for their horses and the enormous bison herds allowed large gatherings. In the winter, when they scattered to smaller camps, individual activities became more important.

Thus, for the nomadic people religion remained largely individualistic. Its meaning and power came through a personal vision, and it was marked by great diversity among tribal members of similar faith and feeling. Although major group ceremonies occurred and drew the tribe or band together, religion among the full-time bison hunters, in keeping with the individualistic emphasis of the people, remained something of a private matter, and the people allowed a great variation of detail in religious form.[20]

Among the Comanches, for example, spiritual activity emphasized commonly accepted displays for obtaining favor from powers in the spirit world. Each individual worshiped above all other spirits his or her own guardian, who had been revealed to him or her during a personal-vision quest. Although they had shamans, the Comanches had no dogma and no priestly class, such as the Pawnees had, to formulate a systematic religion or coherent system of the universe.[21]

For the nomadic tribes the personal-vision quest was a nearly universal religious element.[22] During it a vision seeker went to a lonely spot in solitude. Here the individual, attempting always to remain awake, would fast and thirst for three or four days, pray to the spirits to take pity, and seek a revelation through a dream or trance. Among some people, such as the Crows, the supplicant might cut small pieces from his or her flesh (or on rare occasions cut off a finger joint of the left hand) to encourage the revelation, or vision. Among some groups, elders encouraged children to seek a vision. In others they expected adolescent males to go on the quest. In many tribes an adult man or woman sought a vision whenever a special cause arose. If an individual had difficulty in obtaining a vision, he sought the aid of a shaman, for everyone coveted a revelation and the patron spirit that came with it.

The spirits who befriended a vision seeker varied in character. Bison, elk, bear, eagles, hawks, dogs, and rabbits frequently served as guardian spirits. A Pawnee tradition describes the invocation of mosquitoes, and a Cree legend suggests that a mosquito once provided a man with chieftaincy. Inanimate objects, natural phenomena and events, and fanciful creatures of more or less human shape (manitous) also appeared as guardians in visions. The vision provided personal power (or medicine).[23]

After experiencing a revelation, the vision seeker created a sacred (or medicine) bundle. In the bundle the seeker placed objects, fetishes, and other physical symbols he or she had been directed to collect during the vision. The bundle itself was a skin bag, and its contents reminded the owner and others of mystical powers controlled by its possessor. A Pawnee bundle might contain, for example, a pipe, tobacco, paints, birds, and corn. A Comanche bundle might have any number of items, including a handful of sweet grass, certain herbs, a deer's tail, a bird's claw, small stones, the gristle of a bear's snout, and beaver oil. Each had a special use. The owner opened and renewed the bundle and manipulated its contents according to definite rites at auspicious times for communal and individual good and well-being.

Villages, fraternal organizations, and in several instances the tribe itself also kept medicine bundles.[24] Village bundles were more common among the eastern horticultural peoples, and powers within the bundle ensured prosperity for the village and its inhabitants. The Pawnee and Arikara medicine bundles, for example, played key roles in the regulation of horticulture and in the control of social relations. Among the Pawnees, a priest who had spent years learning its rites, rituals, and secrets manipulated the village bundle (although a patrilineal descendant of the original owner protected it).[25]

Among the Mandans all sacred bundles, whether individual or tribal, were privately owned, and the owners could sell the bundle or transfer its power. Each bundle (personal, fraternal, or tribal) functioned for the good of the people and became associated with a detailed mythology. Each contained objects representing characters and incidents of the myth. A detailed study of Mandan ceremonialism indicates that each bundle included a bison skull with other objects and possessed a secret but ritualistic lore and song. As a social obligation nonowners might give feasts to a bundle, and bundle owners on occasion gave renewal feasts to their own bundles. In that they pertain to specific activities, such as fishing and eagle trapping, some of the bundles with their associated rites proved quite specialized. Others served as general curing bundles; many became linked to fertility, to crops, or to the control of the weather.[26]

Great tribal bundles occurred among several groups. Some of these included the Sacred Pipe bundle of the Blackfeet, the Morning Star bundle of the Skidi Pawnees, the Medicine Arrows bundle and the Sacred Buffalo Hat bundle of the Cheyennes, the Flat Pipe bundle and the Sacred Medicine Wheels of the Arapahos, and the Okipa bundle of the Mandans. Following prescribed rituals in exact detail, the people held annual ceremonies related to their tribal bundles. The grand celebrations sometimes coincided with natural events, such as the summer solstice or the spring or autumn equinox, and they provided opportunities to visit relatives, gossip, find marriage partners, and trade. The purpose of the tribal ceremonies was as much to show respect for the spirits as equal residents of the universe as to worship them; that is, the celebrants wanted to win approval from the spirits as much as to show reverence. The ceremonies reaffirmed the group's cultural identity and renewed its relationship with the spirit world.

Ceremonies associated with the Arapaho Flat Pipe bundle were typical. Wrapped in several pieces of cloth and hung in a large ceremonial tipi located in the center of the camp circle, the Flat Pipe was the Arapaho "holy of holies." In majestic fashion, the people invoked the pipe to grant long life and happiness, at times they presented it with offerings, and its keeper manipulated the pipe in special ways. Regarded with substantial awe, its keeper also directed the Arapaho Sun Dance, in which the pipe played an important role, and other tribal ceremonies. He was the only person familiar with the orthodox version of the complicated tribal origin myth (which took four days to relate) associated with the pipe. The Arapaho Flat Pipe ceremonies were elegant and moving affairs.[27]

The Skidi Pawnee Morning Star ceremony was an elaborate affair. Held every few years and performed well into the nineteenth century (when white pressure and the efforts of a young Skidi leader named Petalasharo [Man Chief] caused the Skidis to abandon the practice), it represented one of the few instances of human sacrifice in North America. Although other Pawnee groups disapproved of the ceremony, the Skidis sacrificed a captured girl (or less often a boy), about thirteen years old, in a ritual whose aim was to renew the earth and the Pawnees as people. In the four-day ceremony the Skidis treated the girl well until after she mounted a special platform at midnight on the final day. Then, with the girl facing the morning star (a bright planet, Venus or Mars) in the east, a warrior shot her through the breast, a priest cut her breast and smeared her blood over his face and body, and the entire community followed by shooting arrows into the corpse. Afterward, as leaders took the body to the plains to dispose of it, the people joined together in feasting and celebrating. "This sacrifice always seemed acceptable to Tirawa," said Eagle Chief, "and when the Skidi made it they always seemed to have good fortune in war, and good crops, and they were always well."[28]

The Mandan Okipa ceremony was likewise a complex and elaborate affair. It required up to a year of preparation. Held annually in the summer, the Okipa observance dramatized the creation of the earth, its people, plants, and animals, and the struggles that the Mandans had endured. Specially trained officers of the Okipa society directed the songs, chants, secrets, and mythology associated with the ritual, but individuals, perhaps as a result of a vision, pledged to offer the ceremony and undergo its elements of self-sacrifice to ensure tribal welfare. Many people participated: Okipa leaders and officers, singers, drummers, impersonators, and others, including a pledger and young men who had volunteered to fast and to participate with the pledger in the special Okipa dances.

The Okipa ceremony lasted four days. The first day leaders repeated tribal and Okipa myths in the ceremonial lodge and around the village. Also on the first day they invested the pledger with the power to perform the rite and dedicated the other dancers. Other rituals and the spectacular Bull Dance began on the second day. Men cut holes through the skin of each dancer's back, breast, and legs. They inserted wooden skewers in the holes, attached rawhide thongs to skewers in the breast and back, and with the thongs hoisted the candidates off the ground, suspended from ceremonial poles. They attached bison skulls to the thongs and skewers in the legs and suspended each dancer until he became unconscious. Then they lowered him until he revived, when they raised him again. Activities on the third day were somewhat similar. The celebration reached its climax on the fourth day when, amidst dancing, chanting, and other rites, relatives lowered the candidates and dragged them around the sacred pole as fast as they could until each dancer fell unconscious. The Okipa ritual ended quickly after the last candidate succumbed, and relatives dressed the wounds. The ceremony revitalized the tribal world and renewed the strength of Mandan society.[29]

Of all the many Plains Indian rituals and ceremonies, the Sun Dance was the most conspicuous. First developed after 1700 by the Arapahos or Cheyennes and perhaps copied from the Mandan Okipa ceremony, the Sun Dance spread rapidly after 1750. It became "the grandest of all" the Plains Indians spiritual celebrations.[30] Suppressed by the U.S. government, it had all but disappeared by the end of the nineteenth century, at which time the Utes and western Shoshonis adopted certain of its features but altered its purpose and practice. Before the 1930s, when the federal government dropped its restrictions, the Sun Dance ceremony had become part powwow and part annual fair.[31]

The spectacular rite was a complex, group ceremony with singers, dancers, musicians, and spectators. Mythology accompanied the usually annual affair. An individual who planned to avenge a death, lead a successful hunt, guarantee a plentiful supply of bison, give thanks for some good fortune of a family member, or ensure the wealth and happiness of the group accepted the Sun Dance. In brief, men who had made special vows danced for from one to four days and nights to the accompaniment of drumming and singing. The dancers often underwent various ritualistic self-sacrifices, including fasting, thirsting, and mutilations, in their quest for power, good health, thanksgiving, success, and general welfare.[32]

The Sun Dance, performed by both semisedentary and nomadic peoples, was remarkable for its homogeneity, despite wide tribal variations in detail. The Mandans, Wichitas, and Tonkawas did not perform the Sun Dance, but a few elements of it appeared among the Omahas and Pawnees. The Arikaras, Assiniboins, Blackfeet, Crows, Gros Ventres, Hidatsas, Kiowas, Kiowa Apaches, Plains Cree, Poncas, Sarsis, eastern Shoshonis, Yanktons, Yanktonais, Santees, and some Plains Ojibwas practiced the Sun Dance. The Comanches performed it at least once (in 1874). It reached its highest degree of elaboration among the Arapahos, Cheyennes, and Lakotas.[33]

In the Lakota Sun Dance a spiritual leader directed the activities. In this role he functioned as a priest learned in the complex rituals and ceremonial aspects of the rite. He guided individuals who had vowed to participate in the dance, selected instructors, marshalls, heralds, and other assistants, oversaw the highly ritualized preparations, and in general took responsibility for the ceremony.

Preparations lasted four days. Merriment, excitement, lively banter, and some licensed sexual promiscuity marked the camp during the period. As described by Ed McGaa (Eagle Man, a Lakota lawyer), Eldon Johnson, and others, during the first and second days of preparation, after all the Indians had assembled, leaders selected heralds and marshalls, female attendants for each dancer, and children who were to have their ears pierced during the Sun Dance. Then the leaders consecrated the dancers and provided them with special clothes and other accoutrements they would use in dancing. At the conclusion of the second day, the participating shamans enjoyed a feast of dog meat, a Lakota culinary delicacy.

Activities on the third day focused on selection of a hunter who would locate the sacred tree for the Sun Dance pole, a digger who would prepare the hole in which to place the tree, and the musicians and singers. Leaders also prepared an escort who would lead a mock war party to the sacred tree and bring it to the Sun Dance circle after it had been symbolically captured and felled. The third day ended with the shamans and dancers feasting on bison tongue, another Lakota delicacy.

During the final day of preparations leaders selected the women who would cut down the sacred tree, and they otherwise completed preliminary activities. Although an atmosphere of general gaiety prevailed in the camp, each dancer, or candidate, kept to himself to prepare for the dancing. He viewed the rising sun each day, received instructions on the ceremony, and took purifying sweat baths.[34]

Then followed the four days of the Sun Dance. The first day began with a large procession through and around the camp and to the area selected for the dance lodge. Mock battles against malevolent spirits followed, and the Lakotas located and counted coup on the sacred spot where the center pole would be erected. They also built a sacred lodge (distinguished from the dance lodge), placing an altar inside dedicated to the Buffalo Spirit. The day ended with dancing around the sacred lodge and a bison feast.

On the second day the Lakotas felled the sacred tree; painted it with four colors, one color on each side; took it to camp in an elaborate procession; and fixed to its top bison and human effigy figures. The next day, following prescribed rituals, they raised the sacred pole and constructed the round, brush-walled dance lodge. As the third day ended, the camp shifted its tone from general good humor and merriment to contemplation of the sacred rites to take place on the final day.

The fourth and final day of the Sun Dance was solemn. The dancers viewed the rising sun before they slowly moved in procession to the dance lodge, where they received final instructions and accepted formal installation. Of the many different dances, the Buffalo and Sun Gaze dances became the most significant, and only certain pledgers participated in them. After the Buffalo Dance, which was part of the dedication to the Buffalo Spirit, children who had been selected for the event had their ears pierced.

Finally the Sun Gaze Dance began. Assistants cut holes, through which wooden skewers could be passed, in the flesh of the backs, breasts, and legs of the pledgers. Rawhide thongs connected the skewers, depending upon the variation of the dance selected, to posts, to bison skulls that dragged on the ground, or to the sacred pole in such a way that the dancer could be raised off the ground. In this way, said Chased by Bears, a Santee-Yanktonai, when a man "gives his body or his flesh, he is giving the only thing that belongs to him."[35]

During the dancing each participant gazed steadfastly at the sacred pole and blew continual short notes on an eagle-bone whistle. Although brief intermissions for rest occurred, the dancing took many hours, sometimes extending well into the night. At the dance's climax the participants jerked and pulled against the rawhide thongs to break free by tearing away their flesh at the skewers. Those who succeeded enjoyed great prestige. Female relatives removed the skewers of those who, because they had fainted, failed to break loose.[36]

The Sun Dance ended after each dancer had been freed and led back to his lodge. Soon afterward the camp broke up, each group leaving for its favorite summer hunting range. No single event, writes Johnson, served to bind the Lakotas together as a unit as did the Sun Dance. During it, he notes, "they came together at one time during the year for a deeply emotional religious experience in which supernatural aid was called upon to assure the tribe a plentiful supply of bison for the coming year."[37]

All plains groups that practiced the Sun Dance believed that the great pain, sacrifice, and supplication experienced in the ceremony were well invested, for at its close, the entire community could again expect good health, fertility, and sustenance. A successful Sun Dance restored tribal harmony, renewed the world, and revived the mysterious powers that ensured the peoples' welfare.

Spiritual activities of the Plains Indians, like most other aspects of their cultures, changed in purpose and practice over the years. New traits appeared and old features declined as intertribal contact increased after 1750. Ranging widely over the plains, the people created channels for the diffusion not only of religious practices and beliefs but also of fundamental social and economic features of their plains cultures. As the power and resources of certain tribes rose while those of others fell, the Plains Indians made new alliances, banding together for defensive purposes or to expand hunting ranges. Nowhere were such changing circumstances more clear than in trade and diplomacy on the plains.

8 : TRADE AND DIPLOMACY

For centuries before the arrival of Europeans, people on the Great Plains had exchanged goods with peoples living on the region's borders. Fairly well-developed trade routes crossed the plains along water courses or through riverine horticultural villages. Foot nomads from the southern plains as early as 1523 showed up at Pueblo villages in the Southwest, and on the northern plains the Missouri River villages attracted hunting peoples to their communities.

The appearance and spread of European goods, especially horses and firearms, and the concomitant arrival of new Indian peoples to the plains, especially after 1700, altered older trading patterns and recast the dynamics of intertribal relationships. While trade routes may not have differed, the people involved, the goods exchanged, and the customs associated with trade and diplomacy underwent a transformation. As they acquired horses, for example, people on the plains became more mobile, covered a greater range of territory, and pressed into other peoples' land. As they intruded on other peoples' hunting grounds, they developed new military sodalities to provide protection and defense through aggression. As dependence on bison grew, the Plains Indians altered their economies. The Plains Cree and Assiniboins, for example, as they acquired horses late in the eighteenth century, shifted away from their long-held positions as middlemen in the Canadian fur trade and turned to hunting bison and to equestrian nomadism.

European contact, dominated at first by French and Spanish nationals, also created new alliances, produced different rivalries, and changed trading contacts. On the central and northern plains and in the bordering aspen parklands, economic motives, stimulated by a growing demand for furs in Europe, influenced French activities. Seeking furs of all kinds, but particularly beaver skins, French voyageurs, coureurs de bois, explorers, and others offered traps, cloth, beads, liquor, and a wide range of other European-made goods, including firearms, to plains and prairie groups for animal pelts, dried meat (pemmican), and other food stuffs. For some northern tribesmen, bison hunting became a commercial activity to supply French and later British traders with dried meat.[1]

Spanish aims, although likewise motivated by economics, included efforts to convert Indian people to Christianity, to educate them in Western traditions, and to bring them into the Spanish system through a process of missionization. The Spanish invited—or coerced—American Indians to join them at missions, on landed estates, or in European-styled villages on the southern plains.

The Spanish system, more tightly controlled, was less lucrative to Indian participants. The Spanish government outlawed the use of liquor in its Indian trade and restricted the exchange of guns and ammunition. Perhaps because they lived on the distant edge of New Spain's material-scarce northern borderlands, Spanish agents in general offered to Indian peoples on the southern plains much less than the French, and later the British, in material goods. In fact, on the southern plains some Indian groups took to raiding pueblos and ranches as an economic activity.

British contact with Plains Indians came later. Except for a few Hudson's Bay Company agents, it did not reach significant proportions until several years beyond the end of the Seven Years War (1754–63), after which the French government surrendered its claims to North America. Then rival traders of the British Northwest Company, which hired displaced French voyageurs, challenged Hudson's Bay men for western lands and Indian trading partners.

Built on mutual need, the fur trade governed many contacts on the northern and eastern plains. Indian people provided beaver skins, of course, but also corn, pemmican, wild rice, bison hides, and buckskin. In return they received traps, guns, powder, shot, textiles, and other European-made items. Watered-down alcohol was plentiful, especially from French and British Northwest Company traders. Indian people received a concoction the traders called "Blackfoot rum"—four or five quarts of 180-proof spirits mixed with enough water to fill a nine-gallon keg. If used as a trade item, the keg might bring thirty beaver skins.

Indian people were effective traders, however, with long traditions in the exchange business. They negotiated carefully, refused to accept inferior goods, and insisted that white traders provide them with specific types and colors of cloth from, for example, English rather than American manufacturers. They sought advantages vis-à-vis competing Indian groups. They intermarried with traders and in the process began developing a large mixed-blood population that now dominates the political and economic life of many reservations.

Trade brought cultural compromises. Indians and Europeans held different concepts involving trade and the exchange of goods. Indian people sought a fair exchange, and their values, ideals, and ethical standards emphasized reciprocity and sharing wealth with relatives and friends. To them, sharing was a virtue, and circulating property often defined one's social position. European traders, more concerned with market values and the acquisition of riches, sought personal gains. To them, property accumulation defined one's social position.

Thus, to American Indians the Europeans seemed odd and unreasonable. The Europeans refused to give up their own remarkable goods, which they possessed in phenomenal amounts and which Indian people themselves wanted, but they nonetheless maintained a limitless lust for beaver skins and bison hides. From an Indian viewpoint the European and later American traders were crude and greedy philistines. The whites saw western Indians as unreasonable in their demands that traders give away large portions of their trading stock. Over time both cultures adjusted their concepts, ethics, and values concerning wealth and exchange.[2]

Trading became a time of celebration. On the northern plains when the European traders appeared at their western posts, Indian people came from distant trapping grounds. A British trader described their arrival at a post on the Saskatchewan River. "At a few yards distance from the gate," he wrote, "they salute us with several discharges of their guns. On entering the house they are disarmed, treated with a few drams and a bit of tobacco." They smoked the calumet (the pipe of peace and friendship) "and plyed [it] about for some time." Indian leaders related the yearly "news with great deliberation and ceremony," relaxing "in proportion to the quantity of Rum they have swallowed, till at length their voices are drowned in a general clamour." After the women erected the tipis, the Indians received "a present of Rum, and the whole Band drink during 24 hours and sometimes much longer."[3] Trading followed.

On the southern plains many Wichita villages became trade centers. After 1746, when Spanish officials closed off the upper Rio Grande trade at Taos and Santa Fe to them, the Comanches quickly worked out a peace accord with the Wichitas, thereby gaining access to French goods at Wichita villages along the Arkansas and Red rivers. About 1750, after the Wichitas secured peace with the Pawnees and mediated a settlement between the Pawnees and Comanches, the villages became centers of a busy southern plains trade. Moreover, with their grass houses tightly packed behind stockades of stakes and earth with loopholes for gunfire, the villages became fortresses able to withstand most raids from Indian enemies.[4]

As trade at the villages grew, the Wichitas found themselves as profitable middlemen. Frenchmen paddled canoes loaded with European goods up the Arkansas and carried away hides, tallow, lard, and farm products. The Comanches on horseback brought in hides, dried meat, horses, and captive slaves. In return they acquired European goods from the French, and from the Wichitas they secured vegetables and other items. The Wichitas took the horses and captives in exchange for their farm products, and they welcomed the French goods that included hoes, kettles, knives, needles, awls, cloth, beads, mirrors, vermilion, and other household conveniences. The trade placed heavy burdens on the Wichita women and their captive helpers, for the increased hunting meant longer hours in preparation of hides. In addition, the French market for their field crops encouraged them to cultivate more ground, and as a result they needed to spend more time in preparation of food for trade.[5]

In response to increasing French trade on its northern borders, Spain directed a flurry of activity in an attempt to control the southern plains, dominate the *Norteños* (Nations of the North), and hold off the French. It did not work. First, the various horse-mounted Apache divisions, particularly the Lipans, blocked Spanish settlement along the expanding fringes of Apacheria. Then, under pressure from Comanche bands, the Lipans moved toward Spanish-claimed territory in Texas, blocking Spanish advance and challenging Spain for the land; on occasion they attacked settlements, terrorized missions, and worried soldiers. Finally, the Comanches, close on Apache heels and an even more difficult foe, pressed deep into Spanish Texas. When it tried to play off one Indian group against the other, Spain suffered disaster from both. Spain never seemed to recognize that the Apaches and Comanches, more than the French, kept it from successful occupation (and even thorough exploration) of the Great Plains.

This misconception did not prevent Spain from trying to maintain peace with the Plains Indians. In 1745 a Lipan band showed up in San Antonio asking for a mission that might protect them from Comanche transgressions. Four years later the Treaty of Alamo Plaza provided for such a mission, and, after some difficulty over location and financial support, Spaniards in 1757 built Mission San Sabá de la Santa Cruz near present-day Menard, Texas, in the heart of Apacheria. They located a presidio (fort) nearby.

The Lipans arrived in large numbers at San Sabá but did not stay, for the Apache-Spanish alliance had antagonized the Comanches and their Wichita friends. One Lipan leader, El Chico, indicated his willingness to enter the mission, but most others, including their headman Casablanca, either wanted revenge against the Comanches or were afraid of an attack. Indeed, the Comanches, led by their powerful leader Cuerno Verde (Green Horn), and Wichitas, led by Grand Sol of the Taovayas, exerted enormous pressure on Spanish positions and on Spain's declining ability to hold the southern Great Plains.[6]

By this time, however, the French government's approach to the plains was largely over. The Seven Years War (1754–63), the last of the great Wars for

Empire, drained the northern prairies and plains of major French activity, for many coureurs de bois turned their efforts from the western Indian trade to the defense of eastern Canada. Thus handicapped, French trade operations on the northern plains withered in the mid 1750s and, by the end of the decade, stopped entirely. On the southern plains French traders, operating out of lower Louisiana, continued their trading activities, but after 1763 under Spanish political control.

In the 1770s Spain again sought peace with the Plains Indians. The governor of Texas in 1779 negotiated a settlement with the Tonkawas and at their urging installed El Mocho as their headman. He had greater difficulty with such Lipan leaders as Roque, El Joyoso, Josef Chiquito, and Manteca Mucho, who wanted to fight the Tonkawas and to assault any Comanches and Wichitas who showed up at San Antonio. The Lipans hunted bison north and west of the Texas administrative center, stole cattle from Spanish ranches, and attacked Comanche camps on the southern plains. When the Comanches struck back, the Lipans sought revenge, and the governor found himself caught in a whirl of crises.

Eventually the governor moved to secure peace with the Comanches. At San Antonio in 1785 he worked out an uneasy truce, sometimes called the Texas Treaty, with three Kotsoteka leaders. But it served neither party well, as younger warriors continued to raid ranches deep in the province. Moreover, Taovaya Wichitas, led by their new headman Guersec and pressed hard by Osages to their north, continued to strike settlements near San Antonio and to war with the Lipans.

More permanent was the Pecos Treaty. In 1786 at Pecos pueblo, a Pueblo community on the upper Pecos River near the edge of the plains, Juan Bautista de Anza and Comanche spokesman Ecueracapa (Leathercloak), a headman "distinguished as much by his skill and valor in war as by his adroitness and intelligence," negotiated the agreement, but not before Ecueracapa assassinated Toro Blanco (White Bull), a leader who opposed the peace. A far-reaching military and commercial alliance, the treaty established peace between western Comanches and the New Mexican settlements, called for a joint war against the Apaches, and allowed Spaniards the right to explore a route between Santa Fe and San Antonio. It also allowed *comancheros,* mainly Pueblos and Hispanics from upper New Mexico, and *ciboleros,* bison hunters, to enter the plains with their ox-drawn, two-wheeled carts to trade with plains people and to hunt bison.[7]

The Comanches, having secured peace with the Spanish, moved toward an accommodation with the Kiowas. In 1790 Pareiya (Afraid of Water), a Comanche headman, invited Gui-k'ati (Wolf Lying Down), a Kiowa leader, to his camp on the Double Mountain Fork of the Brazos River in western Texas.

Gui-k'ati remained through the summer, paving the way for a general council later in the year. At the fall conference the Comanche and Kiowa participants agreed to live together in peace. They strengthed the alliance some years later when Roncon, a Kiowa leader, married the daughter of the headman of the Yamparika Comanches. As the alliances took firm shape, Comanche power and dominance on the southern Great Plains increased.

On the northern plains, in the meantime, British traders occupied several trading posts. Blackfeet and Piegan men who hunted the plains and the northern parklands carried wolf skins, bison hides, and dried meat to the posts, but traders hoped that they might teach them to trap beaver and other valuable fur-bearing animals along the Sasketchewan and Assiniboine river systems. For years the Plains Cree and the Assiniboins had served as middlemen in the northern fur trade, but as they acquired horses, they turned to bison hunting as an economic activity, thus leaving the white traders searching for new partners, such as the Blackfeet, Piegans, and Gros Ventres.

Farther south along the middle Missouri River, Hidatsa, Mandan, and Arikara villages became increasingly important as trade centers. In 1779 David Thompson of the British Northwest Company visited the Mandan villages. Five villages stood scattered along the Missouri, he indicated, the largest containing 113 lodges with an average population of ten people who "lived by the cultivation of corn as well as by hunting the buffalo."[8] He found a Hidatsa village nearby and reported that Gros Ventres were visiting at two of the Mandan villages. Lakotas, he noted, frequently attacked the Mandans, and Cheyennes came in from the west to trade with the Hidatsas. The Mandans owned few horses and fewer firearms. Chief Big White Man, with whom Thompson visited, welcomed trade that might provide guns and ammunition. Thompson encouraged the Mandans to go north to trade, but, fearful of Lakota and Yanktonai war parties, they declined.[9]

Fear of enemy war parties was not the only problem for Plains Indians. European-borne diseases, especially smallpox, measles, and rubella, caused a drastic decline in native populations during the late eighteenth century. The terrible smallpox epidemic of 1780–81 destroyed perhaps two thirds of the Chipewyans, an "edge-of-the-woods" people who once were the largest and strongest Athapaskan group in northern Canada. The epidemic reduced the Cree population as well as the tribe's influence. South and west of them, the Plains Cree with their allies the Assiniboins battled the Blackfeet tribes for the Canadian plains and, after the Blackfeet suffered a heavy death toll in the 1780–81 epidemic, gained a permanent place on the Great Plains.

Not long afterward, American hunter-traders entered the plains. They found the southern plains still dominated by the Comanches and their Wichita allies. Many Comanche and Wichita bands on a regular basis attended trade fairs in San Antonio, and as they pressed their old war against the Lipans deep into south Texas, the Comanches sometimes struck Spanish positions or overland pack trains. Chief Yzazet and other Comanche leaders in Texas struggled to maintain the uneasy Spanish-Comanche peace. Conditions were changing, however; in 1807 Comanches under Chief Cordero with a delegation of Wichita leaders appeared in Natchitoches, Louisiana, to visit with American, as opposed to Spanish, agents. The Comanches sought American trade on the southern plains.

The hunter-traders found the northern plains dominated by the powerful Lakota and Blackfeet groups. The Lakotas sought to control much of the Missouri River Valley as well as access to the bison hunting grounds in the upper Platte. The Blackfeet sought to control access to trade at British posts on the Canadian plains as well as the American Fur Company posts on the upper Missouri and its tributaries, including Fort Union (the largest and perhaps best built trading post on the northern plains) on the Missouri and Fort McKenzie on the Marias River.

Perhaps no activity opened the Great Plains to Americans more than the successful return in 1806 of the Meriwether Lewis and William Clark expedition. For more than two years the Corps of Discovery, as the expedition was called, had traveled up the Missouri River, across the Rocky Mountains, to the Pacific Ocean, and back to St. Louis. The expedition created widespread interest in the American West, its inhabitants, and its possibilities for economic development.

There followed more than half a century of sustained contact with the Plains Indians. Scientists, traders, adventurers, government explorers and soldiers, painters, and others, such as teachers, missionaries, and whiskey peddlers, entered the plains. Most people crossed the plains to get to the Rocky Mountain fur country or to New Mexico, Oregon, or California. Others carved out homesteads on the eastern edge of the plains or pushed into Indian Territory (modern Oklahoma, Kansas, and Nebraska). Indian people were friendly, hospitable, and with few exceptions peaceful at first, but as contacts increased so did friction.

When trouble between Indian groups and white migrants occurred, the government sent federal troops to the plains. The troops were to punish Indian people, if that was necessary, and to impress Indian leaders with the size and strength of the U.S. Army. Sometimes the plans went awry.

In one such instance in 1823, Colonel Henry Leavenworth led 220 men of his Sixth Infantry up the Missouri River from Council Bluffs. Acting in response to a call for help from fur traders who had been attacked (with thirteen of their men killed) and stopped by Arikaras, he planned to force a passage through the Arikara villages, located along the Missouri about six miles above the mouth of the Grand River. Traders and rivermen soon increased his command, and when they saw the expedition as a chance to strike a blow at the Arikaras, Lakota and Yankton warriors joined Leavenworth. A combined force of 1,100 men in August attacked the Arikara villages, but Leavenworth soon convinced the Arikaras to negotiate a truce. Wanting to crush the Arikaras, the fur traders, Lakotas, and Yanktons were disappointed, and the powerful Lakotas interpreted Leavenworth's negotiations as a lack of bravery. As the army began its return to Council Bluffs, the traders set fire to the villages, burning them to the ground.[10]

Fur traders complained that Leavenworth's failure to strike a hard blow at the Arikaras would encourage Indian efforts to block passage up the Missouri. One of them wrote "that instead of raising the American character in the estimation of its inhabitants and impressing them with the power and spirit of our government, the contrary effect has been produced." Leavenworth disagreed, suggesting that if future trouble occurred it would be due to the burning of the villages. His superiors, however, feared that in the absence of a strong show of military force both the Arikaras and Lakotas might attack American traders and scientists along the river.[11]

In response, Colonel Henry Atkinson in 1825 led a peace commission up the Missouri River. With 476 men and eight keelboats, he made a show of military force, fired shells from the big cannon his troops had brought upriver, and met in council with various Missouri River peoples. With Benjamin O'Fallon, an Indian agent appointed as peace commissioner, Atkinson concluded nine treaties, all of them statements of friendship that affirmed the idea of licensed fur traders, return of stolen property, and apprehension of foreign traders. Child Chief of the Poncas, Black Bear of the Yanktons, Little Moon of the Cheyennes, Long Hair of the Crows, and Bloody Hand of the Arikaras signed Atkinson's treaties, as did Standing Buffalo of the Oglala and Little White Bear of the Hunkpapa divisions of the Lakotas. Leaders of the Yanktonais, Mandans, and Hidatsas also consented to treaties.[12]

Hoping also to negotiate with the Blackfeet, Atkinson ascended the Missouri some 120 miles above the mouth of the Yellowstone River. Unsuccessful in contacting Blackfeet leaders, he returned downstream. Back at Fort Atkinson, he signed treaties with Only Chief and Big Female of the Otos and Missouris, Bad Chief and Sun Chief of the Pawnees, and Big Elk of the Omahas.[13]

By the mid 1830s the American government had with limitations extended an effective federal authority to many of the horticultural and hunting peoples of the plains. It had succeeded by using a combination of army posts and roads, military expeditions, peace commissions, and experienced traders. In response to the government action, several Plains Indian groups had agreed to keep trade routes open, and some, such as the Santees, had accepted restrictions on their hunting lands.

The government was less effective in dealing with hostilities between Indian communities. On the plains raiding parties formed, struck, and dispersed before Indian bureau personnel or army officers knew of their existence. Consequently, intertribal raiding on the Great Plains continued, and in some areas even increased, after the mid 1830s.

The Comanches, for example, having agreed in an 1835 treaty (Camp Holmes) to remain away from immigrant Indian groups on the eastern edge of the plains, struck deep into Texas, still a part of Mexico. The raids, the first against American settlements there, began as Texans sought independence. In one of the most destructive raids, occurring in May 1836, a group of Comanche and Kiowa allies attacked Parker's Fort, located east of the Brazos River near modern Groesbeck, and took several captives, including young Cynthia Ann Parker, who grew to womanhood among the Comanches and whose son Quanah became a powerful Comanche chief.[14]

The Lakotas, likewise, continued to expand their range of territory and to increase their population and power. Led by the Oglalas and Brules, they successfully challenged the Pawnees for use of the Platte River Valley, moved into the upper North Platte hunting ranges above Fort Laramie, and became the principal threat to American control of the northern Great Plains. Apparently unimpressed with the U.S. Army's recent demonstrations on the middle Missouri River, the Oglalas and Brules became particularly aggressive in their territorial designs, especially west of the Black Hills.

In the late 1830s perhaps the major development affecting the Plains Indians was the rapid spread of pandemic diseases. The major disease—once again—was smallpox. Carried to the plains by deckhands onboard an American Fur Company steamboat moving up the Missouri, the disease struck Arikara, Mandan, and Hidatsa villages with devastating results in 1837. In a few weeks perhaps one half of the estimated forty-five hundred Arikaras and Hidatsas died, and the disease killed virtually all of the more than sixteen hundred Mandans (138 survived).[15] The neighboring Yanktonais suffered four hundred deaths. From the Missouri River villagers, smallpox swept the northern plains, reaching into Canada, where the Assiniboins lost over one half of their population of eight thousand, and into western Montana, where it killed six thousand to eight thousand Blackfeet, including Piegans, Bloods, and Siksikas. The Crows lost a third (one thousand) of their people. In one division of the Lakotas, one half of the people died. In 1838 the Pawnees acquired the sickness from Lakota scalps and prisoners whom they had taken in a raid. Perhaps two thousand Pawnees died.[16]

Traders carried the disease south, where smallpox spread to Kansa, Omaha, and Osage peoples. From the Osages it spread in the winter of 1839–40 to Kiowa, Kiowa-Apache, Cheyenne, Arapaho, and Comanche bands. The 1837 smallpox pandemic represented one of the more serious cases of disease-related deaths on the Great Plains.[17]

Disease pandemics and the growing white presence also altered geopolitical dynamics. Concerned with the westward displacement of bison herds and the concomitant crowding of Indian peoples into restricted hunting grounds, many Plains Indian groups forged alliances that changed intertribal relationships. Although the plains was a place nearly always in flux, the alliances created peace among some groups, leaving others isolated and turning more and more to the protection of federal troops.[18]

On the northern plains the growing power of the Lakota divisions was the key to the shifting balance of power. The Lakotas, as they expanded their territorial claims, fashioned an alliance with the Southern Cheyenne Dog Soldiers (occasionally called Half-Sioux Cheyenne), Northern Cheyennes, and Northern Arapahos. Then they brought the Yanktonais and much later some of the Assiniboins into their orbit. The alliances were peace agreements that grew more out of rivalry over hunting grounds than out of problems from intertribal war, but difficulties related to tribal devastation from disease also became factors. The Lakotas refused to surrender the bison-rich Platte River country to the Pawnees, and in the 1840s some seven thousand Oglalas and Brules moved toward Fort Laramie on the upper North Platte to be near the bison.

The once powerful Pawnees, weakened by deaths from smallpox, could not counter their northern enemies, and to escape the mounting number of Lakota raids, moved their villages south of the Platte. Shortly afterward, the government ordered the Pawnees back to their Loup River sites, and the Lakota as well as Cheyenne attacks continued.

The Yanktonais resented the Métis presence in their lands. Taking thousands of bison to sell the hides to Hudson's Bay Company agents, the Métis pressed deep into Yanktonai and Yankton territory east of the Missouri River. Suffering from results of the recent smallpox epidemic that crippled their population, the Yanktons could do little. The Yanktonais, however, freed by the recent overtures of peace from destructive Lakota raids, struck at Métis intrusions, forcing the Canadians to reorder their hunting patterns. The Yanktonais also increased their raids on the Assiniboins and later intruded on Assiniboin hunting grounds.

The Northern Cheyennes and Northern Arapahos, likewise freed from Lakota attacks, pursued their own objectives. They concentrated on keeping the Pawnees near their villages below the middle Platte and lower Loup rivers and in defending themselves from the Crows. Moreover, living astride the upper North Platte River, one of the major roads to the Far West, the Cheyennes and Arapahos needed the intertribal stability to adjust to the growing white traffic across the plains.

The Assiniboins needed peace. In 1837 some four thousand of the eight thousand Assiniboins died as a result of smallpox. With fewer warriors, people of the once strong group could no longer launch revenge raids or even defend themselves adequately against concerted strikes from their neighbors. The shifting alliances on the northern plains eventually caused the Assiniboins to split: one group in the 1850s made peace with the Yanktonais and the other made peace with their old Gros Ventre enemies and became friendly with some Crow people.

The same pox that killed many Assiniboins also struck the Blackfeet confederacy. Within four years of the 1837 epidemic, nearly half of the confederacy's population of fifteen thousand had died. In one Piegan camp only two people survived. Blackfeet people north and west of the Big Horn Mountains surrendered some of their best hunting grounds and pulled back toward the Canadian border to be closer to their kinsmen in Alberta.

On the southern plains the problems were more complex, but in 1840 the nomadic groups moved to establish peace among themselves.[19] Each tribe had its own reasons. The Southern Cheyennes wanted more horses, easier access to hunting lands below the Arkansas River, and an end to the recent war with the Kiowas. The war had begun in 1837 when Satank, the brilliant Kiowa *Kaitsenko* leader, and his warriors had killed, stripped, and scalped forty-eight men of the Cheyenne Bow String society on a horse-stealing venture in Kiowa territory near the Antelope Hills. A year later, seeking revenge, a Cheyenne war party that included the young (but future chief) Black Kettle, attacked a large Kiowa camp in the battle of Wolf Creek. The Cheyennes killed some fifty men and women, but in a fight that lasted several hours they were not able to take the camp, losing two important leaders, Gray Thunder and Gray Hair, and a number of important warriors. Peace with the Kiowas would allow the Cheyennes to continue their raids against the hated Pawnees, who in 1830 had captured the Cheyenne Sacred Arrows bundle, and to secure horses through trade from the large Kiowa herds.

The Kiowas wanted greater access to trade at Bent's Fort, located in Cheyenne country on the Arkansas River in southeastern Colorado. Established by William Bent and others about 1834, the trading post had been a major attraction to the Cheyennes and Arapahos, one that played an important role in their reasons for pushing south from the lower Black Hills to the upper Arkansas. Bent married a Southern Cheyenne, Owl Woman, and the couple had five children who drifted between eastern white society and their western Indian world. Bent's Fort, a large adobe fortress, became such a busy place that its visitors and occupants used up the timber for miles along the river. Grass over wide stretches around the post disappeared under heavy grazing from horses, mules, and oxen. Indian people, mountain men, Santa Fe traders, and others all used the post as a rest stop and market place. The Kiowas also wanted to do business there.

The Southern Arapahos, those friendly people of an easy temperament, wanted and needed peace. The recent smallpox epidemic had decimated their already small population, and they had become reluctant to continue fighting the durable Kiowas, even alongside their Cheyenne allies. Indeed, some Arapaho people were in regular contact with the Kiowas, visiting them as far south as Adobe Walls on the Canadian River in the Texas Panhandle, a place where William Bent had established a short-lived trading post. Moreover, the Arapahos may have sought peace based solely on their accommodating disposition.

The Comanche desire for peace related to a growing threat from Texas. After generations of mainly successful raiding in Texas, the Comanches—at least the southern division, the Penatekas—had suffered a major defeat in San Antonio. Twelve Penateka leaders, under the tall old Muguara (Spirit Talker) and accompanied by fifty-three warriors, women, and children, in March 1840 had ridden in to discuss peace. At the meeting with Texas authorities in a stone building afterward called the "Council House," a fight broke out. The twelve chiefs, including Muguara, died, and the Texans captured most of the others. In April Comanche leader Piava negotiated a trade for most of the hostages, but the Council House massacre caused shock, grief, and outrage among all Comanche divisions, provoking daring retaliatory raids. If they were going to make war on the Texans, the Comanches did not need to be fighting Cheyennes on a second front to the north.

The result was a grand council of peace along the Arkansas River several miles downstream from Bent's Fort where timber and grass still existed. Perhaps five thousand Indians with over eight thousand horses attended. Pahayuco and Buffalo Hump (Potsanaquahip) of the Comanches, High Backed Wolf and Yellow Wolf of the Cheyennes, and Eagle Feather, Satank, and Little Mountain of the Kiowas played important roles, as did leaders of the Kiowa Apaches, who initiated the peace feelers. The Comanches and Kiowas gave their northern friends hundreds of horses, with Satank giving away perhaps two hundred head from his personal herd. Leaders from each of the tribes exchanged gifts, feasted on various culinary delicacies, smoked the calumet of peace, and in general established a solid, but not complete, friendship.[20]

Just a few years later, the War with Mexico (1846–48) and the crush of gold seekers to California in 1849 marked the beginning of a period of significant changes for the Plains Indians. When Stephen Watts Kearny, an able and experienced U.S. military officer, in 1846 led his troops toward Santa Fe through the heart of the Great Plains, leaders of the southern plains peoples were startled. Kearny stopped at Bent's Fort, where Indian leaders viewed seventeen hundred soldiers, twenty thousand horses and mules, and scores of canvas-topped wagons stretching for miles along the Arkansas River. With good reason Yellow Wolf, the thoughtful Cheyenne leader, and other plains tribesmen were apprehensive. They recognized that here existed an enormous white presence to which they could provide no adequate response.[21]

Farther north along the sandy Platte River Valley, perhaps forty-five thousand forty-niners raced to California. At the end of the summer migration season in 1849, the valley lay dusty and barren, with wood along the shallow stream cut for fuel, grass along the river lowlands destroyed under the pressure of too many horses, mules, and oxen. Thousands of Mormon migrants who traveled on the north bank of the Platte added to the woes. The ecological devastation in the gutted valley cut a wide swath through the rolling grassland, permanently dividing the bison herds and splitting the Great Plains through its central heartland.

The mounting number of whites ran off game and destroyed root-digging grounds. Washakie, the great Shoshoni leader, complained that "before the emigrants passed through [my] country, buffalo, elk and antelope could be seen upon all the hills; now, . . . [I see] only wagons [and my] people [are] very poor."[22] By the late 1840s, with such well-traveled routes as the Santa Fe Trail to New Mexico and the Oregon Trail along the Platte River, the Great Plains had been cut into three parts, divisions that disrupted migrating bison herds and influenced Plains Indian life.

By this time, too, the United States needed a new policy for dealing with the Plains Indians. From the western prairies of Minnesota to the central hill country of Texas, white people crowded toward the plains, leaving less and less territory for occupation by Indian people. Moreover, lands of the enormous Mexican Cession acquired after the War with Mexico in 1848 needed to be occupied, and that meant military posts and with them soldiers, supply trains, farmers, ranchers, and townspeople—all cutting through, or settling in, western Indian lands.

Various plans for a new policy emerged in the 1840s. Most of them called for a general plan of restricted colonies for American Indians, but not until after the War with Mexico did Congress take action. In November, 1850, Luke Lea, the Commissioner of Indian Affairs, suggested that the hunting peoples of the plains, "our wilder tribes" as he called them, should be "placed in positions where they can be controlled," in a permanent home in a country "of limited extent and well-defined boundaries."[23] Congress agreed and in February 1851 passed the Indian Appropriation Act, a law that sanctioned a new policy of concentration and provided $100,000 to negotiate a set of treaties.

Thomas Fitzpatrick applied the new concentration policy. A master of frontier skills and known as "Broken Hand" to Indian people, Fitzpatrick was the U.S. agent for the Upper Platte and Arkansas Agency. He summoned many of the bison-hunting peoples to a meeting near Fort Laramie, a former fur trade outpost located on the North Fork of the Platte River in present Wyoming. In 1851 almost ten thousand Indian people (the largest gathering of American Indians on the plains up to that time) from nine groups attended. With their tipis and horses stretched for miles across the area, restless young warriors exchanged challenges to races on foot and horseback and boasted bravely to one another, and 270 hopelessly outmanned soldiers nervously stood by, watching the mountain of gifts that would be distributed at the council meeting's conclusion. Fearful that enemies might steal their large horse herds, Comanche and Kiowa bands did not appear.

After moving the huge Indian camp to Horse Creek, about forty miles from the fort, the "Great Council" took place. The meeting, and scores of treaty councils like it, represented a long-established procedure for making peace (or at least negotiating) between various Indian communities on the plains or between Plains Indians and whites. In its Indian diplomacy the U.S. government had long used councils to explain treaties and to persuade Indian spokespersons to sign them.

But cultural differences existed. As explained by Raymond J. DeMallie, although both understood the council meeting as a diplomatic medium for open discussion, Indian and white participants held separate ideas about treaties. To the Plains Indians the council—the coming together—remained the key; the treaty was less important. For the federal government and its representatives, the treaty, signed at the end of the council meeting, mattered above all else; the council served only as a preliminary to the written agreement.

Indian and white council rituals also differed. The meetings included such ritualistic actions as gift giving and pipe smoking. From the Plains Indian point of view, pipe smoking, perhaps the most common ritual, was a pledge to truth and honor in the discussions to follow. Gift giving served as a prelude to bargaining. But whites, as at Horse Creek, often held back mountains of goods and kept them close at hand as a bribe to speed the bargaining, for such gifts would be distributed only at the close of the meeting. The councils usually included ritualistic feasts and dances, and sometimes the younger men offered displays of horsemanship. Although they might consider it silly, or at least redundant, Indian representatives usually signed the treaty, an act they

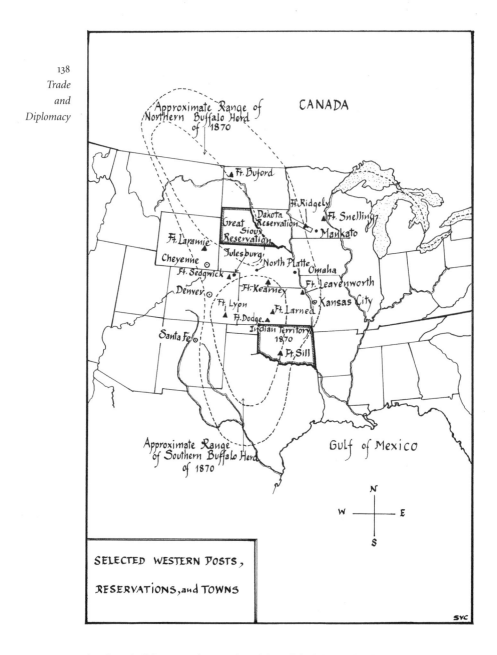

CANADA

Approximate Range of
Northern Buffalo Herd
of 1870

▲ Ft. Buford

▲ Ft. Ridgely

Dakota
Reservation
Great
Sioux
Reservation

▲ Ft. Snelling
• Mankato

Ft. Laramie

Cheyenne ⊙

Julesburg

North Platte

• Omaha

Ft. Sedgwick ▲

Denver ⊙

Ft. Kearney ▲

Ft. Leavenworth ▲

Ft. Lyon ▲

Ft. Larned ▲

⊙ Kansas City

Ft. Dodge ▲

Indian Territory
1870

Santa Fe ⊙

▲ Ft. Sill

Gulf of Mexico

Approximate Range
of Southern Buffalo Herd
of 1870

N
W — E
S

SELECTED WESTERN POSTS,
RESERVATIONS, and TOWNS

SVC

(perhaps) did not understand and (surely) did not think necessary, but one they knew was important to whites—a white ritualism.

Thus, as DeMallie suggests, Plains Indian diplomacy featured gift giving, ritual, and counseling through carefully prepared speeches. Although changes occurred as the councils became less elaborate and the rituals and gift giving declined after the 1851 Horse Creek discussions, the council meeting as an institution of diplomacy remained stable through the last half of the nineteenth century.[24]

At Horse Creek, then, following much ritualism, debate, and extended speeches, the participants signed the Treaty of Fort Laramie. One of the most significant accords between American Indians and the government, the treaty, completed on September 17, 1851, reflected the government's evolving efforts to concentrate the Plains Indians away from main-traveled roads and to establish peace between Indian groups. The Indian peoples received gifts, bounties, promises, and an annuity of $50,000 for fifty years (which the U.S. Senate reduced to ten years). The twenty-one leaders from eight Indian groups who signed the treaty pledged that their warriors would not attack travelers, freight wagons, or mail stages crossing their territory.[25]

More importantly, the Indian participants agreed to accept definite tribal limitations to their land. The Lakotas received the country north of the Platte and west of the Missouri. The Mandans, Gros Ventres, and Arikaras accepted lands east of the lower Yellowstone; the Assiniboins west of it; and the Crows west of the Powder River. The Cheyennes and Arapahos retained the western plains between the North Platte and Arkansas rivers, and later the Shoshonis got land in the Wind River country of Wyoming.[26]

Fitzpatrick did not invite Pawnees, Omahas, Poncas, Otos, or Missouris to the Fort Laramie meeting. To maintain peace he should have, for many of them lived on land the Lakotas hunted. Without a peace agreement the people of these village groups remained subject to Lakota raids. Moreover, the Cheyennes, led by their spokesman Rides on Clouds and still angry over the Pawnee theft of their Sacred Arrows in 1830, refused a postconference offer of peace from Chief Big Fatty of the Skidi Pawnees.

In 1853 Indian leaders of the southern plains signed the Treaty of Fort Atkinson. Broken Hand Fitzpatrick, as sole commissioner for the government, met with the Comanches and their allies the Kiowas and Kiowa Apaches at Fort Atkinson on the Arkansas River near present Dodge City. The participants came to terms on July 27, but only after considerable persuasion on the part of Fitzpatrick. The federal government provided gifts and bounties and agreed to pay an annuity of $18,000 for ten years. The Indian delegates, as they had in an earlier treaty, agreed to allow whites to use the heavily traveled Santa Fe Trail and accepted tribal limitations to their territory. The Comanches, led by Shaved Head and Rides on Clouds, promised to remain below the Arkansas; the Kiowas, led by Chief Little Mountain and their war leader Satank, and Kiowa Apaches, led by Poor Wolf, agreed to stay in the area near the Arkansas west of its Great Bend. Indian leaders also agreed to stop raiding in Mexico.[27]

Two years later the Blackfeet, the principal remaining plains holdout, signed the Judith Treaty. The pact, which they concluded with Isaac Stevens, the governor of the Washington Territory, provided for an annuity of $20,000 for ten years and $15,000 per year for educating Blackfeet children at government-built schools. Under the leadership of Lame Bull, Mountain Chief, and Low Horn of the Piegans; Feather and White Eagle of the Bloods; and Three Bulls of the Siksikas, the Blackfeet accepted a restricted land area about the upper Missouri in western Montana and agreed to military posts and the safe passage of travelers through their lands. Piegan Chief Low Horn warned Stevens, however, that, although they might be willing to establish peace, the older leaders could not restrain the competitive nature of the younger men who, to gain status, needed to achieve success in hunting or raiding.[28]

The Crows and Shoshonis, who had been invited to Stevens's meeting at the junction of the Judith and Missouri rivers in north-central Montana, did not attend. Representing the Plains Crees and Assiniboins, whom the government likewise had invited, was one Cree leader, Chief Broken Arm, who brought tobacco as a token of friendship. From the Blackfeet perspective the absence of the Crows was important. The headman of the Bloods, Seen from Afar, worried that in lieu of peace with their old enemies "our young men will not be persuaded that they ought not to war against the Crows."[29]

Meanwhile, in 1853 George W. Manypenny, the Commissioner of Indian Affairs, began to secure treaties that further restricted Indian land holdings in Kansas or moved American Indians out of the region altogether. The so-called "Manypenny treaties," arranged with the Delaware, Iowa, Kaskaskia, Kickapoo, Miami, Missouri, Oto, Sac and Fox, Shawnee, Peoria, and other tribes, resulted in the forfeiture of over fifteen million acres (their new reservations represented about 1.5 million acres) and in effect liquidated the northern portion of Indian Territory.

In the mid 1850s the Plains Indians' world was changing dramatically. In the north, the Ojibwas, having been forced from much of Wisconsin and Minnesota into the Canadian forests of Manitoba, bumped the Crees westward and pressured the Métis of the lower Red River. At least one band of Ojibwas moved to the edge of the Canadian plains in Alberta. The four Santee divisions, having accepted in the Treaty of Traverse des Sioux (1851) a reservation on the upper Minnesota River, pushed Yanktons and Yanktonais westward up against the Missouri River. When eastern Nebraska opened to white settlement in 1854, Indian groups of western Iowa moved farther west, placing pressure on the Poncas, Omahas, and Otos of the middle Missouri River.

Farther south similar developments occurred as eastern groups pushed into territory inhabited by plains nomads. Bison, although huge numbers of them still remained, became harder and harder to find. To ease the growing scarcity, restless young warriors broke into smaller groups to steal and raid among both Indians and whites. Intertribal wars intensified and became a irritating problem for the federal government. The Pawnees and Lakotas, for example, had fought a series of ferocious battles for years, and they continued to fight one another. The government countered with additional expeditions.[30]

In the mid 1850s American Indians on the plains with no place to retreat had no place to go. Hungry but faced with declining food supplies, beleaguered but faced with increasing white pressure, and dying but faced with mysterious maladies, the exasperated Indian people, as they had always done, moved across the changing plains grasslands and through their familiar, but restricted, hunting grounds without heed to boundaries or borders. Under pressure from a growing number of western settlers, the U.S. Army struck back. There followed a long decade of wars that suddenly turned the Plains Indians from nomadic bison hunters to settled residents on government-run reservations.

9 : WAR AND PEACE

Significant fighting between Plains Indians and government soldiers extended for a little more than a decade. The fighting had its beginning in the turbulent years of the 1850s, intensified in the Civil War years, and reached a peak in the years immediately afterward. In the early period Indian participants accorded themselves well, often achieving a large measure of success. In the later period, the federal troops prevailed, but not before the extension of railroads to the plains and the disappearance of bison. During the military campaigns both Indian and government representatives endeavored to secure a lasting peace, but pressures of an advancing white population thwarted the efforts until the Plains Indians relocated to small reservations scattered throughout the American West.

The increasing white population in the West was staggering. It numbered 1.3 million in 1860, 2.3 million ten years later, and 4.9 million in 1880. The government in 1860 estimated about 350,000 American Indians (about the same number of people who lived on Manhattan Island in New York City) in all the West, but only about 75,000 of them on the Great Plains. Although severely outnumbered, the Plains Indians in 1860 continued to hunt, often undisturbed, over large areas of the plains. The number of bison between the Arkansas and Platte rivers and beyond the Black Hills in the Powder River country remained enormous, if declining.

Trouble came soon enough. New discoveries of gold in Colorado, mounting white migration across the plains, and the government's desire to improve western transportation seriously contracted both Indian land and bison herds. "This country was once covered with buffalo, elk, deer, and antelope, and we had plenty to eat," noted the Shoshoni leader Washakie. "But now, since the white man has made a road across our land and has killed off our game, we are hungry, and there is nothing left for us to eat. Our women and children cry for food and we have no food to give them."[1] Survival of the Indians, at least from the government's perspective, depended upon getting Indian people out of the way of the growing traffic.

To keep the Comanches and Kiowas away from settlers on the southern plains, the federal government in 1853 built a line of military posts along the advancing frontier in Texas. Robert S. Neighbors, an able and honest Indian agent, met with southern Comanche leaders, including Old Owl, Yellow Bird, Senaco, Buffalo Hump, and Ketumseh, and convinced some of them to accept a reservation on the Clear Fork of the Brazos River. In 1855 about three hundred Comanche people lived on the reservation. A few years later Texas frontiersmen drove the Comanches out and opened the reservation, as well as one nearby for other Indian groups, to white settlement.[2]

On the northern plains white traffic along the Oregon Trail resulted in the Grattan affair. A young Miniconjou Lakota, High Forehead, in 1854 shot a lame cow. When a Mormon migrant near Fort Laramie claimed the animal and sought government restitution, Lt. John Grattan, who recently had arrived from the East, rode with thirty men to the Brule camp of Chief Conquering Bear, where High Forehead was visiting, and demanded payment or surrender of High Forehead. The Lakotas delayed, and the impatient Grattan ordered his men to fire. The Brules and other Lakotas at the village countered, killing Grattan with his entire party, and then they widened their activities to immigrant trains and trading depots. A year later Colonel William S. Harney, a white-bearded officer whom Indian people called "Mad Bear," struck several Lakota villages, and in March of 1856 he got the Lakotas to accept a treaty that gave the government authority to name the Lakota (and Yankton) chiefs. The Senate rejected the treaty, but fear of Harney's return kept the Lakotas quiet for several years.[3]

On the central plains the gold rush of 1859 brought 100,000 people to Colorado, most of them through Kansas. So many people flooded Cheyenne and Arapaho lands that Indian people essentially became isolated in their own country. Another treaty seemed needed, and government agents in February 1861 convinced several leaders, including the wise and gentle Black Kettle as well as Left Hand and Lean Bear of the Cheyennes and Little Raven and Storm of the Arapahos, to sign the Treaty of Fort Wise (Fort Lyon). Those who signed agreed to abandon the central plains between the Platte and Arkansas rivers and accept some land bordering the Arkansas River in southeastern Colorado. Because bison and other game were hard to find in the region, many people left to hunt and raid. Federal troops and Colorado militia units went in pursuit. Cheyenne and Arapaho warriors struck back, and the fighting that followed engulfed the entire plains in major war.

Major warfare on the Great Plains lasted from 1864 to 1876, just over a decade. In fact, in 1870 most of the Plains Indians were living on reservations, and much of the fighting afterward occurred between regular army soldiers and Indian warriors who had left the reservations with their families and refused to return. Such fighting in most cases represented cleanup campaigns. When the army adopted its policy of attacking the plains people in their small winter camps, resistance among the Plains Indians broke down and for all practical purposes seemed nonexistent. In the wars on the plains, then, Indian people had no real chance—at least over the long haul.[4]

In the short run, the Plains Indians possessed several advantages. They remained formidable warriors and superb horsemen, and they knew their homeland thoroughly. In some ways they appeared better equipped for fighting on the plains than the soldiers who came against them, for they needed no long wagon trains for supplies and rations, and each warrior could carry dozens of arrows and keep one or more in the air constantly. Their horse-mounted military traditions were unrivaled.[5]

The western army, at least in the early years of the fighting, possessed little experience in dealing with the guerrilla-style, horse-mounted tactics of the Plains Indians. In some of its divisions, such as the state militia and state volunteer units sworn into federal service, the frontier army seemed a sorry collection of sad sacks. It also suffered from poor leadership. The army, however, enjoyed a large industrial base, an increasing number of railroads for quick transportation, and the telegraph (once lines were extended) for rapid communication. In addition, it could exert a united, concerted, and concentrated effort. Its advantages overcame the initial weaknesses of inexperience and poor leadership. After the Civil War the western army, particularly the regular units, gained not only experience but also an aristocracy of talent in its leadership.

The Plains Indians could not prevail in a protracted war. They had no industrial base, and they had no concept of a united, concentrated effort. They could not sustain a fight and could not hold what they had won. Most battles ended with Indian participants in retreat, even when they had won, for their supplies were exhausted and their concept of warfare did not include the idea of controlling an important river crossing, a strategic hill, or a critical mountain pass. For them war remained a series of individual fights in which counting coup seemed more important than killing or capturing the enemy.

Moreover, throughout the wars with whites the Plains Indians remained more interested in raiding other Indian villages and stealing horses than in fighting whites. In the 1850s and 1860s the Lakotas and Yanktonais continued to threaten Ponca, Pawnee, and Omaha villages to the south and east, and expansionist aims of the Lakotas (mainly the Brules and Oglalas) pressured the Crow, Gros Ventre, and Blackfeet people to the west and north. The fighting in part caused the Piegans and Gros Ventres, once allies, to begin raids on one another. Gros Ventres and Crows joined forces in the 1860s to raid Blackfeet villages on the upper Missouri. The Lakotas, Yanktonais, Northern Cheyennes (and eventually some Southern Cheyennes), and Northern Arapahos continued their old alliance, which in the 1860s created a sizable confederation that pushed into the Powder River country. Here their large camps became subject to Crow horse-stealing raids, and when retaliatory strikes followed, Indian fighting continued—but it remained limited war, often confined to small raids, counterraids, and coup-counting usually associated with the Plains Indians' prevailing concepts of war.

The soldier-Indian wars, however, represent a tragic culture clash. Both the Indians and the soldiers held exalted images of themselves, and neither seemed interested in understanding the attitudes and thoughts of the other. Their concepts of warfare, land use, and social structure were different. Indian warriors used many weapons of bone, horn, stone, and wood. The soldiers were concerned with the idea of future progress, with production, and with the use of "modern" technology in combat. Each side considered its own actions justified, the other's wanton and murderous, thus giving rise to such names as the Grattan massacre (in which Indian warriors badly defeated soldiers) and the Sand Creek massacre (in which territorial troops in federal service killed men, women, and children) to their engagements.

Myth sometimes governs perceptions about warfare. Many soldiers did not want to fight. For them Indian campaigns often meant endless days staring at a waterhole, long marches across a dusty prairie for weeks at a time, and few comforts. Although many engagements occurred, there was little that was gallant about Indian fighting on the Great Plains. As confining as life at a frontier fort might be, at least an army post had comforts and an occasional bit of gambling or other amusements, and diversions existed in the little towns that sprang up near the posts. Many of the officers likewise preferred not to fight Indian people, but the army in part determined promotions above the rank of colonel by success in battle. The competition was keen. Thus, to gain one of the few promotions that occurred in the post–Civil War army, men seeking a general officer rank needed to make a name for themselves by gaining a spectacular victory over an enemy in the field.

The nature of the fighting represents a related misconception. Because the horse-mounted Indian warriors rarely stood to fight but preferred hit-and-run, guerrilla-style raids, engagements, when they occurred, were a series of fighting pursuits. At the battle of Beecher's Island on the Arikaree Fork of the Republican River in northeastern Colorado in 1868, soldiers, who had been recently recruited from the frontier, dug in and fought off repeated attacks of horse-mounted warriors. Accounts of the battle filled newspapers of the day, giving the impression that most fighting in the West followed a similar pattern. It did not, but young soldiers saw in the battle their own self-image as Indian fighters: outnumbered and surrounded, but steadfast and heroic under heavy siege as Indian warriors thundered down around them through several days of furious combat. More often soldiers rode for miles to engage the enemy, then watched as Indian warriors scattered to fight when they held the advantage. Very little formal combat took place. For Indian people, engagements with the army were often a series of fighting retreats as they moved their families from one campsite to another. For the army, fighting the Plains Indians proved far more frustrating than heroic.

Barricaded forts became another misconception. Most were not. In the mid 1860s the government did indeed barricade posts along the Bozeman Trail, running north and west from Fort Laramie to the gold fields of western Montana, but the practice generally remained too expensive, for the army designed most military installations as temporary structures. Nor were barricades needed. Plains warriors, in part because of their concepts of warfare, rarely attacked army posts. Indian raiding parties, however, stole horses and ran off livestock that might be grazing nearby.

There also is a myth of large numbers of Indian warriors and soldiers killed. In the 1868 battle of Beecher's Island, unusual in that it lasted nine days, six soldiers died. Indian informants reported nine Indian men killed. Similarly, in 1875 Lt. Col. William R. Shafter led black troops under his command across the Llano Estacado of West Texas and eastern New Mexico following a veritable maze of trails in pursuit of American Indians. When the campaign ended after five long months in the field, Shafter reported one Apache killed, five (four women and a boy) captured. No soldiers died.[6] With such exceptions as the Minnesota Sioux uprising and the Sand Creek massacre, few whites and fewer Indians died in warfare on the Great Plains. Indeed, during the nineteenth century Indian casualties in battles with other Indian groups probably reached numbers higher than losses in campaigns with white soldiers.[7]

In addition, only a few of the more than thirty Indian groups that occupied the western prairies and high plains during the middle of the nineteenth century fought in the wars against whites. A majority of them, including those communities that had been taking a beating from the larger groups, sided with the soldiers. The Pawnees and Crows, for example, provided scouts for the army and in other ways assisted the soldiers. In effect, preexisting patterns of intertribal warfare influenced the fighting against whites.[8]

Finally, it is a misconception to think that Indian people did not adjust to the mounting war with whites. During the period, as we have seen, a few plains groups changed somewhat in social organization from composite tribe to chiefdoms (the idea of a central authority figure). The tribe represented a loose social organization with perhaps several leaders. But under pressure of increasing warfare, Indian people looked to charismatic leaders, such as Sitting Bull, Red Cloud, Crazy Horse, Quanah, or Black Kettle, for guidance.

In the new developing arrangements the leader became a figurehead for his people. He assumed responsibility for their livelihood, their politics, and their relationships with other groups—both Indian and white communities. In addition, as military fraternities, in face of mounting war-related deaths among their members, declined in influence, the leader's role expanded. His powers were not limitless, however, for he had no legalized authority to carry out his decisions; and that lack of authority was a weakness in the new order of things.

Clearly, in the wake of repeated war and peace, internal political economies of Plains Indian communities changed in complicated and important ways. But they did not all change alike. The Araphos, for example, increasingly accommodated themselves to white ideas about tribal organization and leadership, and as early as the 1851 Horse Creek council they appointed Little Owl as their head chief, a concession to federal government representatives who wanted to deal with a single leader rather than several band chiefs. In addition, rather than choose their own range of territory in 1851, Cut Nose, a tribal spokesman, suggested in another concession that white leaders pick out Arapaho lands. But then, in typical Arapaho fashion, he asked that the whites reciprocate by not hunting on their land.

The Lakotas, on the other hand, for as long as they could, refused the appointment of a single leader. They wanted, as Blue Earth, an old Brule chief, said, "a chief for each band," and he indicated to government representatives in 1851, "if you will make one or two chiefs for each band, it will be much better for you and the whites. . . . [We] can't make one chief." Eventually, the Lakotas yielded, and when they did, they created a new political and diplomatic office, one the Lakotas probably had not used earlier.[9]

Thus, changes occurred. But on the plains no significant Indian confederations formed, as they had earlier east of the Mississippi River, to resist mounting white pressure. Nor did the Plains Indians develop a coherent foreign policy as had, for example, the Iroquois and the Cherokees. Defeat came too quickly, for one thing, and animosities over access to restricted bison-hunting ranges remained too inflamed, for another. Moreover, since the beginning of the concentration policy in 1851, when tribal territories had been clearly marked out, the government could—and did—secure additional lands from any one Indian group on the plains without arousing the others.

After the Civil War, the United States Army contained about fifty-six thousand officers and men (a number the army later reduced) serving in three divisions: the Atlantic, Pacific, and Missouri.[10] The division of the Missouri (actually the Mississippi until the army renamed it in 1869), with headquarters first in St. Louis and later Chicago, was responsible for most of the Indian campaigns on the Great Plains. Authorities divided the division into the departments of Dakota, Platte, Missouri, and Arkansas, and later added the Department of Texas. They divided the departments into districts and sometimes subdistricts to oversee operations in the field. The highly centralized but loose chain of command ran from field and district officers through department and division commanders to the General of the Army, the Secretary of War, and the President.

The Plains Indians had no such organization. Their war leaders led only through personal influence. They could offer no overall policy, unity, authority, or centralizing agency. Although when necessary they fought for their land, their homes, and their lives, the Plains Indians participated mainly for personal honor and distinction, and even as they fought the army they continued to place greater emphasis on fighting other Indian groups—their familiar enemies. The Plains Indians, however, possessed spirited military traditions, distinguished histories of combat, and well-defined military institutions that served them well in the campaigns against white soldiers.[11]

The Plains Indians and the United States Army after 1860 fought in several campaigns in which over one hundred pitched battles occurred. The major campaigns began with the Minnesota Sioux uprising in 1862 and ended with the great Sioux war of 1876—although the Sioux "outbreak" of 1890–91 in western South Dakota brought five thousand troops to the region in a final dramatic encounter with Northern Cheyennes and Lakotas. In between occurred the Cheyenne-Arapaho war, the Sioux war of 1866–68, the Washita campaign, the Red River War, and others. With concomitant military operations through the larger American West, they represent a tragic period in U.S.–Indian relations.

The Civil War was the turning point. American military presence on the plains had been large enough until the war to maintain at least a semblance of peace. Indeed, U.S. domination in some ways proved overwhelming up to 1860 and thus prevented much fighting. Shortly after the Civil War started, however, the United States military presence in the West changed. Troops abandoned forts in the region, particularly Texas, and Indian leaders (and some white settlers) moved to destroy them. The number of military personnel in the remaining posts declined as soldiers went east to fight in the Civil War. Many pioneers enlisted in volunteer armies, leaving women, children, and older men to run farms and ranches on the frontier. In response the Plains Indians slowly at first but with greater daring and frequency began raiding outlying settlements, farms, and ranches in their areas. When Indian warriors found that they could defeat the few ill-trained forces remaining, fighting increased, and by 1862 major warfare had begun.

From Minnesota to Texas problems developed. For whites in Texas the trouble became frightful. Lipans, Kickapoos, and others raided from Mexico.

Comanche and Kiowa bands struck from the plains. Some whites fled their homes, and the frontier in Texas moved back as much as one hundred miles in some places. Others sought help by "forting up," crowding into military posts. Texans along the frontier, but as deep into the state as Kerrville in the hill country, created "home guard" units to defend the region from Indian attacks.

In Minnesota the Sioux uprising of 1862 led to the destruction of homes and villages and the heavy loss of lives. More than four hundred whites died as Santee warriors, led by Shakopee, Big Eagle, Mankato, Red Middle Voice, and even the peace advocate Little Crow (Taoyateduta), burned and pillaged over a wide area along the Minnesota River. The Santees suffered few deaths themselves, but when troops finally restored order, the government tried four hundred Santee men for murder, arson, and rape. The courts ordered 306 hanged for the crimes, but President Abraham Lincoln, arguing that the Indian attacks were acts of war, dropped the sentences for all but 39. At Christmas time on a single scaffold in Mankato, Minnesota, authorities hanged 38.[12] Physician William F. Mayo, from nearby Le Sueur, used the skeletal remains of Cut Nose, who had been with Chief Shakopee, to teach his sons anatomy. Later Mayo and his sons established the famed Mayo Clinic in Rochester, Minnesota.[13]

Causes of the Sioux uprising were many. Deep friction, hard feelings, tribal factions, the failure of the federal government to protect Dakota land, the absence of men and troops, and a half century of treaty making that had left the Santees with little that was promised all contributed. The Santees in 1837 had agreed to abandon lands east of the Mississippi River. In the Treaty of Traverse des Sioux in 1851 they had given up lands in Minnesota and Iowa for a reservation along the upper Minnesota River, and in 1858 they had surrendered land on the north side of the river for gifts, food, and an annuity of $70,000 for fifty years.

The immediate cause was the late arrival of the 1862 annuity payment. Short of food and in debt to agency traders, the Santees, who had put off their annual bison hunt until after the annuity distribution, found their credit stopped. According to Jerome Big Eagle (a Santee), when the agent asked traders what Indian people might eat, the unsympathetic Andrew Myrick said that they can "go and eat grass."[14] Hungry and resentful, the Santees broke into the agency warehouse for food, and when other events overtook them, they struck prairie settlements, but not before they had killed Myrick and stuffed his mouth with grass.

In all, the government used some sixty-three hundred federal and militia troops to defeat the Santees. Regular forces under the eccentric Alfred Sully pursued Indian bands as far as the lower Yellowstone River, deep in Lakota lands above the Black Hills. Perhaps ten thousand or more pioneers fled their homes, leaving twenty-three counties devastated and almost empty of people. The Santees surrendered the reservation, moved west to Dakota, lost their annuities for four years, and for many years played a minor role on the Great Plains.[15]

Shortly afterward came the Cheyenne-Arapaho war of 1864–65. During the conflict, which was characterized by raid and counterraid, Lakotas in the north and Comanches and Kiowas in the south joined Cheyenne and Arapaho warriors. Indian raiders attacked wagon and freight trains, mail stages, ranches, towns, and Colorado-bound immigrants. Colorado units, sometimes raised as an excuse to steal Indian ponies, answered by striking villages and Indian hunting parties. The attacks culminated on November 29, 1864, when Colorado volunteers sworn into federal service and under Colonel John Chivington, a barrel-chested elder in the Methodist church, struck the Cheyenne camp of Black Kettle, a peace advocate, along Sand Creek in southeastern Colorado. The "hundred dazers," as Chivington's volunteers were called (because they served for one hundred days), killed at least 163 men, women, and children.[16] Afterward, while a military commission investigated the massacre, Indian warriors renewed their attacks, for a time isolating Colorado from the rest of the nation.[17] Federal troops arrived, but they seemed ineffectual. The army set fires all across the southwestern plains, hoping to starve out Indian people. It did not work, but in 1865 a strong movement for peace among both Indians and whites abruptly ended the war.

Causes of the Cheyenne-Arapaho war can be traced to the heavy intrusion of whites on Indian hunting grounds. Increasing pressure after the Colorado gold rush had encouraged the Southern Cheyennes and Arapahos to abandon Kansas for territory along the Arkansas River, a sterile, barren country. The agent at Fort Lyon noted that in the winter of 1863–64 few bison and little other game could be found within two hundred miles of their camps. Hungry and desperate, Cheyenne and Arapaho bands attacked wagon trains for food and ranches for livestock. Colorado authorities, thinking they had an Indian war on their hands, struck back. Despite efforts for peace, both sides escalated and widened their attacks.[18]

Treaties ending the war came in October 1865. On the southern plains agent Jesse Leavenworth, William Bent, Kit Carson, and four others met with leaders of the Comanches, Kiowas, Kiowa Apaches, Cheyennes, and Arapahos at the mouth of the Little Arkansas River (modern Wichita). The commissioners and the Indians signed three treaties, known collectively as the treaties of the Little Arkansas. The Cheyennes, led by Black Kettle and Little Robe, and Arapahos, led by Little Raven and Storm, agreed to remain on a reservation south of the Arkansas and to stop depredations along travel routes through the central plains. In return they received gifts and annuities and the government's repudiation of the outrages at Sand Creek. The Comanches, led by Rising Sun, Buffalo Hump, and Ten Bears, and Kiowas, led by Stinking Saddle Horn, Satanta (White Bear), and Satank, accepted land below the Cheyennes and retained the right to hunt in the Texas and Oklahoma panhandles. They also received gifts and annuities. The Kiowa Apaches, led by Poor Bear and Iron Shirt, made similar agreements and accepted the same reservation.[19]

On the northern plains Dakota territorial governor Newton Edmunds, Superintendent of Indian Affairs Edward B. Taylor, and four others met at Fort Sully on the Missouri River with leaders of the Lakotas and Yanktonais. The commissioners and Indians, led by Lone Horn, Iron Nation, White Hawk, War Eagle, Yellow Hawk, Buck, and Charging Bear of the Lakotas and Big Head and Tall Soldier of the Yanktonais, signed a series of nine treaties (collectively known as the treaties of Fort Sully), one with each of the seven Lakota divisions and one each with the Upper and Lower Yanktonais. Except for Lone Horn, the Indian participants were peace advocates who had not participated in the recent hostilities, but in exchange for annuity payments they agreed to keep their warriors away from the emigrant trails along the Platte River.[20]

The Cheyenne-Arapaho war cost territorial, state, and federal governments $30 million. Perhaps eight thousand federal and militia troops had participated without much success in bringing Indian leaders to terms, and hundreds of soldiers had died. Indian deaths, including those at Sand Creek, are more difficult to calculate, but the Commissioner of Indian Affairs reported that in the summer of 1865 "fifteen or twenty Indians had been killed at an expense of more than a million dollars apiece."[21] Property destruction and the number of settler-rancher deaths were large. In Dakota and Texas the frontier retreated as settlers left and immigration decreased in face of Indian attacks.[22]

Hardly had the ink dried on the Fort Sully treaties when the Sioux war of 1866–68 broke out. Red Cloud, the great Oglala warrior, and Tasunkakokipapi (or Tashunkasaquipah, Young Man of Whose Horses They Are Afraid), an Oglala chief, led the Lakotas, who with their allies opposed government plans for construction of a road through their game-rich Powder River hunting grounds. The army went ahead anyway, building Fort Reno on the Powder River about 170 miles from Fort Laramie, Fort Phil Kearny seventy miles farther north, and Fort C. F. Smith on the Big Horn River. Indian leaders in 1866 moved to block construction. Slowly at first, they pressed the army and construction workers and then by degrees took control. By November 1866, with Indian war parties attacking wagon trains, troops, workers, and others, people in the forts had become virtual prisoners. On December 21 in a battle called the Fetterman massacre, Indian warriors wiped out an army relief party. By the summer of 1867, keeping the forts open had become expensive, exhausting, time consuming, and unworkable. In the fall the government agreed to abandon the forts and its plan for the road. On May 19, 1868, it made good on its promise.[23]

Causes of the Sioux war can be traced to the desire for a shorter route to the gold fields of western Montana. John M. Bozeman, who in 1862 arrived in the Montana mining country, determined to blaze a trail east along the Yellowstone River and then southeastward on the eastern side of the Big Horn Mountains to Fort Laramie. The route he laid out was practical and profitable, if Indian raiders did not attack travelers on the trail. After getting a treaty from several "stay-around-the-fort" chiefs, the army in 1865 moved to survey the road and build forts to protect it.[24] The people under Red Cloud, who had refused to sign the treaty, struck back.

In a protracted campaign on the plains, the Sioux war of 1866–68 represented the only clear victory of the Plains Indians over federal troops. The high cost of maintaining the forts, continued congressional cuts in military spending, and Red Cloud's unwavering resolve were factors in the government's decision to end the campaign. Both sides endured heavy casualties. In one battle, the Wagon Box fight of August, 1867, the Lakotas and their allies suffered impressive losses when troops, using the new breech-loading, Springfield rifles, turned back repeated Indian charges. Red Cloud said that he "lost the flower of his men" in the fight.[25] Predictably, the Fetterman fight embarrassed the army, and its officers became bent on revenge.

Instead, the war became a catalyst for a general peace policy. Peace, believed such advocates as Cheyenne-Arapaho agent Jesse Leavenworth, was cheaper than war, and at least two investigating groups argued that the concentration policy was not working. The Doolittle committee, a Joint Special Committee of Congress chaired by Senator James Doolittle of Wisconsin, investigated the Sand Creek massacre and reasons for Indian problems in the West. It made several recommendations to ameliorate the sorry conditions and in January, 1867, presented its report. The Sully commission, charged with investigating Indian affairs after the Fetterman fight and headed by General Alfred Sully, found a long list of treaty abuses by both the government and white settlers and called for a general policy of peace in dealing with the Plains Indians. Editors of the *Nation* concluded that "our whole Indian policy is a system of mismanagement, and in many parts one of gigantic abuse."[26]

Partly to blame for the difficulties on the Great Plains was the division of authority between the Department of Interior and the War Department. The

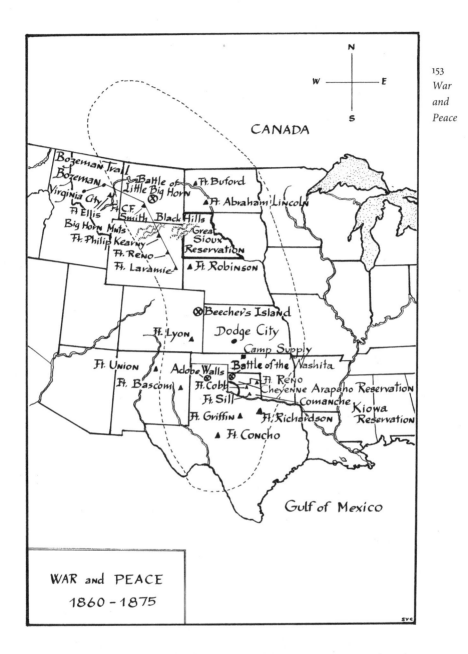

WAR and PEACE
1860 – 1875

Bureau of Indian Affairs in the Department of the Interior attempted to placate tribal leaders with gifts, annuities, and reservations. It demanded a policy of accommodation with Indian tribes. The army in the War Department preferred to punish Indian people for any infraction of the rules. During Hancock's war in the summer of 1867, for instance, troops, in part simply because Indian leaders had refused to negotiate with General Winfield S.

Hancock, destroyed a hastily abandoned Indian camp. Located on the Pawnee Fork of the Arkansas River forty miles west of Fort Larned, the camp contained 250 Cheyenne and Lakota lodges and large quantities of camp and food supplies.[27]

After Hancock's action on the Pawnee Fork, peace advocates won the day. Responding to a recommendation from Commissioner of Indian Affairs Nathaniel G. Taylor, Congress on July 20, 1867, created an Indian Peace Commission to make treaty arrangements and select reservations for the tribes.[28] Headed by Taylor, the commission included military officers, federal legislators, and prominent citizens.

The Peace Commission wanted small reservations carved from two large areas: one below the Arkansas River in Indian Territory for the southern tribes and one above the Platte River for the northern groups. In each of the larger regions the commission planned to assign each tribe to a specific area in which Indian people would be segregated from whites, treated as wards of the government, and taught to live in fixed homes and till the soil; they would begin a transition to lifestyles of the whites. The commission further planned to assign an agent to each reservation.

The commissioners in September, 1867, went to Fort Laramie hoping to meet with northern leaders. Saying he was too busy preparing for the fall bison hunt, Red Cloud, who held enormous influence among his people, refused to talk. Many other Indian leaders agreed with him and stayed away from the fort. The commissioners held some preliminary talks with a few minor leaders and left, indicating that they would return later. They rode south.[29]

The commission met with representatives of the southern groups along Medicine Lodge Creek, located seventy miles below Fort Larned in southwestern Kansas. Perhaps five thousand Indian people attended, and five hundred troops arrived heavily armed and equipped with cannons. With their tipis ranging over a wide area, their camps noisy and busy, and their horses grazing across hundreds of acres, the Indian participants celebrated in the grassy valley. They feasted on dog meat and other culinary delicacies, but most food came from the commissioners, who had wagon load after wagon load of supplies—as well as gifts to be distributed after the council concluded. The meeting became a colorful affair in which Cheyenne warriors staged a mock attack before settling down for discussions.

Both sides argued over peace issues and terms of the treaties. The great witty but tempestuous Kiowa leader Satanta, who in happier days announced dinner by blowing on a French horn, made an impassioned speech. The masterful Comanche orator Ten Bears brought tears to the eyes of those who listened to him talk. But using threats, bribery, and coercion, the commissioners got the headmen and other leaders to accept reservations in Indian Territory.[30]

In the Treaty of Medicine Lodge, October 21, 1867, the Kiowas and Comanches consented to a three-million-acre reservation between the Red and Washita rivers in western Indian Territory. The government promised to provide them with buildings, farm equipment, clothes, cloth, hats, food, and a $25,000 annuity for thirty years and agreed that their people could hunt south of the Arkansas so long as the buffalo ran. Ten Bears, Painted Lips, Horse Back, and Iron Mountain of the Comanches; Satanta, Satank, and Kicking Bird of the Kiowas; and Poor Bear of the Kiowa Apaches were the principal signatories. A week later the Cheyennes and Arapahos, including Black Kettle, Tall Bull, Bull Bear, and Little Robe of the Cheyennes and Little Raven, Yellow Bear, and Storm of the Arapahos, signed a similar treaty giving them a reservation of five million acres just to the north of the Kiowa-Comanche grant—a place so arid that streams dried up each summer.[31]

After Indian leaders had signed, the council ended with the opening of a mountain of boxes filled with gifts, including blankets, clothing, food, guns, ammunition, and knives. As cold weather approached, the Indians headed for their fall bison hunt before going to their winter camps. The commissioners rode back to Fort Laramie to deal with the northern peoples. Because Red Cloud again refused to show, they met with a few friendly Crow leaders and headed east to spend the winter.

In the spring they were back. The commission got the government to agree to close the Bozeman Trail and abandon forts along the road. That done, many of the older Lakota and Yanktonai leaders and headmen, but not Red Cloud, came in for discussions, and on April 29, 1868, they signed the Treaty of Fort Laramie. Over the next few months dozens of additional leaders, including Tasunkakokipapi, signed. Those who signed agreed to quit fighting and received land west of the Missouri River in Dakota Territory—the Great Sioux Reservation. The government guaranteed the Powder River country as "unceded Indian territory" free of whites "so long as buffalo may range thereon in numbers sufficient to justify the chase." It promised to help Indian people by providing money, buildings, tools, equipment, and training in agriculture. A week later the Crows under Pretty Bull signed the treaty, and the Northern Cheyennes and Arapahoes followed them. In November, after his men had destroyed the empty forts, Red Cloud at last signed the treaty.[32]

Despite the treaties, there was no general peace. On the northern plains such leaders as Sitting Bull and Crazy Horse, who had not signed the treaty, continued to live on the rich hunting grounds west of the Black Hills and to raid along the Oregon Trail and the Missouri River. On the southern plains

about a third of the Comanches, including the Quahada band of the celebrated mixed-blood chief Quanah, had not signed the Treaty of Medicine
Lodge, and they did not go to the reservation. Most of the Kiowas went to the
reservation, but Satanta led his band onto the Texas plains. Many of the
Cheyennes, led by Roman Nose and Stone Forehead (Medicine Arrows), and
some Arapahos did not accept the treaty or go to the reservation but remained on the Smoky Hill–Republican rivers bison range. Younger
Cheyenne warriors in 1868 hit Kansas settlements hard, including massive
strikes against their old Indian enemies the Kansas and Pawnees.

The army responded with the idea of "total war." As the raids took place
because Indian people were off their reservations, the army, led by the com-
mander of the Division of the Missouri, William T. Sherman, determined to
use force. It would bring all Indian people, peaceful (those on reservations)
and hostile (those off reservations) alike, back to Indian Territory. The southern Plains Indians, Sherman argued, needed to be "soundly whipped."[33]

The job was not easy. In mid August 1868 a party of about two hundred
Cheyennes, Arapahos, and Lakotas struck white settlers along the Saline and
Solomon rivers in Kansas. They killed fifteen men, raped women, captured
children, and looted and destroyed property. Other raids followed. To catch
the Indians, the army created several lightly provisioned, fifty-man, horse-
mounted units unencumbered by wagons bringing supplies. In mid September perhaps seven hundred Cheyennes and Lakotas clashed with one
of the patrols, led by Major George A. Forsyth, in a fight that became known
as the battle of Beecher's Island. The militant Roman Nose of the Cheyenne
Elk Scrapper society, Cheyenne Dog Soldiers led by Tall Bull, and Lakota
and Arapaho warriors pinned the soldiers down on an island in the Arikaree
Fork of the Republican River in northeastern Colorado. After a nine-day
siege in which Roman Nose died, black troops of the Tenth Cavalry rescued
Forsyth's command.[34]

Now the army turned to winter campaigns and a strategy of "converging
columns." It planned to encircle Indian camps with columns of troops from

different directions during the winter when Plains Indians were less prepared to fight. The most famous engagement was the Washita campaign of late November, 1868. Troops from Fort Bascom, New Mexico; Fort Lyon, Colorado; and Fort Dodge, Kansas, converged on the valleys of the Canadian and Washita rivers in western Indian Territory, where the southern Plains Indians had winter camps. The command of Lt. Col. George A. Custer (Pahuska, or "Long Hair," as Indian people called him) from Fort Dodge, after establishing a base at Camp Supply, struck with devastating results. It attacked the Cheyenne village of the peace advocate Black Kettle in the Washita valley, killing men, women, and children. It destroyed the village's horses, food, lodges, robes, and other possessions.[35]

Winter campaigning, although hard on the troops, brought results. After additional engagements in December and January, most of the Comanches, Kiowas, and Arapahos in early 1869 returned to their reservations. The Cheyennes held out until mid March, when troops under Long Hair Custer found the camp of Little Robe and Stone Forehead along Sweetwater Creek in the eastern Texas Panhandle. After three days of tense negotiations, the Cheyennes promised to return to their reservation and remain there. Most of them went to the reservation, but Tall Bull led one faction northward, hoping to reach villages of the Northern Cheyennes. He did not make it. Troops found the band in Colorado in July and attacked it, killing Tall Bull and forcing those who survived back to Indian Territory.[36]

But now Ulysses S. Grant was President. Under pressure from various eastern groups shocked by the army's handling of western Indians, he embarked on another peace initiative. Known as Grant's "Peace Policy" or the "Quaker Peace Policy," it was a series of laws and executive actions that began in 1869. Its form took shape in January when a group of Quakers, concerned with fraud and corruption in the Indian service, suggested that churchpeople ought to nominate Indian agents and superintendents. Although he did not write it, Grant fostered the official climate in which the policy could take shape. Among its prominent features were a new role for church groups as agents; appointment of a Board of Indian Commissioners composed of wealthy philanthropists (serving without pay) to oversee disbursement of Indian appropriations; concentration of Indian people on reservations where they would be educated, christianized, and helped toward agricultural self-support; and an end to the treaty system by which the government viewed Indian groups as "domestic dependent nations."[37]

Grant's Peace Policy meant continued civilian supremacy in the conduct of Indian affairs. Such a policy clearly disappointed the army. Led by William T. Sherman, the army had lobbied hard during the recent Indian campaigns for the transfer of the Indian bureau back to the War Department, and Grant seemed to support the army's goal. The outgoing commissioner of Indian affairs, Nathaniel Taylor, and Congressman William Windom of Minnesota, chairman of the House Committee on Indian Affairs, led opposition to any transfer from the Interior Department. Once in office Grant shifted his position, favoring now "any course toward [the Indians] which tends to their civilization and ultimate citizenship."[38] Thus, the Interior Department, through its Bureau of Indian Affairs, retained exclusive control and jurisdiction of all Indian people on the reservations. The War Department, through the army, held responsibility for those off the reservations.

The policy had mixed benefits. From the point of view of eastern friends of the Indians, it was effective. They reasoned that it protected Indian families from avaricious white traders and pioneers. Many of them saw it as a means of preserving American Indian rights to life, liberty, and property. From the army's point of view, it did not work. With church domination of Indian management giving the policy a stong nonmilitary complexion, the army could play no significant role in its execution. The policy did not keep Indian people on reservations, and the army had difficulty catching those who slipped away. Indian war leaders, realizing that the soldiers could not pursue them onto Indian Territory, came to use the reservations as sanctuaries from which to raid neighboring settlements.

In Montana, Blackfeet and Lakota raiding parties stole horses and livestock. They hung around overland trails, driving off stock when they could and killing an occasional white who ventured too far from his companions. After whites killed the brother of Mountain Chief, a Piegan headman, the Blackfeet retaliated. For six months Mountain Chief's band intensified their attacks, killing perhaps twelve people. In response Major Eugene M. Baker, under orders from his superiors, led soldiers from Forts Ellis and Shaw in pursuit. At the end of January, 1870, in very cold weather, Baker's troops on the Marias River struck the peaceful Blackfeet village of Chief Heavy Runner. They killed 173 people, including 53 women and children.

The Baker massacre, as it was called, ended Blackfeet resistance. It also caused federal authorities to reorganize its northern Indian administration and to handle Montana Indian peoples at separate agencies. Heavy criticism from the East followed the massacre, but white settlers and military officers in Montana delighted in the murderous attack.

In Texas the raiding became heavy. Lipan and Kickapoo bands continued to cross from Mexico, and Comanche and Kiowa warriors rode out from Indian Territory, sometimes striking ranches in western Texas, sometimes following their old trail to Mexico, and sometimes hunting the bison-rich Llano Estacado of West Texas and eastern New Mexico. Texans complained often and loud, but to little avail—until 1871. In that year Sherman, now General of the Army, toured the state. While his small escort crossed Salt Creek Prairie, in modern Jack County, enroute eastward from Fort Griffin to Fort Richardson, a large Kiowa raiding party led by Eagle Heart, Big Bow, Big Tree, the shaman Mamanti (Sky Walker), and the *Kaitsenko* shirt wearer Satank watched him pass. A few hours later the Kiowas attacked a wagon train. That night an injured survivor told Sherman of the deadly raid in which Indian warriors killed or wounded most of the twelve teamsters. Convinced now of the validity of the Texas appeals, Sherman turned loose the troops.[39]

The soldiers were active. Led by Colonel Ranald S. Mackenzie, considered the most able man of his rank in the Department of Texas, federal troops struck Indian villages everywhere off the reservations. Called "Bad Hand" and "Three Fingers" by Indian people, Mackenzie in 1872 searched out and destroyed Indian camps in the Texas Panhandle. He crossed into Mexico in 1873 to destroy a Kickapoo village, causing international troubles along the border. He kept his troops constantly in the field, thus allowing Indian people little rest. It was not enough, however, as other problems led to a major military campaign in the Panhandle.[40]

The Red River War of 1874–75 was the last major engagement on the southern plains. It brought to the Texas Panhandle some three thousand troops in five converging columns. The columns, coming from different directions, operated more or less independently, but they attacked and burned Indian camps amid the deep canyons and steep breaks on the eastern edge of the Llano Estacado. From August through November the federal troops, under the direction of Colonel Nelson A. Miles, called "Bear Coat" by Indian people, kept up the pressure through fourteen pitched battles. Bad Hand Mackenzie delivered the critical blow when in Palo Duro Canyon with five hundred troops he defeated people from five Comanche, Kiowa, and Cheyenne villages, burning tipis, destroying large quanties of supplies, and capturing over fourteen hundred horses. To avoid the soldiers, Indian people kept constantly on the move, struggling against hunger, cold, and deprivation. Lone Wolf and his Kiowa band in February, 1875, were the first to return to the reservation. Others followed, although several Cheyenne bands attempted to reach Northern Cheyenne villages. In June, when the last Comanche holdout, Quanah, brought his Quahada band to Fort Sill in Indian Territory, the war was over.[41]

Causes of the Red River War can be traced to bison hunters. Having wiped out the large herds in the Arkansas River country, white hunters in 1872 moved south into the Texas Panhandle. Two years later, led by J. Wright and John W. Mooar, they laid out a village at Adobe Walls on the Canadian River, planning to use the place as a base from which to collect hides before hauling them to Dodge City, Kansas. Indian people resented the unwelcomed and, according to treaty promises, illegal intrusion, and on June 27, 1874, stirred into action by the young Comanche shaman Isatai, they attacked. The twenty-eight hide men, using their "big fifty" buffalo guns effectively, held off the charge, returned to Dodge City, and complained to army representatives.[42] The southern Plains Indians, determined to keep whites off their favorite hunting grounds and led by Quanah, renewed their attacks, hitting bison hunters and isolated settlers over a wide area of the southwestern plains and causing the army to respond with force.

The Red River War was a turning point. Not only did it represent one of the two or three largest concentrations of federal troops on the plains, but also it gave the army a greater role in Grant's Peace Policy, and it closed off the great Texas bison herds to Indian people. Military officers had reported seeing many herds of one hundred thousand bison on the Llano Estacado in 1875; three years later not a single animal grazed the high tableland. In 1876 Charles Goodnight, a resourceful trail blazer and Texas plainsman, drove a large herd of cattle from Colorado to the Canadian River in the heart of the Texas Panhandle. Discovering that Hispanic sheep ranchers from New Mexico had already settled there, he moved his animals to Palo Duro Canyon, where just two years before Indian families had maintained five large villages. Before the Red River War, southern Plains Indians had hunted and camped freely over a wide area. After the war, they agreed to remain on the reservations.

In the north the last major campaign was the great Sioux war of 1876. In it Lakotas, Cheyennes, Arapahos, Assiniboins, Yanktonais, and others fought federal soldiers in the "unceded Indian lands" west of the Black Hills. The war included the battle of the Little Big Horn (Greasy Grass), in which Long Hair Custer and over two hundred men of his Seventh Cavalry on June 25, 1876, died in the most famous of all soldier-Indian fights. After Indian warriors defeated Custer, General Philip Sheridan, commanding the Division of the Missouri, ordered new expeditions, which used converging columns and winter campaigning. When Bad Hand Mackenzie, with eleven hundred troops of his Fourth Cavalry, surprised and defeated the Cheyenne village of Morning Star (Dull Knife) and Little Wolf in a Big Horn canyon in terribly cold weather on November 25, the war was essentially over; although Crazy Horse did not surrender until spring, a few remnant bands held out until the next fall, and Sitting Bull took his people to Canada, the Grandmother's Land.[43]

The Sioux war of 1876 had many causes, all of them relating to Fort Laramie treaty violations. Indian people complained of moldy flour, spoiled beef, and moth-eaten blankets that resulted from corruption in the Indian bureau and kept Indian families short of supplies. They resented the steady advance of the Northern Pacific Railroad, whose survey crews, accompanied by fourteen hundred soldiers, injudiciously occupied Indian land. They were angry with the rush of miners to the Black Hills. In the aftermath of an 1874 Custer expedition that had confirmed rumors of gold in the Black Hills, perhaps fifteen thousand whites in the winter of 1875–76 illegally entered Indian country. Indian success in the Sioux war of 1866–68 had left many Lakotas feeling invincible, especially Sitting Bull, a Hunkpapa leader of superior ability; Crazy Horse, an Oglala who was a genius at handling men; and full-chested, thirty-six-year-old Gall, a Hunkpapa war leader and one of the principal chiefs in the battle of the Little Big Horn.

Military authorities touched off the war. They knew that many younger men were leaving reservations to join bands of "non-treaty" people in the region northwest of the Black Hills. Fearing trouble, the army ordered all Lakotas, regardless of treaty guarantees—which allowed them to hunt in the "unceded Indian lands"—to return to the Great Sioux Reservation by February 1, 1876. Sitting Bull, Crazy Horse, and Gall refused, and in the weeks that followed, others joined them. In the spring General Sheridan ordered three columns, about twenty-five hundred men, from three directions to converge in the Yellowstone River Country, where he expected the troops would find the Lakotas and their allies. Shortly thereafter the war began.

When the Sioux war ended several months later, few American Indians rode unrestricted on the Great Plains. They were on reservations or, as in the case of those who followed Sitting Bull, in the Grandmother's Land. The stunning Indian victory over Custer and his famed Seventh Cavalry during the war shocked the United States, which just a few days later on July 4, 1876, celebrated its centennial, and renewed efforts to bring a solution to the "Indian question," as the 1868 Peace Commission had called it.[44] Although military campaigns continued against the Utes in the Rockies, the Nez Percés in the Northwest, and the Apaches in the Southwest, the Sioux war of 1876 ended major campaigns on the Great Plains.

The war also cost the Lakotas the Black Hills—their *Paha Sapa*. After the discovery of gold in the pine-covered mountain country, federal authorities endeavored to secure the region from the Indians. Senator William B. Allison of Iowa in 1875 led a commission that met with Lakota leaders in a grand council attended by some ten thousand Indian people on the White River in northwestern Nebraska, not far from the Red Cloud agency near Fort Robinson. Under threat of being shot by Oglala shirt wearer Little Big Man if they signed away the Black Hills, the leaders refused the $6,000,000 offer as well as an annual rental agreement of $400,000 for mining rights. The council broke up, but government agents continued to negotiate.

The Sioux war changed negotiations. After Custer's defeat, Congress in

August 1876 determined that no additional appropriations would go to the Lakotas until they agreed to relinquish the Black Hills. A new commission met only with headmen and other leaders at the various agencies on the Great Sioux Reservation. Without weapons and horses and faced with starvation, the leaders in 1877 signed an agreement that revised the 1868 Treaty of Fort Laramie. In so doing the Lakotas gave up hunting rights in Montana and Wyoming and surrendered the beautiful and gold-rich Black Hills. For the Lakotas the loss of the Black Hills represented a sad end to the wars on the Great Plains.

The history of warfare on the plains in the period after 1860 is a familiar one, a classic tale of which a hundred books and movies have been fashioned. Although often characterized has having been on the receiving end of a policy of extermination, the Plains Indians, until the army adopted winter campaigning, accorded themselves well in the struggles, sometimes destroying whole army units. Their relocation to reservations came as much from the extension of railroads, the extermination of the bison herds, and the appearance of scattered white settlements as it did from military action or "enlightened" government policy.

Much of the high plains west of the one hundredth meridian was in 1860 Plains Indian country. "I was born upon the prairie, where the wind blew free and there was nothing to break the sun," said the Comanche leader Ten Bears in 1867. Now "the Texans have taken away the places where the grass grew thickest," and "the whites have the country which we loved."[45] Moreover, the decade of war and peace, as we have seen, prompted serious internal cultural change. By 1876 the Plains Indians, living on reservations, had entered a new era in their dynamic societies, one lacking many of the unique traits and social patterns that had characterized the earlier period, but one as fully marked as the others by cultural continuity and vitality.

10 : RESERVATION LIFE

eservation life for most of the horticultural people began in the 1850s. For the nomadic groups it began after the treaties of Medicine Lodge (1867) and Fort Laramie (1868). Reservation life changed through the years as Congress passed laws affecting resident Indians and cutting reservation sizes, and for nomadic peoples it reached a nadir in the years after 1887 when the federal government forced on many reservation people a program of individual allotments of land. In the twentieth century Plains Indians in significant numbers left reservations for large cities and new opportunities made available by the urbanization of America, but, located in the heart of their ancestral homeland, the reservations (or what remained of them) continued to exert a powerful hold on the American Indians of the plains.

The federal government established reservations to get Indian people out of the way, to solve the "Indian question," to maintain a peaceful West, and to appease both western voters and eastern pressure groups. It used reservations to assimilate, or Americanize, Indian people—or tried to. It did not establish or use reservations to benefit the Plains Indians, and from the Indians' view reservation life, at least for the first-generation residents, matched the Cherokees' "trail of tears" for needlessness, want, and suffering.

Reservations were not prisons, of course, and despite some initial malaise, plains people quickly adjusted to reservation life. Even when they sought to become Christian farmers, many lived or camped in rural areas away from towns, traded at the reservation agencies, and hunted or trapped animals for food and hides. Although reservation policy restricted their movement, autonomy, and religious freedom, they did not abandon traditional belief systems, and rarely did they give up traditional songs, dances, ceremonies, and other cultural forms. Where necessary they made cultural accommodations to white-supported reservation living, but changes came.

Whites who supported the reservation system claimed that people on reservations would change from nomadic hunters and raiders to settled farmers and stock raisers. The children would be educated in schools, and missionaries would bring Christianity to all. Arguing from a Eurocentric point of view, they further claimed that the reservations would be the center for tribal management and an Indian transformation.

They were right. Reservation life worked a major transformation, indeed. Although the Plains Indians retained many older customs, myths, folkways, and traditions, significant cultural forms that had marked both village life and plains nomadism disappeared. Two Leggings, a Crow warrior, although he lived forty years after the government placed his people on a reservation, ended his autobiography with the reservation period. "Nothing happened after that," he said. "We just lived. There were no more war parties, no capturing of horses from the Piegans and the [Lakotas], no buffalo to hunt. There is nothing more to tell."[1]

The hunting economies went first and fast.[2] Because after the mid 1870s there were few bison left, the hunt no longer provided direction and order to the seasonal round of band or village activities. Women no longer were preoccupied with tanning hides, preserving meat, fashioning clothing, constructing tipis, or making utensils from bison carcasses. Men, who once used the hunt to increase their wealth and position, no longer rode off to collect meat for the band or hides for trade. The men's societies no longer served to regulate the hunt, and they either took on new roles or lost their meaning altogether. As the hunting economy ended and men turned to farming or stock raising, women lost one of their important sources of power and influence.

The political system changed. War leaders lost their relevance, and headmen could not compete with the reservation agent, whose authority included control over the distribution of rations, especially the significant matter of the issuance of live beef. Agents used their power to make and unmake chiefs until the whole matter of chieftainship became cloudy, thus undermining the prereservation system of native leadership and administration. Indian people continued to elect tribal councils that formulated laws, appointed judges, and held meetings, but because Indian bureau personnel approved (or disapproved) all actions, the meetings and laws meant little. People in a few plains communities, such as the Northern Arapahos, continued to handle many of their own affairs, but the political system came under Interior Department control.[3]

The old system of raids and counterraids ended. War societies that once governed plains fighting became irrelevant. On reservations there was little need to celebrate a raid's success or to mourn its failure. Fraternities, which once provided men with unity of goals and experiences, disappeared. Men discontinued the time-consuming activities that saw them prepare and decorate weapons according to prescribed rituals for hunting and raiding. In a warrior society without war, men lost a common purpose for living. Raiding and warfare could no longer serve as the way to wealth and prestige. An entire status structure crumbled. Radically new avenues to recognition, honor, position, and leadership developed.[4]

Social relationships changed. Men with no bison to hunt and no raiding party to join lost their familiar role in society. The Lakota *tiyospe* relationships shifted. In prereservation days, several Lakota families camped together, forming a band of families that provided support, comfort, and social interaction of all kinds. Because extended families frequently chose, or were assigned, adjacent allotments and the families often camped together on one of them, *tiyospe* remained important on reservations long after individual allotment of land. But as the government encouraged (to the point of insistence) the Plains Indians to take up single family units, the separation of families onto individual plots discouraged the old system, and over time each family of husband and wife came to live with greater independence of the consanguine family. Moreover, under the changed conditions of reservation life, traditions lapsed from memory and were lost.[5]

Spiritual life changed. Through its circular entitled *The Code of Religious Offenses,* the government in 1883 prohibited or curtailed nearly all dances. It outlawed the Sun Dance, driving its practice underground or eliminating it altogether. Once the core spiritual experience for about twenty plains groups, it no longer provided a spiritual unity and tribal wholeness. On reservations the Sun Dance became little more than a summer pageant. Shamans and priests, who after 1883 could be jailed for practicing their craft, often died before they had instructed others. Government policy as reflected in *The Code* illustrated a lack of regard for the principle of religious freedom and separation of church and state. The attitude continued in the Southwest until John Collier became commissioner of Indian affairs in the 1930s.[6]

Attempting to fill the spiritual void, missionaries converted many Plains Indians to Christianity—although few Indian people discarded completely their traditional patron spirits. Likewise the old spiritual link between the bison and the Plains Indians became disconnected. The pre- and posthunt ceremonies that often included the entire band or village in spiritual supplication were no longer pertinent to the yearly round of religious activities. The vision quest, because it was often associated with the hunt or war, changed in meaning.

Education changed. Once grandparents and aunts and uncles dominated a childhood education that saw girls learn skills associated with management of the household and boys learn skills related to preparing them for manhood in a hunting society. On reservations white-oriented day schools appeared with a curriculum that taught arithmetic, emphasized the reading and writing of English, and presented education as a value system to replace Indian ideals.

Many young people left reservations for boarding schools, where local officials cut the children's hair and replaced the Indian clothing in favor of typical white styles. Lone Wolf, who was part Blackfeet, remembered that upon arrival at his boarding school "our belongings were taken from us . . . placed in a heap and set afire." Then our "long hair, the pride of all the Indians" was cut. "The boys, one by one, would break down and cry when they saw their braids thrown on the floor."[7]

Carlisle Indian Industrial School in Carlisle, Pennsylvania, founded in 1879 by Captain Richard H. Pratt, was perhaps the most famous boarding school. Established as a model institution for Americanizing Indian children, its administrators did not allow students to speak in their native tongue and taught them in a vocational and manual labor–dominated curriculum that provided a large dose of Anglo moralizing. It adopted military discipline, with students dressed in uniforms, drilled in military formation, and marched to class. In 1880 thirty-one Lakota leaders, including Spotted Tail, Red Cloud, Red Dog, Two Strike, American Horse, and Crow Dog, visited Carlisle. They did not like what they saw with regard to military uniforms and corporal punishment. Spotted Tail and some of the others took their children out of the school. Sometimes white educators kept the young people away from the reservations for five years or longer, often causing them to lose touch with their native culture.[8]

Boarding school education had its shortcomings, but the institutions taught industrial skills and promoted learning in the liberal arts. Some people enjoyed their boarding school experience. Education at government schools often meant employment advantages, especially in the Indian Service, and the schools promoted pan-Indianism, a significant aspect of American Indian identity in the twentieth century. Students, boys and girls, from varied backgrounds and different cultures speaking different languages, met at residential places like Carlisle and Haskell Institute (founded in 1884) in Lawrence, Kansas, and some of them later married.

Ethnic compositions changed. Plains Indians had always intermarried with outside peoples. Children of Hispanic, Anglo, or African American heritage (or from other Indian ethnic groups) reared in a new band or tribe became wives or husbands of tribal members and produced mixed-blood children. During the reservation period and afterward, marriages with whites increased substantially, resulting in a resident population on the Pine Ridge Reservation in South Dakota that in 1940 stood between 50 and 60 percent mixed blood, ranging from one sixteenth to fifteen sixteenths degrees of Indian birth. In 1950 there were few full-blood Pawnees. In 1980 most Gros Ventres possessed some white ancestry[9]

Many culture traits disappeared. "The happiest days of my life," said Pretty

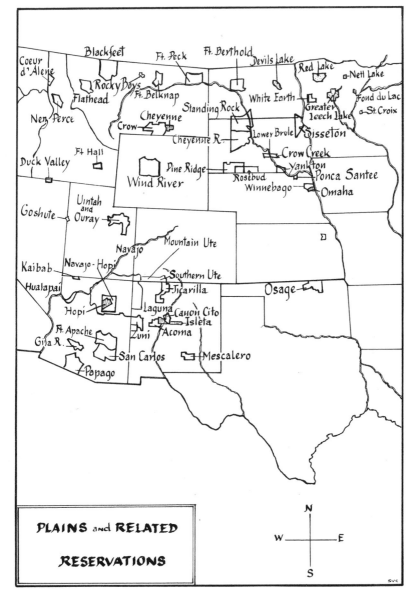

PLAINS and **RELATED**

RESERVATIONS

N

W———|———E

S

SVC

Shield of the Crows, "were spent following the buffalo herds. . . . But how could we live in the old way when everything was gone?"[10]

Lifeways that included tipi-dwelling, horse-mounted nomadism; an absence of horticulture; and the utilization of bison as well as weapons designed for hunting such animals were among the principal traits that had characterized nomadic groups. On reservations such lifeways vanished. One observer, after visiting the Blackfeet reservation in the 1890s, indicated that the people were "crowded into a little corner of the great territory which they once dominated," and they are attempting "to give up inherited habits, ... to break away from all that is natural to them, ... to reverse their whole mode of existence."[11] Early in the reservation period, some men became stock raisers, a few producing very large herds of exceptional quality. Slowly at first and then to a greater degree, they became farmers. The tipi, originally made of bison skins and later of government-issued canvas, gave way to tents and then log or frame homes that in the twentieth century were not so different from Anglo houses. Towns appeared with schools, churches, and stores. By 1940 reservation towns had come to look like many other rural American communities, boasting drugstores, cafes, beauty shops, and motion picture theaters with both white and Indian customers.[12]

Many other culture traits that survived well into the twentieth century changed in function. The Matokiks, a women's society among the Blackfeet, remained active as late as the 1950s, for example, but its function had become one of healing rather than one of providing success in bison hunting. The Blackfeet horse medicine cult, whose original purpose was to influence the actions of horses, became one for curing ill humans.

In short, there developed a mode of life far removed from hunting and raiding. The shift occurred rapidly. "Almost overnight," writes Robert M. Utley, "a whole way of life vanished ... whole clusters of habits and customs, activities, attitudes, values, and institutions lost relevance and meaning."[13] The Plains Indians in 1860 were relatively affluent and independent, with large tribal territories. They had many horses and bison robes and large supplies of dried meat, and bison were numerous, if declining. In 1890, hardly a generation later, the Indians of the plains, suffering from food and other material shortages, were nearly landless and dependent upon the federal government. "Even the Cheyenne," remembered Carl Sweezy, an Arapaho, "began to see that they must take [a] new road. The old one had come to an end."[14]

Deprived of a large land base that had provided economic, political, and military strength and power, Indian people on reservations found themselves stripped of many older life patterns, humiliated by agency impositions, and shorn of tribal moorings. "We began to stay in one place," said Pretty Shield, "and to grow lazy and sicker all the time. . . . Our old men used to be different; even our children were different when the buffalo were here."[15]

Not everything changed. The people retained a strong commitment to older ways, and, when the federal government banned some practices, the Plains Indians performed them in secret. They preserved many traditional symbols, life patterns, myths, values, folkways, and customs, and they kept their own languages even as they learned English. Women continued to manage the household, to care for the tipis or cabins, to prepare the meals. Men continued in their efforts to provide family sustenance. Women and children continued to wear blankets and otherwise dress in Plains Indian styles, and many of the men and some boys, against agency rules, continued to wear their hair long or in braids. Shamans did not always give up older healing practices, and the activities associated with sweath baths remained culturally important. Families traveled around the reservations, visiting kinfolk, enjoying traditional social activities, and spending days or weeks away from home. Intertribal visitations also continued. The racing of horses remained popular, gambling was still a favorite amusement, and Indian people quickly mastered the various games of chance associated with playing cards. In short, people transformed reservations into favored homelands where their cultures and societies not only endured but remained vital.

A favorite activity, one that preserved temporarily an old custom, occurred during the distribution of cattle. Plains Indians transformed the occasions, which took place every two weeks, into simulated bison hunts. "Issue days were big times for all of us," said Carl Sweezy. "All across the prairies, . . . people in bright colors and high spirits came riding to the issue station. There were visiting and excitement and work and feasting. . . ." He noted that "for a few hours, the Arapaho knew once more some of the excitement of the old buffalo hunt. . . . It was a time of plenty and of hospitality for everyone."[16]

Issue days became lively affairs in which men on horseback and with wonderful delight chased the animals across the plains. Young people so admired the affair that a government school official rewarded good conduct by dismissing classes for the event. After pursuing the cattle for two or three miles, men shot the animals, and women and children followed to share in the butchering. Until the issue of live cattle was banned in the 1890s, Plains Indians took pleasure from the event in ways that they had once enjoyed bison hunts. They transformed issue days into times of feasting, gambling, and entertainment.[17]

The Grass Dance became a favorite celebration. The immediate ancestor of the modern Indian encampment (or powwow) and associated with bison and hunting, it grew from older warrior society dances. When reservation people came together for social or religious purposes, it was a popular activity for energetic young men who found its dance vigorous and its songs exciting. Having originated in the 1860s among the Omahas, Poncas, Pawnees, and Lakotas, it spread throughout the plains. It grew in popularity over the next two decades, and on the northern plains, especially among the Oglalas, it became the most important secular dance in the 1890s.[18]

In fact, older song texts and dance traditions proved remarkably resilient on reservations. Some changes occurred, of course, and new dances, such as the Grass Dance, appeared, but older texts and traditions persisted and helped to provide a foundation for much of the American Indian cultural revival that appeared in the twentieth century.[19]

Nonetheless, in the first years of reservation life there was a great deal of idleness. Indian people had a hard time accepting that the "old days" were gone forever, clinging to an empty hope of vast herds, valiant deeds, and vacant prairies. Tales of the old men encouraged the dreams and prolonged the idleness. Although some men took up farming and succeeded, failed crops on the arid reservation lands discouraged agricultural activity. Moreover, government equipment came late or not at all, and too often, especially among the Northern Cheyennes, Northern Arapahos, and Lakotas, there were rumors of reservations being divided and people moved. Under such conditions, men were slow to take to farming, even when they had overcome significant cultural biases against tilling the soil. The eloquent Shoshoni leader Washakie in 1878 spoke of the difficulties. The government, he said, "leaves us without the promised seed, without tools for cultivating the land, without implements for harvesting our crops, without breeding animals better than ours . . . and so after all we can get by cultivating the land, and by hunting and fishing, we are sometimes nearly starved, and go half naked."[20]

Two decades later, little had changed. Hamlin Garland, a popular author, spent several summers at the turn of the century visiting western Indian communities. He visited the Northern Cheyennes, Lakotas, and Blackfeet, reporting that the people "have small, badly-ventilated log or frame hovels of one or two rooms, into which they closely crowd during" the winter. In the summer they use canvas tipis. "They dress in a sad mixture of good old buckskin garments and shoddy clothing, sold by the traders or issued by the government." They are "poor, with very little to do but sit and smoke and wait for ration day." The rations last family members "for a week to ten days and they go hungry till next ration day comes around." Farming, Garland concluded, was "practically useless, and their herds are too small to furnish them support."[21]

Such conditions encouraged new forms of spiritual life. In the south, the Comanches turned to peyote. They had used peyote in a limited way for many years, but sometime after 1875 (after the 1874 Sun Dance had failed them) they began to use it for religious purposes. They held peyote meetings in sacred tipis where they consumed a non-habit-forming hallucinogen found in the "buttons" (the dried top of the plant) of the small, gray-green, spineless peyote cactus (lophophora williamsii). They accompanied the consumption of peyote, which produced a colorful but mild vision, with hymn singing, drum beating, and testimonials. Peyote usage reached the Kiowas,

Wichitas, and Shawnees in the 1880s, and not long afterward it spread through much of the West.

Soon enough the peyote movement became something of a nonviolent means of cultural emancipation. The ceremony, which usually lasted through the night and provided a sense of enhanced perception of reality, showed individuals how to accommodate themselves to the larger white world yet remain spiritually independent. In the twentieth century peyote worship became associated with the Native American Church, where it also became an event to purge the individual of sin. The Plains Indians held peyote ceremonies to cure illnesses and as a thanksgiving for some favorable event or good fortune.[22]

In the north, the Dream Dance appeared. A Dakota woman, Wananikwe, who claimed to have escaped an attack by Long Hair Custer on her camp in 1876, preached friendship among Indian peoples. She claimed that the Holy One Above had given her a large drum and that all who came in peace with a tobacco offering might find contentment. The Dream Dance, which in the 1880s spread through the upper Midwest and to the central Great Plains, brought hope and consolation to those who performed the ritual, but it did not attract much attention among people of the northwestern plains.[23]

Outside pressures also interrupted reservation life. Railroaders, ranchers, farmers, and others, including miners in the North, encouraged Congress to open reservations for Anglo use. When Congress agreed, Indian communities lost some of their land. The Crows, for example, who had been granted territory below the Yellowstone River in 1851, lost the eastern end of their land in the 1868 Fort Laramie treaty. A new agreement in 1875 cut the western end of the reserve, and during 1880–82 they ceded away another 1,688,000 acres from the western end of the reservation.

In Indian Territory, railroaders, ranchers, and farmers ("boomers," they were called) all coveted land. Joined by western business enterprises and large banking firms, they pressed the federal government to open reservations and allow white settlement. In the western end of the territory, they distracted the plains peoples, delaying agriculture there and restricting Indian income.

Sources of income were already limited. The Plains Indians had little training and less experience in agriculture. To keep agents away they plowed some ground and planted some seeds, but poor weather nullified the efforts. With stock raising they enjoyed greater success, but on the northern reservations the cold winter of 1886–87 killed many herds, and afterward Indian cattlemen used their breeding stock to help feed hungry reservation residents. They lived in a rural area where opportunities for industrial work were nonexistent, or practically so. Freighting attracted some, particularly the Pawnees and Lakotas. The latter for a time hauled their own annuities, but freighting alone could not support the large Lakota population, and political pressure from white teamsters kept a regular Indian freighting system from developing.

On the Canadian plains similar problems occurred. Indian people there turned to farming, but government policy sometimes denied them adequate seeds, tools, equipment, and training. Too often, as a result, reserves in western Canada became centers of poverty.[24]

On the southern plains also there were difficulties. During the western cattle boom of the early 1880s Indian representatives leased grazing land to white ranchers, and by 1885 most of the grasslands on Comanche-Kiowa and Cheyenne-Arapaho reservations were under contract to Texas stockmen. The Cheyenne leaders Little Robe, Stone Calf, and White Shield, who opposed the leasing system, in 1883 refused their portion of the first semiannual payment of $31,178, but most accepted the "grass money" and used it to feed and clothe destitute members of their bands.[25]

The controversy over the Cheyenne grass money represented an important aspect of reservation life—the struggle between headmen and agents. The agents normally held the upper hand, but when a powerful leader, such as Red Cloud of the Oglalas or Sitting Bull of the Hunkpapas, challenged picayune rules, Indian people sometimes gained various concessions. When the agent's administration was marked by weakness and incompetence, the headman's influence was more pronounced.

One agent, John D. Miles, faced a different problem. The Indian bureau had determined to remove a number of people to Indian Territory. The Poncas, the Pawnees, and the Northern Cheyennes were among the first to go, with the latter people coming to Miles's agency for the Southern Cheyennes and Arapahos. Reservation life on the southern plains was difficult for the Northern Cheyennes. The more than nine hundred recent arrivals suffered from heat and disease, and they did not always get along with their southern kin. They complained about the rations, some of them threatened to leave, and many of them refused to stay near the agency.

Then, suddenly, a minority of Northern Cheyennes left. In September, 1878, having been on the reservation only a year, Morning Star and Little Wolf led three hundred of their people back toward their northern homeland. During their "Cheyenne Autumn," as the quest has been called, they fought federal troops in a few engagements, stayed away from settlements as much as possible, and crossed the Platte River, where after a dispute they divided. Morning Star with his faction went to Fort Robinson in northwestern Nebraska; Little Wolf kept his people on the plains (along Lost Chokecherry Creek near modern Valentine, Nebraska) all winter. In the spring Little Wolf surrendered and went to Fort Keogh on the Yellowstone River. The federal government allowed Morning Star's people, who had lost about half of the band in attempting a desperate escape from Fort Robinson to avoid a return to Indian Territory, to reunite with Little Wolf at Fort Keogh. On the Tongue River reservation in Montana, the combined band joined the Northern Cheyennes under Two Moons, one of the leaders who had fought against Custer at the Little Big Horn. The flight of the Cheyennes received national attention and brought heavy criticism on the army and the agency system.[26]

The Poncas made a similar break for the North. Having been removed in 1877 from their reservation in Dakota, they received lands in Indian Territory. Homesick and unable to endure their new surroundings, Chief Standing Bear (Mochunozhin) in 1878 led one group northward. Arrested by General George Crook (or "Three Stars," as Indian people called him), Standing Bear entered a local jail, but with the aid of Thomas. H. Tibbles, a newspaperman and former scout who advertised the plight of the Poncas, the chief sought a writ of habeas corpus for his release. The subsequent U.S. Circuit Court case, *Standing Bear v. Crook* (1879), received national coverage, focused attention on the Ponca trouble, galvanized various reform groups into the Friends of the Indians, and defined Indian rights with regard to the government holding American Indians on reservations against their will. Standing Bear won the legal battle, but agency administrators continued to block Indian efforts to come and go from the reservations as they pleased. Standing Bear's band, which had been forced back to Indian Territory, in 1881 finally settled on the Santee agency in northern Nebraska, near their old reservation.[27]

Reservation life created problems over the legal status of Indian people. Because any extension of U.S. authority onto the reservations undermined American Indian treaty guarantees, Congress at first took little action in the matter of legal and political jurisdiction on Indian lands. Although a few individuals opposed it, many people supported the extension of U.S. authority to reservations. As reform groups debated the appropriate congressional course, the Indian bureau usurped Indian legal prerogatives. Wanting greater control on the reservations, the bureau's agents used the principle of "equal privileges and equal responsibilities for all" as its justification for extending government laws onto Indian lands.

To enforce the laws, the federal government adopted an Indian police system. Several agents, including some on the Lakota and Blackfeet reservations, had used American Indians as police with success, and Commissioner of Indian Affairs Ezra A. Hayt in 1877 recommended the general adoption of such a force. It would, Hayt wrote in his annual report, relieve the army of police duty, save lives and property, and "materially aid in placing the entire

Indian population . . . on the road to civilization." The next year Congress authorized a force of 430 privates and 50 officers, and in 1879 it raised the number to 800 privates and 100 officers.[28] Tribal police allowed agents to bypass headmen and other leaders in getting agency instructions carried out, and they enabled agents to control reservation people without calling in federal troops.

Indian police were effective, at least from the white point of view. They were trustworthy and loyal officers who got results, sometimes while performing difficult and dangerous assignments. Among younger men duty as a police officer was popular as the position's association with warriors gave it a cachet of manhood. The Indian police maintained order, expelled intruders, and suppressed the whiskey trade. But they also assisted the agent in curbing the power of traditional leaders and in helping to eliminate tribal religion, dances, and celebrations. In 1890 fifty-nine agencies posessed an Indian law-enforcement squad.

To assist the police the Interior Department created a system of Courts of Indian Offenses. Established by Henry M. Teller in 1883, the courts consisted of three judges, usually chosen from the agency police. The judges were to impose fines or jail sentences on people who persisted in traditional Indian customs, religion, and practices. They also regulated gambling, drunkenness, and a whole series of minor, petty offenses.[29] More difficult for the agents was what to do about major crimes, particularly when treaty guarantees and custom left jurisdiction in the control of Indian people.

The problem came to a head in 1883. Crow Dog, a minor Brule leader and head of the agency police, killed Spotted Tail, the influential headman who lived in a fancy, two-story frame home on the Rosebud Reservation and who received important favors from the agent. Although Spotted Tail, a philanderer of sorts, angered fellow Brules with his activities, the killing was more related to the distribution of range "lease" money than to taking another man's wife. Apparently a cold-blooded murder, the act brought the Crow Dog and Spotted Tail clans together, and in typical Lakota fashion they moved to avoid a feud and resolve the problem. When Spotted Tail's family accepted the compensation that Crow Dog's relatives offered, the Lakotas, as was their custom, believed the matter closed. Territorial officials were not satisfied, however, and they arrested Crow Dog, hauled him to territoral court at Deadwood in the Black Hills, and tried and convicted him before a federal jury. Before the year ended, the Supreme Court heard the case.[30]

In *Ex parte Crow Dog* the Supreme Court ruled that the United States held little jurisdiction over crimes committed on Indian lands by one Indian against another. It was no simple decision. In effect, the Brules on their reservation could resolve according to tribal custom serious disputes among their people. The federal government recognized that Indian tribes enjoyed a legally protected political autonomy, a right it had never extended to other groups (the Mormons in Utah, for example). The decision created a storm of protest among whites. Fearful of losing control, Indian agents led the movement for federal legislation that might establish government jurisdiction.[31]

The Major Crimes Act was the result. Passed by Congress in 1885, the law further extended federal jurisdiction over people on reservations and was a significant encroachment upon traditional tribal autonomy. It listed seven major crimes: murder, manslaughter, rape, assault with intent to kill, arson, burglary, and larceny. An American Indian who committed one of these crimes against another Indian person was subject to legal statutes of the territory or state in which the crime was committed. The law, which despite treaty guarantees the Supreme Court upheld in *United States v. Kagama* (1886), pleased Indian bureau personnel and their backers who supported the "detribalization" and Americanization of Plains Indians.[32]

Meanwhile, in *Elk v. Wilkins* the Supreme Court had ruled on a different matter. John Elk, a Dakota who had left his Santee Reservation along the Missouri River in northern Nebraska, lived and worked in Omaha. When he attempted to vote in the city's fifth ward, the registrar stopped him on grounds that he was not a U.S. citizen. Elk brought suit, contending that he had voluntarily left the reservation, was under the jurisdiction of the United States, was working and living on his own, and was "civilized." Therefore, he was a citizen of the United States in the meaning of the Fourteenth Amendment to the Constitution and entitled to vote. The Supreme Court in 1884 agreed that Elk was under the jurisdiction of the United States but denied that he was a citizen entitled to the right to vote.[33]

Elk v. Wilkins had no immediate impact on reservation Indians, but it was an important contribution toward individual allotment of reservation lands. Senator Henry L. Dawes of Massachusetts, a leading proponent of Indian citizenship and assimiliation, called the decision strange and wicked. Like most Americans, Dawes believed that Indian people became citizens once they had placed themselves under U.S. jurisdiction. In the East, where various reform groups supported a strong humanitarian approach to American Indian affairs, there was widespread disgust with the Supreme Court's ruling. More importantly, the decision transformed American thought from the idea of gradual assimilation and citizenship through education to a plan for immediate citizenship.[34]

An important result of the new attitude was the General Allotment Act of 1887. Often called simply the Dawes Act, the law was meant to benefit American Indians by speeding up assimilation and citizenship. It had plenty of supporters. Western ranchers, railroaders, settlers, and land speculators backed the bill because it meant individual allotment of land to Indians, thus freeing millions of surplus acres to land-hungry whites. Eastern reform groups supported the law because allotment in severalty meant assimilation, citizenship, and other civil liberties, such as the right to vote, for Indian people. Others liked the measure because they believed it would break up tribal bonds, or "mass," as Theodore Roosevelt called it, thus ending the customs, relations, and traditions that American Indians had continued to practice on reservations.

Some whites and many Indian leaders opposed the Dawes Act. Although he signed the bill into law, President Grover Cleveland thought it was just another way for westerners to get Indian lands. Henry M. Teller, a senator from Colorado and former secretary of the interior, warned that Indian people would eventually lose their allotment homesteads. Ethnologists and anthropologists associated with the Smithsonian Institution objected to the law. A minority of the House Committee on Indian Affairs suggested that the real purpose of the law was to secure Indian lands but get them in the name of humanity rather than greed.

Among the Plains Indians, Lone Wolf, the adopted son of the great Kiowa leader of the same name, and Sitting Bull, the patriotic Hunkpapa who after returning from Canada had settled on the Standing Rock Reservation, led the opposition. Lone Wolf attempted to reach Washington, D. C., to protest, but agents arrested him. He escaped, received help from the Creeks, and headed by train for the capital, but arrived too late to prevent passage. Even so, he complained about the law to everyone he met. Back in Indian Territory he called a council of southwestern tribes to protest the General Allotment Act, and the intertribal council adopted a resolution calling upon President Cleveland to halt enforcement of the law. Sitting Bull led a half-dozen Indian leaders on a tour of northern reservations to alert people about the law and to organize efforts to resist its enforcement.

The opposition had little chance, and President Cleveland on February 8, 1887, signed the bill into law. The Dawes Act authorized the President to seek agreements for allotment in severalty (individual allotment) of reservation lands. It was a complicated system in which heads of households received 160 acres (a quarter section) of land for farming, single adults and orphans 80, and children 40. Larger amounts would be allowed for grazing land. The Indians were to select their own property, but if they did not, the government would choose for them. To prevent alienation of the property to acquisitive whites, the government would hold the land in trust for twenty-five years, a period during which the Indians would become assimilated, or so supporters of the law hoped. Upon receiving an allotment, the individual would become a citizen of the United States. The law also provided that surplus, nonallotted territory be opened to settlement, with proceeds from the sale of land set aside in trust for the reservation Indians.[35]

The law was a disaster. It hurt traditional Indian culture wherever it went into effect, it did not facilitate assimilation, and it had a ruinous effect on American Indian populations. It destroyed the Indian land base. Indian lands in 1887 totaled 154 million acres. When the law was repealed in 1934, Indian lands totaled about 48 million acres, a reduction of 70 percent over the lifetime of the measure. Because the law was revised every few years, liberalizing white access to alloted lands through lease or purchase and reducing the trust period, American Indians before 1934 lost an additional 27 million acres, or two thirds of the allotted land. The law impoverished Indian people, and through much of the plains it changed reservations or in some cases effectively ended reservation life.[36]

The allotment process was obtuse. Most plains reservations were grazing lands and so designated, but government surveyors marked out tracts in semiarid regions where 160 acres did not make a worthwhile farm. The federal authorities seemed determined to make agriculturists of Plains Indians by allotting them a quarter section of land where no nineteenth-century farmer should have been. Surplus land ceded for white settlement likewise was divided at first into 160-acre units, but in western South Dakota and on the northwestern plains there were agreements for larger parcels, including allotments of 320 acres to the head of a family and 160 acres for other members of the household.

The land went quickly. In 1887–88, even before the allotment surveys had begun, the government acquired reservation land in Montana. In return for long-term annuities, Indian communities there ceded over 17.5 million acres from the enormous reservation lying north of the Missouri River. The Blackfeet accepted a smaller reserve in the upper Marias River drainage system; the Gros Ventres and some Assiniboins took a reservation along the Milk River; other Assiniboins, Yanktonais, and some Santees, refugees of the Minnesota uprising of 1862, took a reservation in the northeastern part of the territory along the Missouri River.

In western Dakota, federal commissioners in the 1880s sought to divide the Great Sioux Reservation. Led by Three Stars Crook, and under heavy pressure from railroads and cattlemen, they succeeded. In return for long-term annuities and other promises, the Lakotas in 1889 agreed to relinquish a wide area between the Cheyenne and White rivers from the Missouri to the Black Hills and an area west of the 102nd meridian north of the Cheyenne River, together representing about 10 million acres. They allowed the remainder of the great reserve to be divided into five reservations under jurisdiction of five corresponding agencies (Standing Rock, Cheyenne River,

Lower Brule, Rosebud, and Pine Ridge) and agreed to individual allotments. Among the Lakotas little enthusiasm existed for such allotments at the time, and the Indian bureau did not push it.[37]

In eastern Dakota, however, several groups agreed to allotment. The Sisitonwan (Sisseton), among the first tribes to have its lands allotted, in February 1889 accepted, and in 1892 some six hundred thousand surplus acres of rich black loam, scattered with deep lakes and groves of trees, became available for whites. The lush farmland went quickly. Moreover, by 1909 two thirds of the three hundred thousand acres retained by the Sisitonwans had passed out of Indian ownership. The Yankton Reservation opened to settlers in 1895. The Yanktonais and an affiliated Santee tribe on the Crow Creek Reservation took allotment early, and their surplus land also became available for white settlement. Prices for the land varied with each reservation and with such factors as the national depression of the early 1890s, which discouraged high prices.

In Indian Territory, allotment and settlement proceeded together. A rider attached to an Indian appropriation bill in early 1889 allowed for the opening of the Oklahoma District, some 2 million acres of unassigned lands, and on April 22, 1889, perhaps fifty thousand people rushed for a 160-acre homestead or a lot in one of the towns that had already been laid out, occupying the entire region in a few days. After allotments to Sac and Fox, Iowa, and Shawnee-Potawatomi peoples, their reservations in 1891 opened to white settlement. The 4 million acres of surplus land from the Cheyenne-Arapaho Reservation became available on April 19, 1892, and eventually twenty-five thousand settlers claimed quarter-section parcels. But, because the land was arid enough to be considered unfit for farming, several months passed before homesteaders took up the westernmost 2 million acres. The government announced the availability of lands in the Cherokee Outlet as well as the Tonkawa and Pawnee reservations, and on September 16, 1893, in one of the most fantastic episodes on the southern plains, settlers claimed 6.3 million acres in a single day. The Comanches and Kiowas, led by Quanah Parker (who once on the reservation had adopted his mother's family name) and Lone Wolf, with assistance from Texas cattlemen who did not want to lose their leased range land on the reservation, resisted allotment in severalty until after the turn of the century.

In Montana the allotment process also varied from place to place. Indian peoples held onto good portions of some reserves, including all of Rocky Boy's Reservation, created in 1916. Allotment moved ahead on the others. On the Blackfeet, Crow, and Fort Belknap reservations, in the 1990s more than half the land belongs to individual Indians, the tribes control about 25 percent, and whites own the remainder. Tribal governments control about 25 percent of Fort Peck Reservation, and the Northern Cheyennes own about 60 percent of the land on their reserve.

The pressures of allotment, the interference of railroaders and cattlemen, the arrival of white farmers, and the shifting conditions associated with reservation life created a time of unease and despair on the Great Plains. To relieve their woes, many American Indians turned to a messiah named Wovoka, a thirty-five-year-old Paiute who had received an inspiration in 1888 that the Holy One Above had directed him to preach love and peace among his people. Wovoka also preached that the earth was to be regenerated and returned to Indian people, including many of their dead brethren. The miracle would come to pass by repeated performances of a special ceremonial dance, and the more often the people performed it, the quicker the coming of the new age. Many Indians of the plains listened eagerly to Wovoka and his missionaries. A delegation of Lakotas, headed by Kicking Bear of the Cheyenne River Reservation and Short Bull from Rosebud, traveled to Nevada to hear the message. When they returned to South Dakota, they brought the new religion with them.[38]

The Ghost Dance, as Wovoka's religion was called, spread over much of the West. However, Quanah Parker, who was a peyote cultist at the time of the Ghost Dance movement, opposed the Ghost Dance on his reservation and helped prevent its spread there.[39] Nor did it take hold among the Southern Cheyennes. Elsewhere it became a powerful force for uniting the Plains Indians. As the people danced, the excess of their emotions sent many of them into trances in which they saw visions of the new day and sang simple, chanting songs. Men, women, and children all participated. Mrs. J. F. Finley, who witnessed a Ghost Dance at the Pine Ridge Reservation in South Dakota, said that 480 people took part and that it lasted from Friday noon until sundown on Sunday. During that time, she noted, none of the dancers touched food or water and scores succumbed to trances or exhaustion. It was not a war dance, but the new Indian restlessness created alarm among whites in the vicinity of reservations.[40]

In mid October, 1890, there were signs of trouble at Pine Ridge. The new agent, a political hack who had little experience with Indian people, misunderstood the Ghost Dance and its message. Called Young Man Afraid of His Indians, he lost the confidence of the Oglalas before he had been at the agency a week. Beneath their outer garments, the Oglalas began wearing "holy shirts," believed impervious to bullets, suggesting perhaps that they expected trouble. Thinking that the Ghost Dance had to be stopped, the agent called for federal troops to put down the activity, and in mid November he indicated that his agency was out of control—one thousand troops were needed. A week later the government stationed soldiers at the Pine Ridge and Rosebud agencies.[41]

The Sioux "outbreak" of 1890–91 had begun. With the arrival of troops, many Lakotas left their reservations. Led by Two Strike, some eighteen hundred Brules fled the Rosebud agency for Pine Ridge. From there they went with Kicking Bear and Short Bull, the Ghost Dance missionaries, and hundreds of Oglalas to the Stonghold—or O-ona-gazhee, as Black Elk called it— a high plateau in the Badlands about forty miles north of Pine Ridge.[42] Indians from other agencies planned to join them. With Bear Coat Miles in command, the army hoped to end the whole affair without violence and return the people to their agencies.

It was impossible. Sitting Bull, who sided with the Ghost Dancers, died in a wretched attempt by Indian police to arrest him at his isolated camp along the Grand River on the Standing Rock Reservation. Hundreds of additional people, frightened but angry over the affair, headed for O-ona-gazhee, determined now to defend their religion by force of arms. Terribly cold weather and inadequate supplies, however, caused many of them to turn back. One such group, a band of 340 Miniconjous, Brules, and Hunkpapas all under the leadership of Big Foot, a Miniconjou, turned south toward Pine Ridge. On December 28 soldiers of the Seventh Cavalry stopped them and instructed the people to camp at Wounded Knee, about fifteen miles northeast of Pine Ridge. The next day, in a confusion of events, shots rang out and the army opened fire, killing at least 146 men, women, and children and suffering 26 dead themselves.[43]

The Wounded Knee massacre, as the event was called, changed the conflict's direction. Most of the Indians had left O-ona-gazhee and were returning to their agencies on the day of the disaster. Upon learning of the slaughter of their kin at Wounded Knee, they refused to continue, and additional reservation people joined them. On January 1, 1891, some four thousand people, including close to five hundred Cheyennes, were in camp along White Clay Creek about fifteen miles northwest of the Pine Ridge agency. Surrounded by some five thousand troops, the people had no place to go, and a week later they began slowly to shift their camp toward Pine Ridge.

The end came on January 15. Troops waiting at Pine Ridge witnessed an impressive sight. Capt. William E. Daugherty of the First Infantry recalled that the Indian people, including Oglalas, Brules, Hunkpapas, Miniconjous, Cheyennes, and others, in excellent order "moved in two columns up White Clay Creek, one on each side, about [4,000] people in all, with 7,000 horses, 500 wagons and about 250 travois." In the four-mile-long procession there was no sound but that of the bells tinkling on the horses, the clatter of hoofs on the frozen ground, the creaking of the wagons, and the scraping of travois poles. There was no incident. As they rode into Pine Ridge, the people set up their tents and awaited instructions.[44]

The conflict was over. Brief but explosive, the Sioux "outbreak" of 1890–91 was the last major military confrontation between the Plains Indians and the federal army. It included the death of Sitting Bull, perhaps the country's most famous Indian person, and the disaster at Wounded Knee, which continues to symbolize the Plains Indians' struggle to hold their land and to retain their traditional customs. Years later, noting this circumstance, Black Elk said "that something else died there in the bloody mud [at Wounded Knee], and was buried in the blizzard. A people's dream died there. It was a beautiful dream."[45]

Although cultural traditions persisted, failure in the Ghost Dance and tragedy at Wounded Knee turned Plains Indians toward new sodalities and different lifeways. "We had to learn to live by farming instead of by hunting and trading," wrote Carl Sweezy. "We had to learn to cut our hair short, and to wear close-fitting clothes made of dull-colored cloth, and to live in houses, though we knew that our long braids of hair and embroidered robes and . . . tall, round lodges were more beautiful."[46]

In the aftermath of allotment and Wounded Knee came hunger, disease, malnutrition, and population decline. Allotment in severalty eliminated some reservations on the plains altogether and significantly cut the size of others. During the allotment era such problems as poverty, deprivation, shoddy housing, and poor health appeared, and allotment fostered an atmosphere of change and coercion.

But reservation life was not abject wretchedness. Many favorite cultural forms persisted into the twentieth century, and Indian people on the plains adjusted rapidly to the new circumstances. They responded creatively. When grass lease money was to be distributed, for example, people showed up at the agency and, one of them writes, "made a good thing of the gatherings. . . . There was trading at the stores and feasting in the tipis and visiting everywhere, and everybody went away happy." When agents made errors in the distribution of shoes, as another example, "that was reason enough for the men to sell their shoes and wear moccasins." Younger people especially adapted quickly to altered conditions, and some of them, such as Carl Sweezy and Luther Standing Bear (a Lakota), remembered parts of their boarding school experience with fondness.[47]

Nonetheless, reservation life after 1870 represented a transitional period for Plains Indian societies. Without abandoning significant cultural forms that had characterized their traditional ways for generations, the plains peoples shifted away from such dramatic aspects of their economies as horse-mounted, bison-hunting practices to new subsistence modes. Although much had changed in the brief period since the treaties of Medicine Lodge and Fort Laramie, much, indeed, remained the same—as twentieth-century experiences clearly demonstrate.

EPILOGUE : THE TWENTIETH CENTURY

I n the early twentieth century, American Indians of the plains survived population decline, forced assimilation, assaults on tribalism, and in the 1930s hardships associated with severe drought and economic depression. In the second half of the century, they entered a period of sociopolitical change, population growth, and cultural revival. A vigorous renewal of traditional religions, ceremonial structures, and healing practices occurred; a renewed sense of tribalism developed. Plains Indians today display a growing sophistication in dealing with the federal government, some economic development on reservations, greater autonomy over their own tribal affairs, and increasing independence for off-reservation people.

The twentieth century opened, however, as the nineteenth closed—with continued loss of reservation land through allotment. Few Plains Indians supported allotment in severalty, few wanted to take up assigned lands, few saw allotment as beneficial; but few were able to adopt white legal principles or other methods to block the practice. An important exception was the determined Kiowa leader Lone Wolf. When his efforts to block passage of the General Allotment Act failed, he fought practical application of the law in a series of confrontations with the Jerome Commission, the federal body assigned to complete allotment agreements with several tribal groups in the Oklahoma Territory (formerly western Indian Territory).

The Jerome Commission worked fast. By 1896 it had completed allotment agreements with many of its assigned tribes and had arranged for opening the surplus lands to settlement. Lone Wolf, arguing in council and sending petitions to Congress, led efforts to block allotment of the Kiowa-Comanche reserve, but finally in 1901 the commission, over Lone Wolf's opposition, completed the task and gained 2 million acres of surplus lands. The federal government set aside three large areas—Fort Sill Military Reservation of 56,000 acres, the Wichita Mountain Forest Reserve of 58,000 acres, and the Big Pasture Reserve of 400,000 acres—and opened most of the remainder for white settlement. Unwilling to quit, Lone Wolf now brought suit against Secretary of the Interior Ethan Allen Hitchcock.

Lone Wolf v. Hitchcock reached the Supreme Court in 1902. Lone Wolf believed that the 1867 Treaty of Medicine Lodge (specifically Article 12) provided that no part of the Kiowa-Comanche Reservation could be ceded without the approval of three fourths of the adult males. Therefore, congressional action that approved the sale of excess tribal lands without the three-fourths approval was illegal and beyond the power of Congress. The Supreme Court, when it handed down its opinion on January 5, 1903, refused to rule on the three-fourths provision but declared that Congress did indeed have the power to pass laws abrogating treaty stipulations as well as complete authority over Indian relations.[1]

The decision had broad implications. A major setback for Indian legal and civil rights, it supported the doctrine of plenary powers of Congress over Indian affairs and implied that Congress could abrogate certain parts of treaties. The decision reaffirmed the concept that American Indians were wards of the government and dependent upon the United States. Recognizing the significance of the Lone Wolf decision, the Indian Rights Association, which had been founded in 1882 by Herbert Welsh, complained that "it is now distinctly understood that Congress has a right to do as it pleases; . . . the Indians have no rights that command respect."[2] In subsequent years *Lone Wolf v. Hitchcock* served to establish congressional right to take lands without regard to treaties.

Citing the Lone Wolf decision, Congress in 1906 opened the Big Pasture Reserve without Kiowa or Comanche consent. The Big Pasture, 400,000 acres of grazing land reserved for the benefit of the Kiowas and Comanches along the Red River, had been leased to Texas cattlemen for over twenty years, bringing to the plains tribes in 1905 about $136,295 annually.

When farmer-settlers sought access to the grazing land, Congress in 1906 passed a measure to open the Big Pasture for settlement. After President Theodore Roosevelt on June 5 signed the bill into law, Big Pasture land sold so rapidly that in September the Kiowas and Comanches owned land solely as individuals. The General Allotment Act, within twenty years of its 1887 passage, had divested the Kiowa and Comanche tribes of all reservation lands.[3]

On occasion the Plains Indians gained ground. One of their most important successes in the early twentieth century occurred in *Winters v. United States*. The case involved water rights on Gros Ventre and Assiniboin lands on the Fort Belknap Reservation in Montana, an arid region where farming was nearly impossible without water. As white farmers and other settlers began diverting water of the Milk River (along the northern border of the reservation) and its tributaries, less and less water flowed to the reservation. Tribal leaders brought suit, their attorneys arguing that where land was reserved for an Indian tribe, there was an implied reservation of water necessary for the irrigation of tribal lands or for other development of the reservation.

In its decision of January 6, 1908, the Supreme Court agreed. It held that a "reserved" water right constitutes a special right that differs from either a riparian right (which resides with owners of land bordering a stream) or a right of prior appropriation (which emphasizes beneficial use based on priority and which has been adopted in some form by all western states, including Montana). Indian people, the court determined, were entitled to the water that passed through the reservation, and it further ruled that those who had diverted water before it had reached the Fort Belknap Reservation must stop the practice until the needs of the reservation inhabitants were satisfied. Moreover, the "reserved rights" doctrine continued unimpaired even if Indian people discontinued their use of the water.[4]

Perhaps more symbolic than real, victory in the Winters case was nonetheless important. In theory it created a solid Indian claim to the precious water resources in arid lands of the West, and it established precedent for Indian water rights through the remainder of the century. The Winters doctrine expanded Indian legal rights at a time when such rights were being lost one after another.[5] In practice the decision made little difference—at first. Farmers, cattlemen, and settlers continued to redirect Milk River water, using the courts to delay application of the Winters decision. But in the 1960s and 1970s, Indian people in Montana and other parts of the West "rediscovered" *Winters v. United States.* They have since used it to protect both reservation water and mineral rights.

World Wars I and II also influenced the lives of Plains Indians. The wars introduced many people to life outside the reservations, and many of them gained employment in non-farm-related jobs. Those who served in the military traveled extensively, many of them to battlefronts in Europe, Africa, and the Far East. "Indian boys," wrote Ella Deloria (Lakota) in 1944, were "in every branch of the service. . . . Indian girls [were] Red Cross nurses, WACs, and WAVEs. They, too, [went] everywhere." More people learned English. Some Indian people, following off-reservation fashions, began to change their hair and dress styles, and some even changed their cultural traditions. High wartime prices for livestock, especially cattle and sheep, encouraged Indian stockmen to sell their animals. Unfortunately, after World War I too many people spent their income without buying livestock, leaving them with neither herds nor money.[6]

During World War II the government's rationing program also produced shortages of some essential goods. Shortages in rubber tires, for example, left many Plains Indian people without the use of automobiles. Many reservation school systems discontinued bus service. Material scarcity modified the services that hospitals and community centers provided, and sometimes the government closed agency offices on reservations.

On the Pine Ridge Reservation, the federal government in 1942 forced the Oglalas to surrender over 400,000 acres of land for use as an aerial gunnery range. Some 128 families who owned three fourths of the land received only about seventy-five cents per acre for their property, and the government leased the remainder from the tribe. Given only thirty days to vacate the land, the Oglalas had to leave before they could harvest their crops.[7]

As Indian people left home for war-related employment opportunities, changes in reservation living patterns emerged. The Sisseton agency in South Dakota, for example, reported that by 1944 over one fourth of the tribal population had moved away from the reservation permanently. For other people the transition from rural reservations in Montana and North and South Dakota proved more difficult. Cut off from familiar customs and traditions, some of them did not remain long in their new positions. For many others, especially for those from the Dakotas, a pattern of travel emerged in which Indian people moved easily between reservations and urban areas.[8]

The great wars also sparked a revival of traditions and institutions that had lapsed. Following World War I, for example, Kiowa women reestablished two war societies, and during World War II, Dakota people renewed some older victory dances. These developments, in turn, sparked additional sodality revivals, such as the Kiowa Black Legs in 1956. Clearly, World War I inspired much of the American Indian reform movement that occurred in the 1920s and afterward.

Between the wars a radical transformation in thinking about American Indians occurred. From the days of Thomas Jefferson, the dominant idea held by whites about Indian people was that American Indians would one day be assimilated, that they would no longer exist as distinctive peoples. In the 1920s, however, Indian reform advocates pushed to end the Americanization process, and in the 1930s they achieved some success.

John Collier, who in 1933 became commissioner of Indian affairs in President Franklin D. Roosevelt's administration, led the way. A strong advocate of self-determination, he wanted to restore American Indian values, functional tribal councils, and traditional religious practices. The primary prerequisite to ethnic and cultural survival, he believed, was retention of reservation land, and therefore he fought for an end to allotment in severalty and for a new Indian policy. He got both.

Congress in 1934 passed the Indian Reorganization Act. The law, popularly known as the Wheeler-Howard Act, stopped allotment and encouraged a new policy of tribal organization. It promoted cultural pluralism by guaranteeing Indians rights to traditional practices, improved Indian education and access to health care, and in general attempted to fulfill many popular recommendations and proposals for reform. It was a comprehensive law, one designed to improve the material life of American Indians and protect their traditional lifeways. Its most controversial aspects were those provisions (Sections 16 & 17) that called for formal tribal governments with written constitutions. Here the law allowed Indian tribes a semblance of self-rule in conducting elections, creating courts with jurisdiction over local offenses, and performing other local government functions.[9] Because its provisions would apply only after tribal members had voted acceptance, the Indian Reorganization Act became the subject of many tribal elections. In the elections some 189 communities accepted the law, and 77 others rejected it. Subsequently, 135 of the 189 approving groups drafted constitutions.

On the Great Plains acceptance was mixed. In the Dakotas the people on some reservations (Crow Creek, for example) rejected the Indian Reorganization Act, those on some (Standing Rock, for example) approved the law but did not write a constitution, and those on some (Rosebud, for example) took full advantage of the measure. That is, they approved the law, organized a federal corporation, adopted a constitution, and created a tribal council to govern themselves. In Montana, except on the Crow and Fort Peck reservations, all the plains people took full advantage of the law.[10]

The Indian Reorganization Act did not apply to most American Indians in Oklahoma, largely because of the opposition of Senator Elmer Thomas, but also because much of their land had been liquidated by allotment. But in 1936 Congress in the Oklahoma Indian Welfare Act extended principles of the law to the so-called "tribeless Indians" there. The law permitted Indian people in Oklahoma to form corporations and to obtain money for various projects from a special revolving loan fund of $2 million.[11]

The Plains Indians also benefited in other ways. Collier urged Congress to include Indian people in its New Deal legislation. The aim was to provide emergency relief to Indian people, whose 1933 per capita income was $81, and to allow American Indians to participate in the New Deal work programs. Congress agreed, and federal programs provided relief and offered employment at comparatively high wages.

Various New Deal agencies extended health care to reservations. Other agencies built new roads and public buildings. Men who enrolled in the Indian Civilian Conservation Corps (CCC-ID) worked in soil conservation, reforestation, and water and wind erosion projects. They built roads, dug wells, constructed dams, and reseeded overgrazed rangelands. Indian families, especially those gathered at CCC-ID camps, enjoyed some basic instruction in reading, writing, and arithmetic, and the children received vocational training in agriculture, forestry, and animal husbandry. Congress also provided educational loans for young people to attend college, and for those people, including adults, who stayed on the reservation, it offered

cattle raising and other farm programs.[12] In short, the Indian Reorganization
Act and Collier's other programs produced significant Indian policy reforms,
or as some have called it, an "Indian New Deal." Both left their marks on the
people of the plains.

For years scholars hailed Collier and the New Deal policies, especially the
Indian Reorganization Act, as benefiting American Indians. In the 1980s,
however, they came under criticism for their failure to restore health and
prosperity to the reservations, for Collier's authoritarian tendencies, and for
their neglect of treaty guarantees.[13] Because World War II interrupted his
efforts, perhaps Collier had little time to fully implement his policies.

In the aftermath of World War II, the Plains Indians struggled with the
federal government over new policy goals designed to terminate all federal
responsibility for Indian welfare. The central idea of one, "termination," was
to integrate Indian people into the mainstream of American life by ending
the federal government's trust responsibilities for tribes. It gained wide acceptance (even among some Indian leaders) after World War II, but by the
early 1960s it had lost favor. Shortly afterward the government discontinued
the policy.[14]

A second postwar policy goal hoped to settle Indian claims against the
United States. Accordingly, Congress in 1946 created the Indian Claims Commission, an agency designed to relieve the overloaded Court of Claims
docket by hearing and adjudicating all valid claims regarding treaties, con-
tracts, and agreements between the United States and Indian communities
before 1946.[15] An independent, quasi-judicial body, the commission exam-
ined more than 850 claims that Indian leaders filed with it. Most of the claims
involved land issues; the principal argument of the Indian claiments was that
either no or not enough compensation had been received for their lands. If the
commission agreed, the United States became liable for the unpaid amount.[16]

Before it went out of business in 1978, the commission had awarded plains
tribes compensation that totaled tens of millions of dollars. Then, in 1979, the
Court of Claims granted the Lakotas $102 million for the Black Hills. Because
they want the land back, the Lakotas have not accepted the money, which the
federal government now holds in trust for them, and which, through interest
accumulation, now totals over $210 million.

In the meantime, as Plains Indians struggled for just compensation before
the Indian Claims Commission, the "Red Power" movement made gains. A
pan-Indian effort, it brought American Indians together to seek support for
themselves, to gain a place for Indian people in the larger white world, and to
achieve various other goals, including enforcement of old treaty guarantees.
In getting Congress to pass a number of important laws that benefited American Indians, the movement achieved some success in the 1970s.

The pan-Indian nature of the Red Power movement can be seen in a whole series of events in the 1960s and 1970s. It was demonstrated in the broad-based, intertribal makeup of the Native American Church and in the 1961 Conference of American Indians in Chicago, where some five hundred people from sixty-seven tribes came together. It is exemplified in the commitment of Robert Burnette, who as chairman of the Rosebud Tribal Council said in 1969, "one of these days, the Sioux will rise up again, and when we do, we'll be fighting for all tribes, not just our own."[17]

A few years later the Plains Indians tested the commitment. In 1972 Dennis Banks, a Chippewa and one of the founders of the American Indian Movement (AIM); several other AIM leaders; and Russell Means, a Lakota and a masterful orator who was brilliant at staging media events, came to western South Dakota to help reservation people at Pine Ridge protest a whole series of injustices. The problems included the actions of police authorities in nearby Gordon, Nebraska, where whites had stripped, intimidated, and murdered Raymond Yellow Thunder, an Oglala from Pine Ridge. AIM organizers in early 1972 led thirteen hundred Indians to Gordon, where they occupied the town for three days before police arrested two suspects. Then in April, Richard Wilson, using bribes and intimidation, won election as the Oglala tribal chairman. His high-handed tactics and his "brazen indifference to his people's opinions" soon turned many on the reservation against him. In addition, there was a problem over a new housing project in which some Oglalas suspected collusion between Wilson and the non-Indian contractors. Finally, in January 1973 authorities in Custer, South Dakota, freed on $5,000 bail the murderer of Wesley Bad Heart Bull, an Oglala. Wesley's mother, who protested the low bail, received a sentence of three to five years in jail for assaulting a police officer. Her son's murderer received two months' probation.[18]

In response, AIM leaders took over Wounded Knee, a tiny crossroads hamlet located about fifteen miles from Pine Ridge. For seventy-one days from mid February to late May, 1973, they staged a highly visible occupation of the historic Lakota site. Iroquois, Ojibwas, Apaches, and others—about 250 American Indians—were part of the demonstration. Non-Indians, including national African American leaders, came to Wounded Knee to show their support for AIM's position and for American Indian concerns in general. They faced a growing number of federal agents. When the govenment tightened its ring around Wounded Knee and agreed to discussions with Oglala representatives, the protesters dispersed and the siege ended.[19]

The results were mixed. Richard Wilson, AIM's chief target, remained as Oglala chairman, and little was accomplished for those who had asked AIM to help them on the Pine Ridge Reservation. Russell Means and Dennis

Banks, however, became national figures, and their "media event" turned American attention to Indian problems and policies far beyond those at Pine Ridge or even the Great Plains. The occupation of Wounded Knee was a pan-Indian event that focused attention on pan-Indian concerns.

The remarkable pan-Indian success aside, on reservations of the American Great Plains, a number of long-standing problems persisted. Housing was often wretched, and poverty remained a consistent difficulty. Too many people suffered from alcohol and drug abuse, low self-esteem, health problems, and unemployment. For lack of funds and personnel, reservation agencies established to deal with such concerns often proved inadequate. Moreover, many tribal members who had left the reservations faced their own dilemmas, including discrimination, periodic unemployment, alcoholism, and inadequate housing.

On the Canadian plains of Manitoba, Saskatchewan, and Alberta, similar problems existed. Road and railway accessibility was limited; and many homes on Indian reserves were without electricity, sewage disposal, and running water. In Manitoba less than 10 percent of reserves in the 1980s had sufficient fire-fighting equipment. Poor health and high mortality rates were characteristic of several reserves, reflecting perhaps a general lack of health care, few medical facilities, poor sewage systems, and problems with disease. Indian people on or near reservations in western Canada also suffered from inadequate job opportunities.[20]

In the 1980s Plains Indians on reservations sought to improve local economic conditions. Because wheat growing and cattle raising could not support the increasing reservation populations, they turned to other sources for employment and income. Some people sought the establishment of light-industry manufacturing. Some, especially those in Wyoming and Montana, demanded improved royalty payments and greater control over mineral resources under their reservations. Although most plains reservations were too far from urban centers to exploit America's fasination with casino gambling, some Indian communities, such as the Yanktons with facilities on "the hill" near Pickstown, South Dakota, enjoyed success with tourism and gambling, earning in 1997 tens of millions of dollars.

Plains Indians also encouraged the growth and popularity of powwows. First developed in the late nineteenth century, powwows by the late 1990s had become gatherings, usually held on summer weekends, in which people from many tribal groups participated. Part social dance, part dance contest, part family reunion, part celebration, and part cultural revival, powwows brought people together to sing, dance, gamble, and visit with family and friends. They are traditional rather than religious events, free of alcohol and full of the spirit of Indian resurgence. The dancing from time to time is interrupted for "specials" or "giveaways," in which a family might honor someone in speech and celebration and then also in the person's honor provide gifts to many of the attendees.

Intertribal, or pan-Indian, powwows—with scores of them held in the open each year—attract people from across the Great Plains and elsewhere. They represent a popular celebration of Plains Indian history and culture. One of the largest is Crow Fair, held annually at Crow Agency, Montana. More than a large gathering of Indian people, it is also an effort to preserve the Crows' customs, traditions, and culture. Dale Old Horn, its director, is a professor of Indian studies at Little Big Horn College and a popular master of ceremonies at many other powwows.[21]

Other bright spots appeared. Indian education on western reservations continued to improve. Saint Labre Indian School at Ashland, Montana, and Saint Francis Mission School on the Rosebud Reservation in South Dakota represent two of the best, modern Indian schools on the Great Plains. Most Plains Indians, however, attended public schools in 1997, and those institutions, while they lagged behind some of the modern suburban schools associated with metropolitan centers, had improved over their earlier counterparts.

More important was the growth after 1978 of tribally controlled colleges, such as Little Big Horn College on the Crow Reservation. One of the schools, Oglala Lakota College, although located in an isolated region (near Kyle) of the Pine Ridge Reservation, enrolled in 1992 nearly nine hundred students. The same year Sinte Gleska University at Mission, South Dakota, attracted in addition to Rosebud Reservation Indians a large number of off-reservation white students, and as early as 1988 it had awarded nine students with graduate degrees in education.

Such achievements bode well for the future. Plains Indian populations are increasing on reservations, in small towns, in middle-sized and large cities, and in the capitals of many plains states, with the latter development suggesting that Plains Indians are gaining access to government and professional careers.

Indeed, some have held high political office. Charles Curtis, a Kansa-Osage, for example, was a member of the U.S. House of Representatives from Kansas before holding a Senate seat. A Republican, he was also vice president of the United States in the Herbert Hoover administration (1929–33). In the 1960s Ben Reifel, a Brule with a Ph.D. from Harvard University, served several terms in the House of Representatives as a Republican congressman from South Dakota. Born at tiny Parmelee on the Rosebud Reservation, he was for many years director of the Aberdeen, South Dakota, area office of the Bureau of Indian Affairs before representing the state's First (East) District in Washington. Ben Nighthorse Campbell, a Northern Cheyenne and a U.S.

Olympic athlete (judo) in 1964, served three terms as a Democrat in Congress before the citizens of Colorado in 1992 elected him to the United States Senate. Three years later he switched to the Republican party.

The Plains Indians have also produced many successful writers.[22] They include Charles A. Eastman, a Santee with an M.D. degree from Boston University; Francis La Flesche, an Omaha ethnologist with the Smithsonian Institution and one of the first American Indian scholars; Gertrude Bonnin (Zitkala Sa), a Yankton; Nicholas Black Elk, an Oglala holy man; John Joseph Mathews, an Osage; and James Welch, a Blackfeet–Gros Ventre; and there are many others. They have produced history, poetry, prose fiction, autobiography, commentary, and other literary forms, often with critical acclaim.

Perhaps the most famous twentieth-century Plains Indian author was N. Scott Momaday, a Kiowa-Cherokee with a Ph.D. degree from Stanford University. His *House Made of Dawn,* which for mastery of language has few rivals, won the Pulitzer Prize for literature in 1969. It is about a Pueblo soldier who returns from World War II and finds that he cannot recover his tribal identity, an experience not uncommon among American Indian soldiers in 1945.

Artists, particularly painters, have also achieved critical acclaim. In the 1920s and 1930s "traditional" painters from Oklahoma influenced many Indian artists. The "Kiowa 5," as they have been called (Monroe Tsatoke, Stephen Mopope, Jack Hokeah, James Auchiah, and Spencer Ash), emphasized American Indian subjects, used flat colors with no shading and little background, and adopted what is called "stylized, linear, and representational art." The work of others, such as Acee Blue Eagle and Allan Houser, continues to impact Indian art forms.[23]

Perhaps the most influencial Plains Indian artist was Oscar Howe, a Yankton from the Crow Creek Reservation in South Dakota. Howe, who holds an Master of Fine Arts degree from the University of Oklahoma, was the first serious painter to combine traditional and modern forms in his paintings. Thus, he is credited with pioneering a new phase of artistic expression in American Indian art, one that allowed many Indian painters to find their own means of individual expression, whether traditional or avant garde. While a professor of art at Dakota Wesleyan University, Howe called his own work, which became increasingly abstract, Indian Cubism.

In international ballet, the Plains Indians have also made contributions. Yvonne Chouteau performed at the age of fourteen for the Ballet Russe de Monte Carlo. A member of the famous group for fourteen years, she served eight years as the leading ballerina. Maria Tallchief, an Osage, was a principal ballerina in the United States, and she also danced with the Company Ballet Russe de Monte Carlo. Her sister Marjorie Tallchief danced with the Paris

Ballet Company. The Tallchiefs changed ballet in America, and in 1951 *Mademoiselle* magazine named Maria its Woman of the Year.

Although Plains Indians today are often suburban-dwelling teachers, doctors, plumbers, factory employees, lawyers, or accountants, the legacy of older customs and traditions endures. Particularly on reservations, older healing practices are still popular, and extended family ties continue to be close. Intertribal powwows are again enjoying popularity and are increasing in number. The lure of the land remains strong. Indeed, anyone alone during a gentle summer evening on the rolling range country of the Great Plains, where the winds blow through still sacred points, becomes a dreamer—a mystic—reconnected with the past, its spirits, and the prominent role of the Plains Indians in American history.

As part of that history, the Plains Indians' traditional cultures emerged at a time when horses and material goods from alien peoples contributed to a growing complexity in plains life and society. A century and a half later, influenced by unrelenting contact with those same peoples, the Plains Indians entered a period of transformation—"an incredible metamorphosis"—into participants in the modern era. Some plains peoples, such as the Pawnees, Wichitas, and Missouri Basin groups, had lived in the region hundreds of years before white contact. Others, such as the Arapahos, Cheyennes, Comanches, and Lakotas, arrived with or after white contact. The dramatic, flamboyant societies they created on the plains appeared nowhere else in North America, but they captured the world's imagination. As we have seen, however, their unique way of life as equestrian bison hunters lasted only a few generations.[24]

Historical accounts, although often dominated by romance and high adventure, reveal the significant contributions that Indian people of the plains have made to American civilization. The Plains Indians supplied whites with furs, hides, dried meat (pemmican), and other goods. They served government explorers and soldiers as guides, scouts, and allies. They marked trails, hunted game, and warned of danger. Indeed, they were indispensable to government agents who utlimately conquered the Indians' homeland. In medicine, whites used Plains Indian herbs and drugs for curing practices and sometimes turned to shamans for medical help. Americans borrowed Indian words for the names of cities, states, lakes, rivers, and other geographical sites on the plains. European languages adopted dozens of words, such as the French "apache," "gros ventres," "travois," "nez perce," and "cache," that come from the plains.

The Plains Indians contributed to American culture in other ways as well. They provided a manual sign language that in part was adopted for communication among modern hearing-impaired persons. They provided ideas and forms for modern signaling systems. Their governments and societies offered models for decentralization, local self-rule, and voluntary associations. The larger white society today admires the Plains Indians' sense of hospitality, graciousness, and personal freedom. America's current fascination with conservation and ecology and its various environmental movements have roots among the Plains Indians.

Motion pictures and television programs also reflect, albeit often inaccurately, the influence of Plains Indian life. The larger American public has only recently begun to appreciate and utilize the rich mythology and folklore of the Plains Indians, and there have been important contributions in drama, dance, art, and literature. Such works as Momaday's *House Made of Dawn* and Charles Eastman's *Indian Boyhood* suggest that many Plains Indian themes await discovery and creative expression.

Moreover, Reifel and Campbell, Oglala Lakota and Sinte Gleska, Momaday and Howe all demonstrate that in the late twentieth century the Plains Indians continued to play a prominent role in American society. They suggest, too, that the Plains Indians, although many features of their traditional societies and cultures have changed, are in a period of renewal that is characterized by a reemerging tribalism and by a heightened desire for an American Indian identity, including a distinctive place for themselves in their own country. Clearly, in a nation marked by an emerging cultural pluralism, the Plains Indians will continue to make substantial contributions to American life.

Notes

CHAPTER 1

1   Clark Wissler, *North American Indians of the Plains*, pp. 18–20; Clark Wissler, *The American Indian*, pp. 220–22. See also Alfred L. Kroeber, *Cultural and Natural Areas of Native North America*, p. 76.

2   Robert H. Lowie, *Indians of the Plains*, pp. 4–10; Symmes C. Oliver, *Ecology and Cultural Continuity as Contributing Factors in the Social Organization of the Plains Indians*, map opposite p. 1; E. Adamson Hoebel, *The Plains Indians: A Critical Bibliography*, pp. 26–27, 40–41; W. W. Newcomb, Jr., *The Indians of Texas: From Prehistoric to Modern Times*, pp. 109, 133–53.

3   See Eldon Johnson, "The Great Plains," in Robert F. Spencer, Jesse D. Jennings, et al., *The Native Americans: Ethnology and Backgrounds of the North American Indians*, pp. 314–15; Alvin M. Josephy, Jr., *The Indian Heritage of America*, pp. 114–15; Roderick Wilson, "The Plains—A Regional Overview," in R. Bruce Morrison and C. Roderick Wilson, eds., *Native Peoples: The Canadian Experience*, pp. 353–58; Harold E. Driver, *Indians of North America*, pp. 16, 27–28.

4   See, Frederick E. Hoxie, *Parading through History: The Making of the Crow Nation in America, 1805–1935*, p. 41; Dale Old Horn, "Crow Kinship Systems," in Walter C. Fleming and John G. Watts, eds., *Visions of an Enduring People: Introduction to Native American Studies*, p. 47.

5   Lowie, *Indians of the Plains*, pp. 5–7; Wissler, *American Indian*, p. 220; Josephy, *Indian Heritage of America*, pp. 114–15, 119–20; Wissler, *North American Indians of the Plains*, pp. 18–20.

6   See Johnson, "The Great Plains," in Spencer, Jennings, et al., *Native Americans*, p. 312; Hoebel, *Plains Indians*, pp. 7–12; Josephy, *The Indian Heritage of America*, pp. 114–15; Alice B. Kehoe, *North American Indians: A Comprehensive Account*, pp. 298–310; Evan M. Maurer, ed., *Visions of the People: A Pictorial History of Plains Indian Life*, pp. 12–13; Harold E. Driver and James L. Coffin, *Classification and Development of North American Indian Cultures: A Statistical Analysis of the Driver—Massey Sample*, pp. 5, 12–20; Dean Snow, *The Archaeology of North America*, p. 96.

7   Robert F. Spencer, "Language—American Babel," in Spencer, Jennings, et al., *Native Americans*, pp. 46–47.

8   Walter Prescott Webb, *The Great Plains*, p. 74.

9   James Mooney, "Calendar History of the Kiowa Indians," *Seventeenth Annual Report of the Bureau of Ethnology, 1895–96*, pt. 1, *passim*; Newcomb, *Indians of Texas*, pp. 218–19; Maurer, ed., *Visions of the People*, pp. 19–20, 29, 40, 51, 65; Joyce M. Szabo, *Howling Wolf and the History of Ledger Art*, pp. 7–9.

10 See Russell Thornton, *American Indian Holocaust and Survival: A Population History since 1492*, pp. xvi, 24–25, 29, 32; David E. Stannard, *American Holocaust: The Conquest of the New World*, pp. 11, 266–68.

11 Francis Jennings, *The Invasion of America: Indians, Colonialism, and the Cant of Conquest,* p. 24. See also Wilbur R. Jacobs, "The Tip of the Iceberg: Pre-Columbian Indian Demography and Some Implications for Revision," *William and Mary Quarterly,* 3d ser., 21 (1974): 123–32; and Calvin Martin, *Keepers of the Game: Indian-Animal Relations and the Fur Trade,* pp. 99–100; Karl H. Schlesier, ed., *Plains Indians, A.D. 500–1500: The Archaeological Past of Historic Groups,* p. xx. For a different view see James A. Clifton, ed., *Being and Becoming Indian: Biographical Studies of North American Frontiers,* p. 5.

12 Thornton, *American Indian Holocaust and Survival,* pp. 95–99.

13 Jennings, *Invasion of America,* pp. 15–31; Stewart, *People of America,* pp. 29–35; D'Arcy McNickle, *They Came Here First: The Epic of the American Indian,* pp. 22–24; Josephy, *Indian Heritage of America,* pp. 52–55; Henry F. Dobyns with William R. Swagerty, *Their Number Became Thinned: Native American Population Dynamics in Eastern North America,* pp. 15–20; Henry F. Dobyns, "Estimating Aboriginal American Population: An Appraisal of Techniques with a New Hemisphere Estimate," *Current Anthropology* 7 (1966): 414–15; Thornton, *American Indian Holocaust and Survival,* pp. 96, 100, 127; A. L. Kroeber, "Native American Population," *American Anthropologist,* n.s., 36 (1934): 1–25.

14 Earl H. Elam, "The Native Texans," in Donald W. Whisenhunt, ed., *Texas: A Sesquicentennial Celebration,* p. 27; Dan L. Flores, "Bison Ecology and Bison Diplomacy: The Southern Plains from 1800 to 1850," *Journal of American History* 78 (September, 1991): 465–85; Thomas W. Kavanagh, *Comanche Political History: An Ethnohistorical Perspective, 1706–1875,* pp. 6–7.

15 Neven N. Fenneman, *Physiography of Western United States,* pp. 61–79.

16 Waldo Wedel, *Prehistoric Man on the Great Plains,* p. 28.

17 Ibid., pp. 28–29; Fenneman, *Physiography of Western United States,* pp. 11–25, 50–60.

18 Webb, *The Great Plains,* p. 28.

19 Ibid., p. 29.

20 Wedel, *Prehistoric Man on the Great Plains,* pp. 36–40; Virgil J. Vogel, *American Indian Medicine,* pp. 106–109; Johnson, "The Great Plains," in Spencer, Jennings, et al., *Native Americans,* pp. 322, 356–57; Lowie, *Indians of the Plains,* pp. 17–18, 105.

21 See, for example, Kelly Kindscher, *Medicinal Wild Plants of the Prairie: An Ethnobotanical Guide,* pp. 32–35, 84–94, 113–17; 126–29.

22 Quoted in Peter Nabokov, ed., *Native American Testimony: A Chronicle of Indian—White Relations from Prophecy to the Present, 1492–1992,* p. 184.

23 Ernest Wallace and E. Adamson Hoebel, *The Comanches: Lords of the South Plains,* p. 70.

24 Webb, *Great Plains,* p. 41.

25 Cited in Nabokov, ed., *Native American Testimony,* p. 174.

26 Tom McHugh, *The Time of the Buffalo,* pp. 16–17. See also Ralph H. Brown, *Historical Geography of the United States,* pp. 378–82; Francis Haines, *The Buffalo: The Story of American Bison and their Hunters from Prehistoric Times to the Present,* pp. 36–37; and E. Douglas Branch, *The Hunting of the Buffalo,* pp. 54–57.

27 Daniel P. Mowrey and Paul H. Carlson, "The Native Grasslands of the High Plains of West Texas: Past, Present, Future," *West Texas Historical Association Year Book* 63

(1987): pp. 25–35; Flores, "Bison Ecology and Bison Diplomacy," pp. 470–71, 476–78, 480–83. See also William A. Dobak, "Killing the Canadian Buffalo, 1821–1881," *Western Historical Quarterly* 27 (spring, 1996): 33–52.

CHAPTER 2

1 Gordon R. Willey, *An Introduction to American Archaeology*, 1: 12–16, 26–37; Alex D. Krieger, "Early Man in the New World," in Jesse D. Jennings and Edward Norbeck, eds., *Prehistoric Man in the New World*, pp. 23–51; McNickle, *They Came Here First*, pp. 7–8; Alan L. Bryan, "Early Man in America and the Late Pleistocene Chronology of Western Canada and Alaska," *Current Anthropology* 10 (1969): 339–48; and Jesse D. Jennings, "Perspective," in Spencer, Jennings, et al., *Native Americans*, pp. 6–12.

2 Dean R. Snow, *Native American Prehistory: A Critical Bibliography*, p. vii. For different time periods, see Kehoe, *North American Indians*, pp. viii, 1–9; Brian M. Fagan, *Ancient North America: The Archaeology of a Continent*, pp. 66–166.

3 C. W. Ceram, *The First American: A Story of North American Archaeology*, pp. 287–97; David M. Hopkins, "Landscape and Climate of Beringia during Late Pleistocene and Holocene Time," in William S. Laughlin and Albert B. Harper, eds., *The First Americans: Origins, Affinities, and Adaptations*, pp. 15–41.

4 Paul S. Martin, "The Discovery of America," *Science* 179 (1973): 969–74.

5 Willey, *Introduction to American Archaeology*, 1: 37–51; Krieger, "Early Man in the New World," in Jennings and Norbec, eds., *Prehistoric Man in the New World*, pp. 51–68; Hopkins, "Landscape and Climate of Beringia during Late Pleistocene and Holocene Time," in Laughlin and Harper, eds., *First Americans*, pp. 28–53.

6 See Jennings, "Perspectives," in Spencer, Jennings, et al., *Native Americans*, pp. 12–22.

7 Kehoe, *North American Indians*, p. 16.

8 Jennings, "Perspective," in Spencer, Jennings, et al., *Native Americans*, pp. 22–24; Wedel, *Prehistoric Man on the Great Plains*, p. 134; E. B. Renaud, "Prehistoric Cultures of the Cimarron Valley, Northeastern New Mexico and Western Oklahoma," *Colorado Scientific Society Proceedings*, 12, no. 5 (1930): 122–35; T. D. Stewart, *The People of America*, pp. 170–75; James B. Griffin, "The Origins and Dispersion of American Indians in North America," in Laughlin and Harper, eds., *First Americans*, pp. 43–56.

9 Kenneth M. Stewart, "The Southwest," in Spencer, Jennings, et al., *Native Americans*, pp. 252–60; Josephy, *Indian Heritage of America*, pp. 150–61; Erik K. Reed, "The Greater Southwest," in Jennings and Norbeck, eds., *Prehistoric Man in the New World*, pp. 175–91.

10 Timothy R. Pauketat, *The Ascent of Chiefs: Cahokia and Mississippian Politics in Native North America*, pp. 5–7, 40–43, 68, 72; "Cache in the Cornfield," magazine clipping, 1973, and "Mounds May Give Clues to Modern Survival," newspaper clipping, 1977, in Temple Mounds File, Southwest Collection, Texas Tech University; Willey, *Introduction to American Archaeology*, 1: 292–304.

11 Wedel, *Prehistoric Man on the Great Plains*, pp. 92–100, 133–37.

12 Ibid., pp. 285–90. See also Karl H. Schlesier, "Commentary: A History of Ethnic Groups in the Great Plains, A.D. 150–1550," in Schlesier, ed., *Plains Indians, A.D. 500–1500*, pp. 308–81; George C. Frison, *Prehistoric Hunters of the High Plains*,

pp. 1–15, 243–50; and David Mayer Gradwohl, *Prehistoric Villages in Eastern Nebraska*, pp. 19–28, 136–42.

13 Kehoe, *North American Indians*, p. 295; Guy Gibbon, "Cultures of the Upper Mississippi River Valley and Adjacent Prairies in Iowa and Minnesota," in Schlesier, ed., *Plains Indians*, A.D. *500–1500*, pp. 137–39.

14 Wedel, *Prehistoric Man on the Great Plains*, pp. 94–97; Waldo Wedel, "The Great Plains," in Jennings and Norbeck, eds., *Prehistoric Man in the New World*, pp. 205–15; Roger T. Grange, Jr., *Pawnee and Lower Loup Pottery*, pp. 6–10, 14–16; Patricia J. O'Brien, "The Central Lowland Plains: An Overview A.D. 500–1500," in Schlesier, ed., *Plains Indians*, A.D. *500–1500*, pp. 199–223.

15 Snow, *Archaeology of North America*, pp. 86–90; George E. Hyde, *Indians of the High Plains: From the Prehistoric Period to the Coming of Europeans*, pp. 3–4.

16 Hyde, *Indians of the High Plains*, pp. 4–7.

17 Snow, *Archaeology of North America*, p. 90.

18 Cited in Theodore C. Blegen, *Minnesota: A History of the State*, p. 47. See also Preston Holder, *The Hoe and the Horse on the Plains: A Study of Cultural Development among North American Indians*, pp. 5–9.

19 See George E. Hyde, *The Pawnee Indians*, pp. 151, 366–67. For a different view see Schlesier, "Commentary," in Schlesier, ed., *Plains Indians*, A.D. *500–1500*, pp. 352–61.

20 Schlesier, "Commentary," in Schlesier, ed., *Plains Indians*, A.D. *500–1500*, pp. 335–36, 339–44.

21 Holder, *The Hoe and the Horse*, pp. 28, 30, 40–43.

22 Ibid.; Gibbon, "Cultures of the Upper Mississippi," in Schlesier, ed., *Plains Indians*, A.D. *500–1500*, pp. 137–39.

23 Schlesier, ed., *Plains Indians*, A.D. *500–1500*, p. xxv.

24 Schlesier, "Commentary," in ibid., pp. 324–35; Hyde, *Indians of the High Plains*, pp. 7–8; Wedel, *Prehistoric Man on the Great Plains*, p. 104; Newcomb, *Indians of Texas*, pp. 103–109.

25 Elizabeth A. H. John, *Storms Brewed in Other Men's Worlds: The Confrontation of Indians, Spanish, and French in the Southwest, 1540–1795*, p. 114.

26 Kavanagh, *Comanche Political History*, pp. 70, 73, 146–48; Wallace and Hoebel, *Comanches*, pp. 6–12, 286; Hyde, *Indians of the High Plains*, pp. 52–62, 93–116.

27 Newcomb, *Indians of Texas*, p. 109.

28 C. Ewers, *The Blackfeet: Raiders of the Northwestern Plains*, pp. 3–29; Hyde, *Indians of the High Plains*, p. 153.

CHAPTER 3

1 Peter Farb, *Man's Rise to Civilization: The Cultural Ascent of the Indians of North America*, pp. 108–10.

2 Wallace and Hoebel, *Comanches*, p. 11; Rupert N. Richardson, *The Comanche Barrier to South Plains Settlement*, pp. 19, 24–28.

3 Donald E. Worcester, "The Spread of Spanish Horses in the Southwest," *New Mexico Historical Review* 19 (1944): 225–32; Frank Gilbert Roe, *The Indian and the Horse*, pp. 72–134; Clark Wissler, "The Influence of the Horse in the Development

of Plains Culture," *American Anthropologist* 16 (1914): 2, 5–6, 10; Webb, *Great Plains,* p. 51.

4   Snow, *Archaeology of North America,* pp. 91–96; Lowie, *Indians of the Plains,* pp. 116–17, 198–200; Josephy, *Indian Heritage of America,* pp. 118–19.

5   Roe, *Indian and the Horse,* pp. 153–55; Robert F. Spencer, "Western North America—Plateau, Basin, California," in Spencer, Jennings, et al., *Native Americans,* p. 195.

6   Royal B. Hassrick, *The Sioux: Life and Customs of a Warrior Society,* p. 85; Richard White, "Making the World Whole Again," in Betty Ballantine and Ian Ballantine, eds., *The Native Americans: An Illustrated History,* p. 222.

7   Anthony McGinnis, *Counting Coup and Cutting Horses: Intertribal Warfare on the Northern Plains, 1783–1889,* p. 66.

8   Ibid., p. 74.

9   Roe, *Indian and the Horse,* pp. 175–80; Wissler, "Influence of the Horse in the Development of Plains Culture," p. 12; Richardson, *Comanche Barrier to South Plains Settlement,* pp. 25–27; Robert Moorman Denhardt, *The Horse of the Americas,* p. 106. See also J. Frank Dobie, "Indian Horses and Horsemanship," *Southwest Review* 35 (autumn, 1950): 265–75.

10 For a detailed study of the horse in Plains Indian society, see John C. Ewers, *The Horse in Blackfoot Indian Culture: With Comparative Material from Other Western Tribes,* pp. 216–18, 225–50, 299–329, 336–40.

11 Quoted in Wayne Moquin with Charles Van Doren, eds., *Great Documents in American Indian History,* p. 62.

12 Tom McHugh, *The Time of the Buffalo,* p. xxii. See also Randolph B. Marcy, *Thirty Years of Army Life on the Border,* pp. 28–29; Theodore R. Davis, "The Buffalo Range," *Harper's Magazine* 38 (1869): 147–163; and Roe, *Indian and the Horse,* pp. 332–75.

13 McHugh, *Time of the Buffalo,* p. xxii.

14 Michael Stephen Kennedy, ed., *The Assiniboines: From the Accounts of the Old Ones Told to First Boy (James Larpenteur Long),* pp. 63–69, 78–79; McHugh, *Time of the Buffalo,* pp. 21, 156–57, 173–74, 177, 191–92; Kehoe, *North American Indians,* p. 311.

15 Roe, *Indian and the Horse,* p. 351. See also McHugh, *Time of the Buffalo,* pp. 61–62, 69; and Wallace and Hoebel, *Comanches,* pp. 202–209.

16 McHugh, *Time of the Buffalo,* pp. 62–64.

17 Ibid., pp. 71–73. See also Wallace and Hoebel, *Comanches,* pp. 59–60; Roe, *Indian and the Horse,* pp. 343–44.

18 Alan M. Klein, "Political Economy of the Buffalo Hide Trade: Race and Class on the Plains," in John H. Moore, ed., *The Political Economy of North American Indians,* pp. 140–42.

19 John G. Neihardt, ed., *Black Elk Speaks: Being the Life Story of a Holy Man of the Oglala Sioux,* p. 154.

20 McHugh, *Time of the Buffalo,* p. 73.

21 Wallace and Hoebel, *Comanches,* p. 60; Carl Coke Rister, "Indians as Buffalo Hunters," *Frontier Times* 5 (April, 1928): 456, 494–95.

22 Lowie, *Indians of the Plains*, pp. 13–16, 155; McHugh, *Time of the Buffalo*, pp. 50–59.

23 Neihardt, ed., *Black Elk Speaks*, pp. 53–60; McHugh, *Time of the Buffalo*, pp. 83–84.

24 See Richard White, "The Winning of the West: The Expansion of the Sioux in the Eighteenth and Nineteenth Centuries," *Journal of American History* 65, no. 2 (1978): 319–43.

25 Roe, *Indian and the Horse*, p. 219; Richardson, *Comanche Barrier to South Plains Settlement*, p. 209.

26 Hassrick, *Sioux*, p. 74

27 Ibid., p. 75.

28 See Robert L. Brooks, "Warfare on the Southern Plains," in Douglas W. Owsley and Richard L. Jantz, eds., *Skeletal Biology in the Great Plains: Migration, Warfare, Health, and Subsistence*, pp. 321–22; John C. Ewers, "Women's Roles in Plains Warfare," in ibid., pp. 325–32; Douglas W. Owsley, "Warfare in Coalescent Tradition Populations of the Northern Plains," in ibid., pp. 341–42.

29 Lowie, *Indians of the Plains*, pp. 104–12; Roe, *Indian and the Horse*, p. 227. See also Jean Louis Berlandier, *The Indians of Texas in 1830*, p. 68; White, "Winning of the West," pp. 319–43; and Richard Lancaster, *Piegan: A Look from Within at the Life, Times, and Legacy of an American Indian Tribe*, pp. 121, 186–87.

30 Cited in William P. Clark, *The Indian Sign Language*, p. 131.

31 Thomas B. Marquis, ed., *Wooden Leg: A Warrior Who Fought Custer*, pp. 119–22.

32 Quote in Moquin with Van Doren, eds., *Great Documents*, p. 69.

33 Hassrick, *Sioux*, pp. 73–74.

34 Ibid., p. 74.

35 Quoted in Benjamin Capps, *The Great Chiefs*, p. 142.

36 Quote in Moquin with Van Doren, *Great Documents*, p. 52.

37 Hassrick, *Sioux*, p. 90. See also Wallace and Hoebel, *Comanches*, pp. 246–50; Lowie, *Indians of the Plains*, pp. 108–109, 111–12.

38 Cited in McGinnis, *Counting Coup and Cutting Horses*, p. 60.

39 Quoted in Colin G. Calloway, ed., *Our Hearts Fell to the Ground: Plains Indian Views of How the West Was Lost*, p. 85.

40 McGinnis, *Counting Coup and Cutting Horses*, p. 49. See also Frank Raymond Secoy, *Changing Military Patterns on the Great Plains (17th Century through Early 19th Century)*, p. 39.

41 Frank B. Linderman, *Plenty Coups: Chief of the Crows*, p. 118.

42 Neihardt, ed., *Black Elk Speaks*, p. 9.

43 Richard Irving Dodge, *Thirty-three Years among Our Wild Indians*, p. 248.

44 Farb, *Man's Rise to Civilization*, pp. 105, 108–109.

45 See Ernest L. Schusky, *The Forgotten Sioux: An Ethnohistory of the Lower Brule Reservation*, p. 29.

46 First quote in Calloway, ed., *Our Hearts Fell to the Ground*, p. 156; second quote cited in Gretchen M. Bataille and Kathleen Mullen Sands, *American Indian Women: Telling Their Lives*, p. 45; third quote, Linderman, *Plenty Coups*, p. 118. See also Thomas H. Lewis, *The Medicine Men: Oglala Sioux Ceremony and Healing*, pp. 1–3.

CHAPTER 4

1   Snow, *Archaeology of North America*, pp. 93–96; John C. Ewers, *Indian Life on the Upper Missouri*, pp. 4, 34–44; Wallace and Hoebel, *Comanches*, pp. 105–106; Josephy, *Indian Heritage of America*, pp. 118–19; Henry Easton Allen, "The Parilla Expedition to the Red River," *Southwestern Historical Quarterly* 43 (1939): 43–71.

2   See Farb, *Man's Rise to Civilization*, pp. 110, 119; and Harriet J. Kupferer, *Ancient Drums, Other Moccasins: Native North American Cultural Adaptation*, p. 181.

3   Farb, *Man's Rise to Civilization*, p. 119; Lowie, *Indians of the Plains*, pp. 40–42; Eldon Johnson, "The Great Plains," in Spencer, Jennings, et al., *Native Americans*, p. 330; and Roe, *Indian and the Horse*, pp. 267–331.

4   Ewers, *Horse in Blackfoot Indian Culture*, pp. 28–32; Johnson, "The Great Plains," in Spencer, Jennings, et al., *Native Americans*, pp. 361–63.

5   Farb, *Man's Rise to Civilization*, p. 119.

6   Willard H. Rollings, "Prairie Hegemony: An Ethnohistorical Study of the Osage, from Early Times to 1840" (Ph.D. diss., Texas Tech University, 1983), p. 173. See also Martin, *Keepers of the Game*, pp. 1–3, 8–9, 11n, 64–65; and Willard H. Rollings, *The Osage: An Ethnohistorical Study of Hegemony on the Prairie-Plains*, pp. 81–82, 95.

7   Snow, *Archaeology of North America*, p. 96.

8   Earl H. Elam, "The History of the Wichita Indian Confederacy to 1868" (Ph.D. diss., Texas Tech University, 1971), pp. 60–61; Kupferer, *Ancient Drums, Other Moccasins*, pp. 150, 184; Roe, *Indian and the Horse*, pp. 267–82.

9   Lowie, *Indians of the Plains*, p. 117. See also Holder, *Hoe and the Horse*, p. xii; Bataille and Sands, *American Indian Women*, p. 77; and Neihardt, ed., *Black Elk Speaks*, p. 62.

10   Newcomb, *Indians of Texas*, pp. 150, 152; Noah Smithwick, *The Evolution of a State*, pp. 245–46; McHugh, *Time of the Buffalo*, p. 86; Lowie, *Indians of the Plains*, pp. 13–23; Roe, *Indian and the Horse*, pp. 275–77.

11   Johnson, "The Great Plains," in Spencer, Jennings, et al., *Native Americans*, p. 323. See also Lowie, *Indians of the Plains*, pp. 18–23; and Kupferer, *Ancient Drums, Other Moccasins*, pp. 134–35; Gilbert L. Wilson, *Agriculture of the Hidatsa Indians: An Indian Interpretation*, p. 13.

12   Quoted in Nabokov, ed., *Native American Testimony*, p. 182.

13   Johnson, "The Great Plains," in Spencer, Jennings, et al., *Native Americans*, pp. 322–23; Holder, *Hoe and the Horse*, pp. 47–48; Newcomb, *Indians of Texas*, pp. 113–14, 238–39, 292.

14   McHugh, *Time of the Buffalo*, p. 85. See also Wallace and Hoebel, *Comanches*, p. 72.

15   Herman Lehmann, *Nine Years among the Indians, 1870–1879*, pp. 105, 116. See also Neihardt, ed., *Black Elk Speaks*, pp. 57–58, 64.

16   Wallace and Hoebel, *Comanches*, p. 74. See also Lowie, *Indians of the Plains*, p. 25; McHugh, *Time of the Buffalo*, pp. 89–90; Newcomb, *Indians of Texas*, pp. 139–40.

17   Flores, "Bison Ecology and Bison Diplomacy," pp. 479–81.

18   Johnson, "The Great Plains," in Spencer, Jennings, et al., *Native Americans*,

p. 324; McHugh, *Time of the Buffalo*, pp. 100–103; Lowie, *Indians of the Plains*, pp. 34–35, 45.

19 Roe, *Indian and the Horse*, pp. 16–32; Lowie, *Indians of the Plains*, pp. 38–42; Gilbert L. Wilson, "The Horse and the Dog in Hidatsa Culture," *Anthropological Papers of the American Museum of Natural History* 15 (1924): 206–209, 216–27; Clark Wissler, "Material Culture of the Blackfoot Indians," *Anthropological Papers of the American Museum of Natural History* 5 (1910): 89–92.

20 Roe, *Indian and the Horse*, p. 27.

21 Robert H. Lowie, "The Assiniboin," *Anthropological Papers of the American Museum of Natural History* 4 (1909): 15. See also Richardson, *Comanche Barrier to South Plains Settlement*, p. 78; and Wilson, "The Horse and Dog in Hidatsa Culture," pp. 206–15, 227, 252.

22 Edwin Thompson Denig, *Five Indian Tribes of the Upper Missouri*, pp. 43–44; Lowie, *Indians of the Plains*, pp. 32–35; Kupferer, *Ancient Drums, Other Moccasins*, p. 131.

23 Elam, "History of the Wichita Indian Confederacy to 1868," pp. 56–57; Newcomb, *Indians of Texas*, pp. 255–56; Lowie, *Indians of the Plains*, p. 35; George Wilkins Kendall, *Narrative of the Texan—Santa Fe Expedition*, 1: 138; José María Sánchez, "A Trip to Texas in 1828," *Southwestern Historical Quarterly* 29 (April, 1926): 265.

24 See John Joseph Mathews, *The Osages: Children of the Middle Waters*, pp. 85, 487–88, 599.

25 Wissler, *American Indian*, p. 222; Robert F. Spencer, "Western America," in Spencer, Jennings, et al., *Native Americans*, pp. 169–70; Lowie, *Indians of the Plains*, p. 37.

26 Reginald Laubin and Gladys Laubin, *The Indian Tipi: Its History, Construction, and Use*, pp. 19–25, 48–74; Lowie, *Indians of the Plains*, pp. 30–32; Wallace and Hoebel, *Comanches*, pp. 86–91; Lancaster, *Piegan*, p. 66.

27 See Christopher H. Bentley, "The Comanche Shield: Symbol of Identity," in Clifford E. Trafzer, ed., *American Indian Identity: Today's Changing Perspectives*, pp. 22–29.

28 Dodge, *Thirty-three Years*, p. 420.

29 Reginald Laubin and Gladys Laubin, *American Indian Archery*, pp. 111–12, 114–17; "Indian Bow and Arrow," *Frontier Times* 8 (1930): 141–42; H. W. Baylor, "Recollections of the Comanche Indians," *Frontier Times* 6 (1929): 374; George Bird Grinnell, *The Cheyenne Indians*, 1: 178–81; Lehmann, *Nine Years among the Indians*, p. 94.

30 For superb discussions of Plains Indian creativeness in such fields as graphic arts and sculpture in both wood and stone with illustrations, see John C. Ewers, *Plains Indian Painting: A Description of an Aboriginal American Art*, pp. 1–67; and John C. Ewers, Plains Indian Sculpture: A Traditional Art from America's Heartland, pp. 9–223. See also Szabo, *Howling Wolf*, pp. 3–13; and John C. Ewers, *Plains Indian History and Culture: Essays on Continuity and Change*, pp. 61–81.

31 Wallace and Hoebel, *Comanches*, pp. 77–79.

32 George Catlin, *Letters and Notes on the Manners, Customs, and Conditions of North American Indians*, 1: 145–46. See also Lowie, *Indians of the Plains*, pp. 46–50; and Wallace and Hoebel, *Comanches*, pp. 77–79.

33 Sánchez, "A Trip to Texas in 1828," p. 269.

34 Newcomb, *Indians of Texas*, pp. 110, 138.

35 Lowie, *Indians of the Plains*, p. 55.

36 Catlin, *Letters and Notes*, 1: 49–51; Berlandier, *Indians of Texas in 1830*.

37 Newcomb, *Indians of Texas*, pp. 110, 196; Lowie, *Indians of the Plains*, pp. 51–53.

38 Johnson, "The Great Plains," in Spencer, Jennings, et al., *Native Americans*, p. 336.

CHAPTER 5

1 Lowie, *Indians of the Plains*, pp. 90–94; Newcomb, *Indians of Texas*, p. 141. For three divisions of the Crows, see Hoxie, *Parading through History*, p. 41.

2 Lowie, *Indians of the Plains*, pp. 89–96; Newcomb, *Indians of Texas*, pp. 119–22, 141–45, 168–71, 201–203, 265–68; Johnson, "The Great Plains," in Spencer, Jennings, et al., *Native Americans*, pp. 323–25, 339–44; Fred Eggan, *The American Indian: Perspectives for the Study of Social Change*, pp. 45–77; and Fred Eggan, ed., *Social Anthropology of North American Tribes*, pp. 35–172.

3 Kupferer, *Ancient Drums, Other Moccasins*, pp. 129–30.

4 For the Gros Ventres, see Eggan, ed., *Social Anthropology*, pp. 37, 38.

5 Newcomb, *Indians of Texas*, p. 258.

6 Farb, *Man's Rise to Civilization*, pp. 128–29.

7 Lowie, *Indians of the Plains*, p. 94.

8 Johnson, "The Great Plains," in Spencer, Jennings, et al., *Native Americans*, pp. 344–45; Clark Wissler, *Societies and Ceremonial Associations in the Oglala Division of the Teton–Dakota*, pp. 8, 11–12; and Josiah Gregg, *Commerce on the Prairies*, p. 343.

9 Moquin with Van Doren, eds., *Great Documents*, p. 52.

10 Quote in Johnson, "The Great Plains," in Spencer, Jennings, et al., *Native Americans*, p. 345. See also Berlandier, *Indians of Texas in 1830*, pp. 38–39.

11 Wallace and Hoebel, *Comanches*, pp. 210–11. For a different view see Kavanagh, *Comanche Political History*, pp. 14–15.

12 Wallace and Hoebel, *Comanches*, pp. 214–15.

13 Ibid. See also M. M. Kenney, "Tribal Society among Texas Indians," *Quarterly of the Texas Historical Association* 1 (1897): 31; Stanley Noyes, *Los Comanches: The Horse People, 1751–1845*, pp. 294–95.

14 See Robert M. Utley, *The Lance and the Shield: The Life and Times of Sitting Bull*, pp. 22, 26; Robert M. Utley, *The Indian Frontier of the American West, 1846–1890*, p. 179.

15 Christopher H. Bentley, "The Comanche Shield: Symbol of Identity," in Clifford E. Trafzer, ed., *American Indian Identity*, pp. 22–29.

16 Lowie, *Indians of the Plains*, pp. 161–64.

17 Ibid., p. 164.

18 Ibid., p. 114; see also Berlandier, *Indians of Texas in 1830*, pp. 40, 59.

19 See Lowie, *Indians of the Plains*, pp. 114–15; Old Horn, "Crow Kinship Systems," in Fleming and Watts, eds., *Visions of an Enduring People*, pp. 45–56.

20 Lowie, *Indians of the Plains*, p. 101. Anthropologists often use "sodality," "society," and "associations" as synonyms for voluntary organizations of people in

contrast to involuntary membership in clans or age grades, which technically are also sodalities.

21 Ibid., pp. 97, 104, 172.

22 Ibid., pp. 100–102; Johnson, "Great Plains," in Spencer, Jennings, et al., *Native Americans*, p. 350.

23 Wissler, *Societies and Ceremonial Associations*, pp. 8, 11–12, 30–38; Johnson, "Great Plains," in Spencer, Jennings, et al., *Native Americans*, pp. 350–51.

24 Lowie, *Indians of the Plains*, pp. 100–101.

25 William H. Leckie, *The Military Conquest of the Southern Plains*, p. 153.

26 Johnson, "Great Plains," in Spencer, Jennings, et al., *Native Americans*, p. 325; Lowie, *Indians of the Plains*, pp. 96–100.

27 Neihardt, ed., *Black Elk Speaks*, pp. 188, 189–93; Johnson, "Great Plains," in Spencer, Jennings, et al., *Native Americans*, p. 351.

28 Cited in Lowie, *Indians of the Plains*, p. 104. See also Lewis, *Medicine Men*, p. 149.

29 Wilcomb E. Washburn, *The Indian in America*, p. 106. See also Stewart, *People of America*, pp. 19–20, 35–55; Thornton, *American Indian Holocaust and Survival*, p. 95; and William H. McNeill, *Plagues and People*, pp. 199–234.

30 Washburn, *Indian in America*, p. 106; Wallace and Hoebel, *Comanches*, p. 149.

31 Washburn, *Indian in America*, p. 109. See also Thornton, *American Indian Holocaust and Survival*, pp. 65–66; James Axtell, *The European and the Indian: Essays in the Ethnohistory of Colonial North America*, pp. 257–59; and Wilbur R. Jacobs, *Dispossessing the American Indian: Indians and Whites on the Colonial Frontier*, p. 33.

32 See Berlandier, *Indians of Texas in 1830*, p. 62.

33 Thornton, *American Indian Holocaust and Survival*, pp. 45, 54, 65–66.

34 See Michael K. Trimble, "The 1837–1838 Smallpox Epidemic on the Upper Missouri," in Owsley and Jantz, eds., *Skeletal Biology in the Great Plains*, pp. 81–89; John C. Ewers, "The Influence of Epidemics on the Indian Populations and Cultures of Texas," *Plains Anthropologist* 18 (1973): 104–15.

CHAPTER 6

1 Cited in Benjamin Capps, *Indians*, pp. 88–89.

2 John C. Ewers, "Women's Roles in Plains Indians Warfare," in Owsley and Jantz, eds., *Skeletal Biology in the Great Plains*, pp. 325–32; Bataille and Sands, *American Indian Women*, p. 131; Kehoe, *North American Indians*, pp. 312–13.

3 Neihardt, ed., *Black Elk Speaks*, pp. 15, 59–60.

4 Cited in Nabokov, ed., *Native American Testimony*, pp. 220–21.

5 Quoted in Capps, *The Indians*, p. 88.

6 Even the Comanches may have been tall people, or at least medium in height. See Noyes, *Los Comanches*, pp. 183–84; Berlandier, *Indians of Texas*, p. 115; Wallace and Hoebel, *Comanches*, p. 149.

7 Quote in Moquin with Van Doren, eds., *Great Documents*, p. 45.

8 Wallace and Hoebel, *Comanches*, p. 142. See also John C. Ewers, "Contraceptive Charms among the Plains Indians," *Plains Anthropologist* 15 (1970): 216–18; and Rupert N. Richardson, "The Culture of the Comanche Indians," *Texas Archeological and Paleontological Society Bulletin* 1 (1929): 63.

9   See Severt Young Bear and R. D. Theisz, *Standing in the Light: A Lakota Way of Seeing*, pp. 8–13.

10 Berlandier, *Indians of Texas in 1830*, p. 33.

11 Neihardt, ed., *Black Elk Speaks*, p. 13.

12 Lowie, *Indians of the Plains*, p. 81; Newcomb, *Indians of Texas*, pp. 120, 145–45, 166–68, 199–200, 259–62; Johnson, "Great Plains," in Spencer, Jennings, et al., *Native Americans*, pp. 352–55; Ruth Murray Underhill, *Red Man's America: A History of Indians in the United States*, pp. 157–58.

13 Kennedy, ed., *Assiniboines*, p. xii.

14 Young Bear and Theisz, *Standing in the Light*, p. 38.

15 Lowie, *Indians of the Plains*, p. 81; Johnson, "Great Plains," in Spencer, Jennings, et al., *Native Americans*, p. 353.

16 Washburn, *Indian in America*, p. 52; Johnson, "Great Plains," in Spencer, Jennings, et al., *Native Americans*, p. 353; Lowie, *Indians of the Plains*, p. 84. Because there was some fear that menstrual blood might contaminate sacred objects, in several tribes women during menstruation went into seclusion. Wallace and Hoebel, *Comanches*, pp. 144–45.

17 Quote in Capps, *Indians*, p. 89. See Lowie, *Indians of the Plains*, p. 78.

18 Neihardt, ed., *Black Elk Speaks*, pp. 67–69, 75–76.

19 Kennedy, ed., *Assiniboines*, pp. 30–32.

20 Cited in Moquin with Van Doren, eds., *Great Documents*, p. 39.

21 Underhill, *Red Man's America*, pp. 157–58; Bataille and Sands, eds., *American Indian Women*, pp. vii—viii.

22 Wallace and Hoebel, *Comanches*, p. 141.

23 Johnson, "Great Plains," in Spencer, Jennings, et al., *Native Americans*, pp. 342–43; Lowie, *Indians of the Plains*, pp. 82–83; Newcomb, *Indians of Texas*, p. 171; Dale Old Horn, "Crow Kinship Systems," in Fleming and Watts, eds., *Visions of an Enduring People*, pp. 45–53.

24 Kennedy, ed., *Assiniboines*, p. 32.

25 Young Bear and Theisz, *Standing in the Light*, p. 110. See also Johnson, "Great Plains," in Spencer, Jennings, et al., *Native Americans*, p. 341; Sánchez, "A Trip to Texas in 1828," p. 262.

26 Moquin with Van Doren, eds., *Great Documents*, p. 41.

27 Johnson, "Great Plains," in Spencer, Jennings, et al., *Native Americans*, p. 339.

28 Ibid., p. 352; Will Roscoe, "'That is My Road': The Life and Times of a Crow Berdache," *Montana: The Magazine of Western History* 40 (winter, 1990): 46–55; Johnson, "Great Plains," in Spencer, Jennings et al., *Native Americans*, p. 352.

29 See Teresa D. La Fromboise, Anneliese M. Heyle, and Emily J. Ozer, "Changing and Diverse Roles of Women in American Cultures," in Fleming and Watts, eds., *Visions of an Enduring People*, pp. 9–28.

30 Wallace and Hoebel, *Comanches*, pp. 111–18; Lowie, *Indians of the Plains*, pp. 118–29; Sánchez, "A Trip to Texas in 1828," p. 266.

31 Wallace and Hoebel, *Comanches*, pp. 151, 268. See, for example, William T. Hagan, *Quanah Parker, Comanche Chief*, pp. 49–50.

32 *Arkansas Intelligencer*, January 6, 1844, as cited in Stan Hoig, *Tribal Wars of the Southern Plains*, p. 22.

33   Kennedy, ed., *Assiniboines,* pp. 166–67; Hagan, *Quanah Parker,* pp. 49–50; Lowie, *Indians of the Plains,* pp. 84–85; Johnson, "Great Plains," in Spencer, Jennings, et al., *Native Americans,* p. 355; and Newcomb, *Indians of Texas,* pp. 174, 263–64.

34   Cited in McGinnis, *Counting Coup and Cutting Horses,* p. 76.

35   Wallace and Hoebel, *Comanches,* p. 150.

36   Newcomb, *Indians of Texas,* p. 263.

37   Lowie, *Indians of the Plains,* p. 85; Johnson, "Great Plains," in Spencer, Jennings, et al., *Native Americans,* p. 355.

CHAPTER 7

1   Thomas Henry Tibbles, *Buckskin and Blanket Days,* p. 69.

2   Catlin, *Letters and Notes,* 2: 3, 59.

3   Quotes cited in Nabokov, ed., *Native American Testimony,* pp. 182, 184.

4   Quote in Moquin with Van Doren, eds., *Great Documents,* p. 210. See also Hoebel, *Plains Indians,* p. 7.

5   Cited in Nabokov, ed., *Native American Testimony,* p. 210.

6   Calvin Martin, "The Metaphysics of Writing Indian-White History," in Calvin Martin, ed., *The American Indian and the Problem of History,* p. 29.

7   See Holder, *Hoe and the Horse,* pp. 126–27; Newcomb, *Indians of Texas,* pp. 128–30, 149–52, 185–91, 210–20, 270–76, 308–13; Neihardt, ed., *Black Elk Speaks,* p. 59; and Wallace and Hoebel, *Comanches,* pp. 185–208.

8   See, for example, Schusky, *Forgotten Sioux,* p. 29.

9   Holder, *Hoe and the Horse,* pp. 41–44; J. R. Walker, "The Sun Dance and Other Ceremonies of the Oglala Division of the Teton Dakota," *American Museum of Natural History, Anthropological Papers* 16 (1917): 79.

10   Quote in Moquin with Van Doren, eds., *Great Documents,* p. 52.

11   Johnson, "Great Plains," in Spencer, Jennings, et al., *Native Americans,* p. 356.

12   Newcomb, *Indians of Texas,* p. 274; Lowie, *Indians of the Plains,* p. 154; Edward D. Morton, *To Touch the Wind: An Introduction to Native American Philosophy & Beliefs,* pp. 37–38, 40–41.

13   Quotes in Neihardt, ed., *Black Elk Speaks,* p. 194.

14   Lowie, *Indians of the Plains,* p. 26.

15   Quoted in Capps, *Indians,* p. 26.

16   Wallace and Hoebel, *Comanches,* pp. 180–82; Lowie, *Indians of the Plains,* pp. 26–27.

17   Wallace and Hoebel, *Comanches,* p. 181.

18   Holder, *Hoe and the Horse,* pp. 31–32. See also Adina de Zavala, "Religious Beliefs of the Tejas or Hasinias Indians," *Publications of the Texas Folklore Society* 1 (1916): 39–45.

19   Holder, *Hoe and the Horse,* pp. 41–42, 127; Lowie, *Indians of the Plains,* pp. 163–64.

20   Holder, *Hoe and the Horse,* p. 127.

21   Wallace and Hoebel, *Comanches,* p. 155.

22   Sometimes the Plains Indians called it the guardian-spirit quest. Although common among nomadic groups and generally considered a plains diagnostic trait, in some tribes individuals acquired supernatural partners or helpers without the quest. Newcomb, *Indians of Texas,* p. 309; Josephy, *Indian Heritage of America,*

pp. 114–15; Washburn, *Indian in America*, pp. 13, 52–53. For a detailed discussion of the Plains Indians and the vision quest, see Lee Irwin, *The Dream Seekers: Native American Visionary Traditions of the Great Plains*, pp. 98–184.

23 Lowie, *Indians of the Plains*, p. 159.

24 Ibid., pp. 160, 170–72; Holder, *Hoe and the Horse*, pp. 41–43; Johnson, "Great Plains," in Spencer, Jennings, et al., *Native Americans*, p. 355; Thomas C. Battey, *The Life and Adventures of a Quaker among the Indians*, pp. 332–33.

25 Holder, *Hoe and the Horse*, p. 43. See also Bernhard E. Richert, Jr., "Plains Indian Medicine Bundles" (M. A. thesis, University of Texas, Austin, 1969), pp. 1–40.

26 Alfred W. Bowers, *Mandan Social and Ceremonial Organization*, p. 107.

27 Lowie, *Indians of the Plains*, p. 171. See also Johnson, "Great Plains," in Spencer, Jennings, et al., *Native Americans*, p. 355; and Morton, *To Touch the Wind*, pp. 38–41.

28 Quoted in Capps, *Indians*, p. 124.

29 Bowers, *Mandan Social and Ceremonial Organization*, pp. 107–13, 149–50; Johnson, "Great Plains," in Spencer, Jennings, et al., *Native Americans*, pp. 325–28; Howard L. Harrod, *Becoming and Remaining a People: Native American Religions on the Northern Plains*, pp. 63, 65, 69; Reginald Laubin and Gladys Laubin, *Indian Dances of North America: Their Importance to Indian Life*, pp. 299–306.

30 Joseph G. Jorgensen, *The Sun Dance Religion: Power for the Powerless*, p. 17.

31 Leslie Spier, "The Sun Dance of the Plains Indians: Its Development and Diffusion," *Anthropological Papers of the American Museum of Natural History* 16 (1921): 498; Harold E. Driver and A. L. Kroeber, "Quantitative Expression of Cultural Relationships," *University of California Publications in Archeology and Ethnology* 31 (1932): 235; Demitri B. Shimkin, "The Wind River Shoshone Sun Dance," *Bureau of American Ethnology Bulletin 151*, Anthropological Paper No. 41 (1953), pp. 406–407; Lowie, *Indians of the Plains*, pp. 178–80; Wilbur S. Nye, "The Annual Sun Dance of the Kiowa Indians," *Chronicles of Oklahoma* 12 (September, 1934): 34–58; and Holder, *Hoe and the Horse*, pp. 129–30.

32 Jorgensen, *Sun Dance Religion*, pp. 17–18. See also Johnson, "Great Plains," in Spencer, Jennings, et al., *Native Americans*, pp. 357–60; and Laubin and Laubin, *Indian Dances of North America*, pp. 306–22.

33 Lowie, *Indians of the Plains*, pp. 7, 178; Johnson, "Great Plains," in Spencer, Jennings, et al., *Native Americans*, p. 357.

34 Ed McGaa, *Mother Earth Spirituality: Native American Paths to Healing Ourselves and Our World*, pp. 84–96; Johnson, "Great Plains," in Spencer, Jennings, et al., *Native Americans*, pp. 357–60. For a description of the Crow Sun Dance, see Michael Oren Fitzgerald, *Yellowtail, Crow Medicine Man and Sun Dance Chief: An Autobiography*, pp. 158–76.

35 Quoted in Fitzgerald, *Yellowtail*, p. 176.

36 Johnson, "Great Plains," in Spencer, Jennings, et al., *Native Americans*, pp. 357–60. See also Neihardt, ed., *Black Elk Speaks*, pp. 95–99; Hassrick, *The Sioux*, pp. 239–48; McGaa, *Mother Earth Spirituality*, pp. 91–96; and Laubin and Laubin, *Indian Dances of North America*, pp. 275–98.

37 Johnson, "Great Plains," in Spencer, Jennings, et al., *Native Americans*, p. 360. See also McGaa, *Mother Earth Spirituality*, p. 95.

CHAPTER 8

1   Kehoe, *North American Indians,* p. 291.

2   Richard White, "Of Furs, Buffalo, and Trade," in Ballantine and Ballantine, eds, *Native Americans,* p. 232.

3   Cited in Ogden Tanner, *Canadians,* pp. 37–38.

4   John, *Storms Brewed in Other Men's Worlds,* p. 317.

5   Ibid.

6   Kavanagh, *Comanche Political History,* pp. 79, 73–93.

7   Noyes, *Comanches,* pp. 80–81; John L. Kessell, "'To See Such Marvels with My Own Eyes:' Spanish Exploration in the Western Borderlands," *Montana: The Magazine of Western History* 41 (autumn, 1991): 75.

8   David Thompson, *David Thompson's Narrative,* p. xxiv.

9   Ibid., pp. 226–37.

10 Francis Paul Prucha, *The Sword of the Republic: The United States Army on the Frontier, 1783–1846,* pp. 153–57.

11 Quote in Hiram Martin Chittenden, *The American Fur Trade of the Far West,* 2: 603; Denig, *Five Indian Tribes,* pp. 54–57.

12 Charles J. Kappler, comp. and ed., *Indian Affairs: Laws and Treaties,* 2: 225–46.

13 Ibid., 2: 256–62; Prucha, *Sword of the Republic,* pp. 158–61; Roger L. Nichols, *General Henry Atkinson: A Western Military Career,* pp. 89–94.

14 Wallace and Hoebel, *Comanches,* p. 267.

15 Thornton, *American Indian Holocaust and Survival,* pp. 95–96.

16 See Linea Sundstrom, "Smallpox Used Them Up: References to Epidemic Disease in Northern Plains Winter Counts, 1714–1920," *Ethnohistory* 44 (spring, 1997): 305–44.

17 Thornton, *American Indian Holocaust and Survival,* pp. 94–99. See also Donald R. Hopkins, *Princes and Peasants: Smallpox in History,* p. 272; Catlin, *Letters and Notes,* 2: 257–59; Ralph K. Andrist, *The Long Death: The Last Days of the Plains Indians,* pp.14–15; John S. Milloy, *The Plains Cree: Trade, Diplomacy and War, 1790–1870,* p. 71.

18 See White, "Winning of the West," pp. 319–43.

19 See Flores, "Bison Ecology and Bison Diplomacy," pp. 465–85.

20 Wallace and Hoebel, *Comanches,* p. 294; Noyes, *Comanches,* pp. 274–79; Kavanagh, *Comanche Political History,* pp. 248, 284; Capps, *Indians,* pp. 15–35; Hoig, *Tribal Wars,* pp. 110–15.

21 Utley, *Indian Frontier,* pp. 1–3.

22 Quoted in Capps, *Great Chiefs,* p. 143.

23 Luke Lea, *Annual Report of the Commissioner of Indian Affairs,* November 27, 1850, in Francis Paul Prucha, ed., *Documents of United States Indian Policy,* pp. 81–83.

24 See Raymond J. DeMallie, "Touching the Pen: Plains Indian Treaty Councils in Ethnohistorical Perspective," in Frederick C. Luebke, ed., *Ethnicity on the Great Plains,* pp. 38–53.

25 The federal government paid the annuities for fifteen years. When the Senate amended the treaty, the Indians needed to approve the change. They had scattered to their various homes and could not be brought together for such action. Thus, some American Indian leaders never ratified the amended treaty.

26 Treaty of Fort Laramie, September 17, 1851, in Prucha, ed., *Documents*, pp. 84–85; Kappler, comp. and ed., *Indian Affairs*, 2: 594–96; LeRoy R. Hafen and W. J. Ghent, *Broken Hand: The Life of Thomas Fitzpatrick, Mountain Man, Guide and Indian Agent*, pp. 284–301; Philip Weeks, *Farewell, My Nation: The American Indian and the United States, 1820–1890*, pp. 62–63; Utley, *Indian Frontier*, pp. 60–63; Andrist, *Long Death*, pp. 18–20.

27 The Senate changed the treaty to say that the money could be used to train Indian people for farming and a settled existence. Wallace and Hoebel, *Comanches*, p. 300. See also Hafen and Ghent, *Broken Hand*, pp.309–12; Kappler, comp. and ed., *Indian Affairs*, 2: 600–602.

28 Lancaster, *Piegan*, pp. 79–80.

29 Quoted in McGinnis, *Counting Coup and Cutting Horses*, p. 94; see also Ewers, *Blackfeet*, pp. 211–19.

30 Prucha, *Sword of the Republic*, pp. 379–81; Wallace and Hoebel, *Comanches*, p. 298; Thomas R. Wessel, "Market Economy and Changing Subsistence Patterns: A Comment," *Agricultural History* 66 (spring, 1992): 61–62.

CHAPTER 9

1 Quoted in Calloway, ed., *Our Hearts Fell to the Ground*, p. 8.

2 Kenneth F. Neighbours, "Robert S. Neighbors and the Founding of the Texas Indian Reservations," *West Texas Historical Association Year Book* 31 (1955): 65–74; Richardson, *Comanche Barrier*, pp. 211–32.

3 Robert M. Utley, *Frontiersmen in Blue: The United States Army and the Indian, 1848–1865*, pp. 112–20, quote on p. 120; Utley, *Lance and the Shield*, pp. 45–47; George E. Hyde, *Spotted Tail's Folk: A History of the Brule Sioux*, pp. 48–53; Lloyd E. McCann, "The Grattan Massacre," *Nebraska History* 37 (1956): 1–26.

4 Farb, *Man's Rise to Civilization*, p. 105.

5 Catlin, *Letters and Notes*, 1: 33–34, and 2: 65–66; Randolph B. Marcy, *Thirty Years of Army Life on the Border*, pp. 28–29; Webb, *Great Plains*, pp. 68–68; Utley, *Frontiersmen in Blue*, p. 7.

6 Shafter to J. H. Taylor, Asst. Adj. Gen., Dept. of Texas, Jan. 4, 1876, in Martin L. Crimmins, ed., "Shafter's Exploration in West Texas," *West Texas Historical Association Year Book* 9 (1933): 82–96; Hans Gasman, 2d Lt., Tenth Cavalry, "Itinerary of Scout," Nov. 26, 1875, U.S. Dept. of War, Records of United States Army Commands, Letters Sent, Dept. of Texas, Record Group 93, National Archives.

7 Don Russell, "How Many Indians were Killed? White Man versus Red Man: The Facts and the Legend, *The American West* 10 (July, 1973): 62.

8 See John C. Ewers, "Intertribal Warfare as the Precursor of Indian-White Warfare on the Northern Great Plains," *Western Historical Quarterly* 6 (1975): 397–410; White, " Winning of the West," pp. 319–43.

9 Quote in Raymond J. DeMaille, "Touching the Pen: Plains Indian Treaty Councils in Ethnohistorical Perspective," in Luebke, ed., *Ethnicity on the Great Plains*, pp. 43–44.

10 Congress repeatedly cut the size of the army. In 1874 it contained about 27,000 officers and men. See Utley, *Frontier Regulars*, pp. 11–15.

11 Ibid., p. 6. See also Wallace and Hoebel, *Comanches*, pp. 245–84; Donald J.

Berthrong, *The Southern Cheyennes*, pp. 41–43; David G. Mandelbaum, *The Plains Cree: An Ethnographic, Historical, and Comparative Study*, pp. 239–58.

12 Gary Clayton Anderson, *Little Crow: Spokesman for the Sioux*, pp. 135–61, 163–64, 165.

13 See Andrist, *Long Death*, p. 65.

14 Jerome Big Eagle, "A Sioux Story of the War," in Calloway, ed., *Our Hearts Fell to the Ground*, p. 95.

15 Utley, *Frontiersmen in Blue*, pp. 261–80; Andrist, *Long Death*, pp. 27–68.

16 George E. Hyde, *Life of George Bent: Written from His Letters*, pp. 137–63; Utley, *Frontiersmen in Blue*, pp. 294–97; Berthrong, *Southern Cheyennes*, pp. 195–223.

17 Congress also investigated the Sand Creek massacre, condemning the white participants because "those Indians were there encamped under the direction of our own officers, and believed themselves to be under the protection of our flag." Report of the Doolittle Committee, January 26, 1867, in Prucha, ed., *Documents*, p. 103.

18 Andrist, *Long Death*, p. 75.

19 Kappler, comp. and ed., *Indian Affairs*, 2: 887–95; Utley, *Frontiersmen in Blue*, pp. 336–40.

20 Kappler, comp. and ed., *Indian Affairs*, 2: 896–908; Utley, *Frontiersmen in Blue*, pp. 336–40.

21 Quoted in Andrist, *Long Death*, p. 95.

22 Berthrong, *Southern Cheyennes*, pp. 224–44.

23 George E. Hyde, *Red Cloud's Folk: A History of the Oglala Sioux*, pp. 134–61; Robert M. Utley, *Frontier Regulars: The United States Army and the Indian, 1866–1891*, pp. 93–107.

24 Hyde, *Spotted Tail's Folk*, pp. 115–17.

25 Quoted in Andrist, *Long Death*, p. 131; Russell, "How Many Indians Were Killed?" p. 47.

26 See Report of Doolittle Committee, January 26, 1867, in Prucha, ed., *Documents*, pp. 102–105; *Nation* 5 (October 31, 1867): 356; Weeks, *Farewell, My Nation*, p. 134. Quote in Ray Allen Billington and Martin Ridge, *Westward Expansion: A History of the American Frontier*, p. 598.

27 Utley, *Frontier Regulars*, pp. 115–18; Donald J. D'Elia, "The Argument over Civilian or Military Indian Control," *Historian* 24 (1961–62): 207–25. See Resolutions of the Indian Peace Commission, October 9, 1868; Secretary of War (J. M.) Schofield on Transfer of the Indian Bureau, November 20, 1868; Indian Commissioner (N. G.) Taylor on Transfer of the Indian Bureau, November 23, 1868, all in Prucha, ed., *Documents*, pp. 116–23.

28 Creation of an Indian Peace Commission, July 20, 1867, in Prucha, ed., *Documents*, pp. 105–106.

29 Utley, *Frontier Regulars*, pp. 130–39; Utley, *Indian Frontier*, pp. 108–109.

30 Douglas C. Jones, *The Treaty of Medicine Lodge: The Story of the Great Treaty Council as Told by Eyewitnesses*, pp. 110–16, 129, 130–34; Alfred A. Taylor, "Medicine Lodge Peace Council," *Chronicles of Oklahoma* 2 (June, 1924): 98–118; Berthrong, *Southern Cheyennes*, pp. 289–302.

31 Wallace and Hoebel, *Comanches*, pp. 309–11; Berthrong, *Southern Cheyennes*, pp. 297–300.

32 Treaty of Fort Laramie, April 29, 1868, in Prucha, ed., *Documents*, pp. 110–14, quote p. 113; Weeks, *Farewell, My Nation*, p. 139; Utley, *Frontier Regulars*, pp. 134–36.

33 Quoted in Weeks, *Farewell, My Nation*, p. 143.

34 George A. Forsyth, "A Frontier Fight," *Harper's New Monthly Magazine* 91 (1895): 42–62; Utley, *Frontier Regulars*, pp. 147–48.

35 Utley, *Indian Frontier*, pp. 123–28; Weeks, *Farewell, My Nation*, pp. 144–48; Wilbur S. Nye, *Carbine and Lance: The Story of Old Fort Sill*, pp. 60–70; Berthrong, *Southern Cheyennes*, pp. 324–29.

36 Utley, *Frontier Regulars*, pp. 155, 157.

37 Report of the Doolittle Committee, January 26, 1867, in Prucha, ed., *Documents*, p. 104; Utley, *Indian Frontier*, pp. 129–34; Weeks, *Farewell, My Nation*, pp. 155–59.

38 Quoted in Weeks, *Farewell, My Nation*, p. 154.

39 Rupert N. Richardson, Adrian Anderson, and Ernest Wallace, *Texas: The Lone Star State*, pp. 265–66; Carl Coke Rister, "The Significance of the Jacksboro Indian Affair of 1871," *Southwestern Historical Quarterly* 29 (1926): 181–200.

40 U. S. Congress, House, *Testimony Taken by Committee on Military Affairs in Relation To Texas Border Troubles*, 45th Cong., 2d sess., 1879, H. Exec. Doc. 64, pp. 1–35; Ernest Wallace, *Ranald S. Mackenzie on the Texas Frontier*, pp. 9, 77–89, 105–11; Ernest Wallace and Adrian Anderson, "R. S. Mackenzie: The Raid into Mexico in 1873," *Arizona and the West* 7 (summer, 1965): 105–26.

41 Wallace, *Ranald S. Mackenzie on the Texas Frontier*, pp. 128–46, 170; Utley, *Frontier Regulars*, pp. 219–33; William H. Leckie, *The Buffalo Soldiers: A Narrative of the Negro Cavalry in the West*, pp. 125–33; Hagan, *Quanah Parker*, pp. 13–15; Berthrong, *Southern Cheyennes*, pp. 389–405.

42 T. Lindsay Baker and Billy R. Harrison, *Adobe Walls: The History and Archeology of the 1874 Trading Post*, pp. 44–45, 49–74.

43 Utley, *Frontier Regulars*, pp. 236–62; Andrist, *Long Death*, pp. 239–300; Hyde, *Red Cloud's Folk*, pp. 291–92; Robert M. Utley, *Cavalier in Buckskin: George Armstrong Custer and the Western Military Frontier*, pp. 165–93.

44 Report of the Indian Peace Commission, January 7, 1868, in Prucha, ed., *Documents*, p. 108.

45 Quoted in Wallace and Hoebel, *Comanches*, pp. 282–84.

CHAPTER 10

1 Peter Nabokov, *Two Leggings: The Making of a Crow Warrior*, p. xii.

2 Some of the discussion presented here is based on Utley, *Indian Frontier*, pp. 236–43. See also Gordon MacGregor, *Warriors without Weapons: A Study of the Society and Personality Development of the Pine Ridge Sioux*, pp. 22–28; Erik Homburger Erickson, "Observations on Sioux Education," *Journal of Psychology* 7 (1939): 101–56; Washburn, *Indian in America*, pp. 209–10, 214–32.

3 Loretta Fowler, *Arapahoe Politics, 1851–1978: Symbols in Crises of Authority*, pp. 2–3, 21; MacGregor, *Warriors without Weapons*, pp. 35–36; Hassrick, *The Sioux*, p. 302. For a different view see Vine Deloria, Jr., and Clifford M. Lytle, *American Indians, American Justice*, pp. 92, 93–97; Donald J. Berthrong, *The Cheyenne and Arapaho Ordeal: Reservation and Agency Life in the Indian Territory, 1875–1907*, p. 28.

4   Utley, *Indian Frontier,* pp. 236–37; Hassrick, *The Sioux,* pp. 302–303.

5   Hassrick, *The Sioux,* p. 301; MacGregor, *Warriors without Weapons,* pp. 52–57; George Bird Grinnell, *Pawnee, Blackfoot and Cheyenne: History and Folklore of the Plains,* p. 36.

6   Utley, *Indian Frontier,* p. 243.

7   Quoted in Nabokov, ed., *Native American Testimony,* p. 220.

8   Richard Henry Pratt, *Battlefield and Classroom: Four Decades with the American Indian, 1867–1904,* pp. 215–17, 238–39, 268, 275–77, 282–85; George E. Hyde, *A Sioux Chronicle,* pp. 54–56; Washburn, *Indian in America,* pp. 229–30.

9   See George E. Hyde, *The Pawnee Indians,* p. 5; MacGregor, *Warriors without Weapons,* p. 25; Loretta Fowler, *Shared Symbols, Contested Meanings: Gros Ventre Culture and History, 1778–1984,* p. 125.

10   Frank B. Linderman, *Pretty-shield, Medicine Woman of the Crows,* pp. 248–51.

11   Grinnell, *Pawnee, Blackfoot and Cheyenne,* p. 86.

12   MacGregor, *Warriors without Weapons,* p. 22.

13   Utley, *Indian Frontier of the American West,* p. 236.

14   Cited in Calloway, ed., *Our Hearts Fell to the Ground,* p. 128.

15   Quoted in ibid., p. 131.

16   Cited in Nabokov, ed., *Native American Testimony,* p. 211.

17   Charles A. Eastman, *From the Deep Woods to Civilization,* pp. 79–80; Washburn, *Indian in America,* p. 228; Wallace and Hoebel, *Comanches,* p. 338; Francis Paul Prucha, *American Indian Policy in Crisis: Christian Reformers and the Indian, 1865–1900,* p. 212.

18   Kehoe, *North American Indians,* p. 337; Young Bear and Theisz, *Standing in the Light,* pp. 56, 98.

19   See, for example, Hoxie, *Parading through History,* pp. 209–25.

20   Quote in Moquin with Van Doren, eds., *Great Documents,* p. 236. See also Erickson, "Observations on Sioux Education," p. 7; and MacGregor, *Warriors without Weapons,* p. 26.

21   Cited in Lonnie E. Underhill and Daniel F. Littlefield, Jr., eds., *Hamlin Garland's Observations on the American Indian,* pp. 167–69. See also Grinnell, *Pawnee, Blackfoot and Cheyenne,* pp. 35, 36, 86.

22   Washburn, *Indian in America,* pp. 222–25; Wallace and Hoebel, *Comanches,* pp. 332–37; Omer C. Stewart, *Peyote Religion: A History,* pp. 30, 32–33, 51–83.

23   Kehoe, *North American Indians,* p. 327.

24   Sarah Carter, *Lost Harvests: Prairie Indian Reserve Farmers and Government Policy,* pp. 13–14.

25   MacGregor, *Warriors without Weapons,* pp. 49–50; Berthrong, *Cheyenne and Arapaho Ordeal,* pp. 92–94, 97.

26   Berthrong, *Cheyenne and Arapaho Ordeal,* pp. 30–31, 33–34, 37–40; Utley, *Frontier Regulars,* pp. 283–84; Secretary of the Interior (Carl) Schurz on Reservation Policy, Extract from the *Annual Report of the Secretary of the Interior,* November 1, 1880, in Prucha, ed., *Documents,* p. 154. See also Mari Sandoz, *Cheyenne Autumn,* pp. 194–211, 269–72; Peter M. Wright, "The Pursuit of Dull Knife from Fort Reno," *Chronicles of Oklahoma* 46 (1968): 141–54; *New York Tribune,* October 5, 1878.

27 *Standing Bear v. Crook,* May 12, 1879, in Prucha, ed., *Documents,* pp. 151–52; Edward E. Hill, ed., *The Office of Indian Affairs, 1824–1880: Historical Sketches,* p. 139; Kenneth R. Jacobs, "A History of the Ponca Indians to 1882" (Ph.D. diss., Texas Tech University, 1977), pp. 157–62; William T. Hagan, *American Indians,* p. 122.

28 Indian Commissioner (Ezra A.) Hayt on Indian Police, Extract from the *Annual Report of the Commissioner of Indian Affairs,* November 1, 1877, in Prucha, ed., *Documents,* p. 151; *U.S. Statutes at Large,* 20: 86, 315, as cited in ibid., p. 151.

29 Courts of Indian Offenses, Extract from the *Annual Report of the Secretary of the Interior,* November 1, 1883, in Prucha, ed., *Documents,* pp. 160–62; William T. Hagan, *Indian Police and Judges: Experiments in Acculturation and Control,* pp. 10–50.

30 Deloria and Lytle, *American Indians, American Justice,* pp. 168–70; *Ex Parte Crow Dog* in Robert N. Clinton et al., *American Indian Law: Cases and Materials,* pp. 33–38; Loring Benson Priest, *Uncle Sam's Stepchildren: The Reformation of United States Indian Policy, 1865–1887,* pp. 201–203.

31 Clinton et al., *American Indian Law,* p. 36. See also Sidney L. Harring, *Crow Dog's Case: American Indian Sovereignty, Tribal Law, and United States Law in the Nineteenth Century,* pp. 118–34.

32 Major Crimes Act, March 3, 1885, in Prucha, ed., *Documents,* pp. 167–68; *United States v. Kagama,* May 10, 1886, in ibid., pp. 168–69; Harring, *Crow Dog's Case,* pp. 134–74.

33 *Elk v. Wilkins,* November 3, 1884, in Prucha, ed., *Documents,* pp. 166–67; Washburn, *Indian in America,* pp. 241–42; Priest, *Uncle Sam's Stepchildren,* pp. 206–208.

34 Priest, *Uncle Sam's Stepchildren,* pp. 207–209.

35 General Allotment Act (Dawes Act), February 8, 1887, in Prucha, ed., *Documents,* pp. 171–74.

36 Although scholars offer a variety of figures as to the amount of land allotted and lost, the numbers are startling by any measure. See Washburn, *Indian in America,* p. 243; Henry E. Fritz, *The Movement for Indian Assimilation, 1860–1890,* pp. 211–15; Deloria and Lytle, *American Indians, American Justice,* pp. 220–21.

37 Utley, *Indian Frontier,* pp. 246–51; Herbert S. Schell, *History of South Dakota,* pp. 139, 247, 315, 317–18.

38 T. J. Morgan, "Report of the Commissioner of Indian Affairs," in *Annual Report of the Secretary of the Interior,* 1891, 52d Cong., 1st sess., H. Exec. Doc. I, pt. 5, pp. 123–27; Russell Thornton, *We Shall Live Again: The 1870 and 1890 Ghost Dance Movements as Demographic Revitalization,* pp. 6–10, 45, 48–50; Washburn, *Indian in America,* pp. 192–93, 217–22; James Mooney, "The Ghost Dance Religion and the Sioux Outbreak of 1890," in *Fourteenth Annual Report of the Bureau of Ethnology, 1892–93,* pt. 2, pp. 24–25, 30, 34, 73, 114–20; Weston La Barre, *The Ghost Dance: Origins of Religion,* pp. 227–30, 300, 304.

39 Hagan, *Quanah Parker,* pp. 59–61; Washburn, *Indian in America,* p. 222.

40 Cited in Paul I. Wellman, *Death on the Prairie,* p. 186; Utley, *Frontier Regulars,* pp. 401–403; Raymond J. DeMallie, "The Lakota Ghost Dance: An Ethnohistorical Account," *Pacific Historical Review* 51 (1982): 385–405.

41 D. F. Royer to Robert V. Belt, Acting Commissioner of Indian Affairs, Nov. 15,

1890, cited in Robert M. Utley, *The Last Days of the Sioux Nation,* p. 111; Neihardt, ed., *Black Elk Speaks,* pp. 242–44. See also L. W. Colby, "The Sioux Indian War of 1890–91," *Transactions and Reports of the Nebraska State Historical Society* 3 (1892): 180; and Kehoe, *Ghost Dance,* pp. 105–11.

42   Neihardt, ed., *Black Elk Speaks,* p. 267.

43   Morgan, "Report," *Annual Report of the Secretary of the Interior,* 1891, 52d Cong., 1st sess., pt. 5, p. 130; Utley, *Last Days,* pp. 227–29; Mooney, " Ghost Dance Religion," pt. 2, pp. 855–71; Utley, *Frontier Regulars,* pp. 404–405. Some scholars put the number of Indian dead at over 250. See Richard E. Jensen, R. Eli Paul, and John E. Carter, *Eyewitness at Wounded Knee,* pp. 20, 110–12.

44   Capt. W. E. Daugherty, "The Recent Messiah Craze," *Journal of the Military Service Institute of the United States* 12 (1891): 577.

45   Neihardt, ed., *Black Elk Speaks,* p. 270.

46   Cited in Nabokov, ed., *Native American Testimony,* p. 208.

47   Quotes in Althea Bass, *The Arapaho Way: A Memoir of an Indian Boyhood,* pp. 40, 45–55. See also Luther Standing Bear, *My People the Sioux,* pp. 133–49.

EPILOGUE

1   *Lone Wolf v. Hitchcock,* January 5, 1903, in Prucha, ed., *Documents,* pp. 202–203.

2   Cited in William T. Hagan, *United States–Comanche Relations: The Reservation Years,* pp. 262–85. See also Deloria and Lytle, *American Indians, American Justice,* pp. 43–44.

3   Hagan, *United States–Comanche Relations,* pp. 265–67, 263–85.

4   *Winters v. United States,* January 6, 1908, in Prucha, ed., *Documents,* pp. 319–20; Norris Hundley, Jr., "The *Winters* Decision and Indian Water Rights: A Mystery Reexamined," *Western Historical Quarterly* 13 (January, 1982): 17–42; Deloria and Lytle, *American Indians, American Justice,* pp. 49–50.

5   Deloria and Lytle, *American Indians, American Justice,* p. 49.

6   Quote in Moquin with Van Doren, eds., *Great Documents,* p. 315. See also Hagan, *American Indians,* p. 146.

7   Alison R. Bernstein, *American Indians and World War II: Toward a New Era in Indian Affairs,* p. 81.

8   Ibid., pp. 74–75, 79. See also Donald L. Parman, *Indians and the American West in the Twentieth Century,* pp. 107–22.

9   Wheeler-Howard Act (Indian Reorganization Act), June 14, 1934, in Prucha, ed., *Documents,* pp. 222–25; Thomas Biolsi, *Organizing the Lakota: The Political Economy of the New Deal on the Pine Ridge and Rosebud Reservations,* pp. 61–84.

10   Ben Reifel (Brule) to Joseph H. Cash, summer, 1967, in Peter Iverson, ed., *The Plains Indians of the Twentieth Century,* pp. 111, 113; Kenneth R. Philp, *John Collier's Crusade for Indian Reform, 1920–1954,* pp. 172–74; Michael P. Malone and Richard B. Roeder, *Montana: A History of Two Centuries,* p. 271.

11   Oklahoma Indian Welfare Act, June 26, 1936, in Prucha, ed., *Documents,* pp. 230–31.

12   Reifel to Cash, in Iverson, ed., *Plains Indians of the Twentieth Century,* p. 119; Antoine Roubideaux (Brule) to Joseph H. Cash, summer, 1967, in ibid., pp. 121–22, 126; Donald L. Parman, "The Indian and the Civilian Conservation Corps," in Norris Hundly, Jr., ed., *The American Indian,* pp. 127–45.

13   See Philp, *John Collier's Crusade*, pp. 240–42.

14   Donald L. Fixico, *Termination and Relocation: Federal Indian Policy, 1945–1960*, pp. 91–110; Parman, *Indians and the American West*, pp. 136–39.

15   Indians Claims Commission Act, August 13, 1946, in Prucha, ed., *Documents*, pp. 231–33; Parman, *Indians and the American West*, pp. 126–28; Fixico, *Termination and Relocation*, p. 31; Harvey Daniel Rosenthal, "Their Day in Court: A History of the Indian Claims Commission" (Ph.D. diss., Kent State University, 1976), pp. 10–26.

16   Fixico, *Termination and Relocation*, p. 31; Ernest Wallace, "The Great Spirit Did Not Put You Here to Steal Our Land," public address, April 25, 1975, in Ernest Wallace, Papers, Southwest Collection, Texas Tech University (revised version in *Studies in History* 6 [1976]: 11–26); Hagan, *American Indians*, p. 167.

17   Cited in Alvin M. Josephy, Jr., *Now That the Buffalo's Gone: A Study of Today's American Indians*, p. 215.

18   Ibid., pp. 235–45.

19   Ibid.; Washburn, *Indian in America*, pp. 273–74; Parman, *Indians in the American West*, pp. 155–59; Kehoe, *Ghost Dance*, pp. 71–72, 78–85. For a somewhat different view, see Young Bear and Theisz, *Standing in the Light*, pp. 150–55.

20   James S. Frideres, *Native People in Canada: Contemporary Conflicts*, pp. 177, 181.

21   Young Bear and Theisz, *Standing in the Light*, pp. 57–63, 65–69, 77, 101–103; Kehoe, *Ghost Dance*, pp. 124–25; Michael Parfit, "Powwow: A Gathering of the Tribes," *National Geographic* 185 (June, 1994): 88–113.

22   See Walter C. Fleming, "Native American Literature Comes of Age," *Montana: The Magazine of Western History* 42 (spring, 1992): 73–76.

23   Joan Frederick, "Traditional Painting in Oklahoma," *Native Peoples: The Journal of the Heard Museum* 8, no. 4 (1995): 48.

24   Quote in ibid.; Colin G. Calloway, ed., *Our Hearts Fell to the Ground*, p. 2.

Bibliography

ARCHIVES, MANUSCRIPTS, THESES, AND DISSERTATIONS

Botsford, E. M. Wild West Show Papers. Southwest Collection, Texas Tech University.

Britten, Thomas. "American Indians in World War I: Military Service as Catalyst for Reform." Ph.D. diss., Texas Tech University, 1994.

Broce, Gerald L. "Cultural Continuity in the Transformation of Comanche Society." Master's thesis, Wichita State University, 1966.

Brown, William. "Comancheria Demography, 1805–1830." Manuscript, 1983, in Comanche File. Southwest Collection, Texas Tech University.

Elam, Earl H. "The History of the Wichita Indian Confederacy to 1868." Ph.D. diss., Texas Tech University, 1971.

Fillpot, Elise A. "The Tribally Controlled Community Colleges Act of 1978." Master's thesis, Texas Tech University, 1989.

Flynn, Sean J. "Western Assimilationist: Charles H. Burke and the Burke Act." Master's thesis, Texas Tech University, 1988.

Gibson, Joe D. "United States Peace Commission on the Northern Plains, 1866–1868, and the Treaty of Fort Laramie." Master's thesis, Texas Tech University, 1974.

Indian Schools. Collection, 1929–45. Southwest Collection, Texas Tech University.

Jacobs, Kenneth R. "A History of the Ponca Indians to 1882." Ph.D. diss., Texas Tech University, 1977.

Magazine Clippings. Temple Mounds File. Southwest Collection, Texas Tech University.

McLoughlin, James. Papers, 1842–1923 (microfilm). University Library, Texas Tech University.

Parker, Cynthia Ann. Reference File. Southwest Collection, Texas Tech University.

Parker, Quanah. Reference File. Southwest Collection, Texas Tech University.

Richert, Bernhard E., Jr. "Plains Indian Medicine Bundles." Master's thesis, University of Texas, Austin, 1969.

Rister, Carl Coke. Papers, 1834–1962. Southwest Collection, Texas Tech University.

Roe, Mason Gordon. "A Comparative Study of Selected Ceremonies of Five American Tribes." Master's thesis, University of Southern California, 1956.

Rollings, Willard H. "Prairie Hegemony: An Ethnohistorical Study of the Osage, from Early Times to 1840." Ph.D. diss., Texas Tech University, 1983.

Rosenthal, Harvey Daniel. "Their Day in Court: A History of the Indian Claims Commission." Ph.D. diss., Kent State University, 1976.

United States. Department of Interior. Records of the Bureau of Indian Affairs. Record Group 75. National Archives.

United States. Department of War. Records of the United States Army Commands. Letters Sent. Dept. of Texas. Record Group 93. National Archives.

Wallace, Ernest. Papers, 1834–1962. Southwest Collection, Texas Tech University

Abel, Annie Heloise. "The History of Events Resulting in Indian Consolidation West of the Mississippi." *Annual Report of the American Historical Association for the Year 1906.* 2 vols. Washington, D.C.: Government Printing Office, 1908. I: 233–450.

———. "Proposals for an Indian State, 1778–1878." *Annual Report of the American Historical Association for the Year 1907.* 2 vols. Washington, D.C.: Government Printing Office, 1908. I: 87–104.

Baker, O. E. *Atlas of American Agriculture.* Washington, D.C.: Government Printing Office, 1936.

Dodge, Henry. *Report on the Expedition of Dragoons under Col. Henry Dodge, to the Rocky Mountains in 1835.* 24th Cong., 1st sess., 1837, H. Exec. Doc. 181.

Dorsey, J. O. "Siouan Sociology." *Fifteenth Annual Report of the Bureau of American Ethnology,* 1894. Washington, D.C.: Government Printing Office, 1894.

Ewers, John C. *The Horse in Blackfoot Indian Culture: With Comparative Materials from Other Western Tribes.* Bureau of American Ethnology Bulletin 159. Washington, D.C.: Government Printing Office, 1955.

Hodge, Frederick Webb. *Handbook of American Indians North of Mexico.* 2 vols. Bureau of American Ethnology Bulletin 30. Washington, D.C.: Government Printing Office, 1907.

Kappler, Charles J., comp. & ed. *Indian Affairs: Laws and Treaties.* 5 vols. Washington, D.C.: Government Printing Office, 1904–41.

La Flesche, Frances. "The Osage Tribe Rite of the Wa–xo'–Be." *Forty-fifth Annual Report of the Bureau of American Ethnology,* 1927–28, pp. 523–857. Washington: Government Printing Office, 1928.

Mallery, Garrick. "Pictographs of the North American Indians: A Preliminary Paper." *Fourth Annual Report of the Bureau of Ethnology to the Secretary of the Smithsonian Institution, 1882–1883.* Washington, D.C.: Government Printing Office, 1886.

Mooney, James. *The Aboriginal Population of America North of Mexico.* Edited by John R. Swanton. Smithsonian Miscellaneous Collections, vol. 80, no. 7. Washington, D.C.: Government Printing Office, 1928.

Mooney, James. "Calendar History of the Kiowa Indians." *Seventeenth Annual Report of the Bureau of Ethnology,* 1895–96, pt. 1. Washington, D.C.: Government Printing Office, 1898.

Mooney, James. "The Ghost Dance Religion and the Sioux Outbreak of 1890." *Fourteenth Annual Report of the Bureau of Ethnology.* Washington, D.C.: Government Printing Office, 1896.

Morgan, T. J. "Report of the Commissioner of Indian Affairs." *Annual Report of the Secretary of the Interior,* 52d Cong., 1st sess., 1891. H. Exec. Doc. 1, pt. 5.

Shimkin, Demitri B. *The Wind River Shoshone Sun Dance.* Bureau of American Ethnology Bulletin 151, Anthropological Paper no. 41 (1953): 397–484.

Swanton, John R. *Some Material on the History and Ethnology of the Caddo Indians.* Bureau of American Ethnology Bulletin 132. Washington, D.C.: Government Printing Office, 1942.

United States. Congress, House. *Sioux Indians, Wounded Knee Massacre.* Hearings before the House Sub-Committee on Indian Affairs, March 7 and May 12, 1938. 75th Cong., 3d sess., 1938, H. Rept. 2535.

United States. Congress, House. *Special Committee of the House of Representatives to Investigate Texas Frontier Troubles.* 44th Cong., 1st sess., 1876. H. Rept. 343.

United States. Congress, House. *Testimony Taken by Committee of Military Affairs in Relation to Texas Border Troubles.* 45th Cong., 2d sess., 1879. H. Misc. Doc. 64.

United States. Department of Commerce. Bureau of the Census. *1980 Census of Population: American Indians, Eskimos, and Aluets on Identified Reservations and in the Historic Areas of Oklahoma.* Washington, D.C.: Government Printing Office, 1980.

United States. Department of Interior. *Annual Reports of the Secretary of Interior.* Washington, D.C.: Government Printing Office, 1870–1970.

United States Indian Claims Commission. *Annual Report for 1974.* Washington, D.C.: Government Printing Office, 1974.

BOOKS AND ARTICLES

Ahern, Wilbert H. "An Experiment Aborted: Returned Indian Students in the Indian School Service, 1881–1908." *Ethnohistory* 44 (spring, 1997): 263–304.

Albers, Patricia, and Beatrice Medicine. *The Hidden Half: Studies of Plains Indian Women.* Lanham, Md.: University Press of America, 1983.

Allen, Henry Easton. "The Parilla Expedition to the Red River." *Southwestern Historical Quarterly* 43 (1939): 43–71.

Anderson, Gary Clayton. "Early Dakota Migration and Intertribal War: A Revision." *Western Historical Quarterly* 11 (January, 1980): 17–36.

————. *Kinsmen of Another Kind: Dakota-White Relations in the Upper Mississippi Valley, 1650–1862.* Lincoln: University of Nebraska Press, 1984.

————. *Little Crow: Spokesman for the Sioux.* St. Paul: Minnesota Historical Association Press, 1986.

————. *Sitting Bull and the Paradox of Lakota Nationhood.* New York: HarperCollins, 1996.

Andrist, Ralph K. *The Long Death: The Last Days of the Plains Indians.* New York: Collier Books, 1964.

Axtell, James. *The European and the Indian: Essays in the Ethnohistory of Colonial North America.* New York: Oxford University Press, 1981.

Baker, T. Lindsay, and Billy R. Harrison. *Adobe Walls: The History and Archeology of the 1874 Trading Post.* College Station: Texas A&M University Press, 1986.

Ballantine, Betty, and Ian Ballantine, eds. *The Native Americans: An Illustrated History.* Introduction by Alvin M. Josephy. Atlanta: Turner, 1993.

Bass, Althea. *The Arapaho Way: A Memoir of an Indian Boyhood.* New York: Clarkson N. Potter, 1966.

Bataille, Gretchen M., and Kathleen Mullen Sands. *American Indian Women: Telling Their Lives.* Lincoln: University of Nebraska Press, 1984.

Battey, Thomas C. *The Life and Adventures of a Quaker among the Indians.* Boston: Lee, Shepard and Dillingham, 1875.

Baylor, H. W. "Recollections of the Comanche Indians." *Frontier Times* 6 (June, 1929): 373–75.

Berlandier, Jean Louis. *The Indians of Texas in 1830.* Edited and introduced by John

C. Ewers; translated by Patricia Reading Leclercq. Washington, D. C.: Smithsonian Institution Press, 1968.

Bernstein, Alison R. *American Indians and World War II: Toward a New Era in Indian Affairs.* Norman: University of Oklahoma Press, 1991.

Berthrong, Donald J. *The Cheyenne and Arapaho Ordeal: Reservation and Agency Life in the Indian Territory, 1875–1907.* Norman: University of Oklahoma Press, 1976.

———. *The Southern Cheyennes.* Norman: University of Oklahoma Press, 1963.

———. "Struggle for Power: The Impact of Southern Cheyenne and Arapaho 'Schoolboys' on Tribal Politics." *American Indian Quarterly* 16 (winter, 1992): 1–24.

Billington, Ray Allan, and Martin Ridge. *Western Expansion: A History of the American Frontier.* 5th ed. New York: Macmillan, 1982.

Biolsi, Thomas. *Organizing the Lakota: The Political Economy of the New Deal on the Pine Ridge and Rosebud Reservations.* Tucson: University of Arizona Press, 1992.

Blegen, Theodore C. *Minnesota: A History of the State.* Minneapolis: University of Minnesota Press, 1975.

Bolton, Herbert Eugene. *Coronado: Knight of the Pueblos and Plains.* Albuquerque: University of New Mexico Press, 1949.

———. *The Hasinais: Southern Caddoans as Seen by the Earliest Europeans.* Edited with an introduction by Russell M. Managhi. Norman: University of Oklahoma Press, 1987.

———, ed. *Spanish Exploration in the Southwest, 1542–1706.* New York: Charles Scribner's Sons, 1916.

Bourne, Edward G. "The Travels of Jonathan Carver." *American Historical Review* 11 (January, 1906): 287–302.

Bowers, Alfred W. *Mandan Social and Ceremonial Organization.* Chicago: University of Chicago Press, 1950.

Brackenridge, H. M. *Views of Louisiana, Together with a Journal of a Voyage up the Missouri River, in 1811.* Pittsburgh: Cramer, Spear and Erickbaum, 1814.

Bradbury, John. *Travels in the Interior of America, in the Years 1809, 1810, and 1811. . . .* London: Sherwood, Neely, and Jones, 1819.

Brandon, William. *Indians.* New York: American Heritage Press, 1985.

Branch, E. Douglas. *The Hunting of the Buffalo.* Introduction by J. Frank Dobie. Lincoln: University of Nebraska Press, 1962.

Britten, Thomas A. *American Indians in World War I: At War and at Home.* Albuquerque: University of New Mexico Press, 1997.

Brown, Jennifer S. H., and Elizabeth Vibert, eds. *Reading Beyond Words: Contexts for Native History.* Toronto: Broadview Press, 1996.

Brown, Joseph Epes, ed. *The Sacred Pipe: Black Elk's Account of the Seven Rites of the Oglala Sioux.* Norman: University of Oklahoma Press, 1953.

Brown, Ralph H. *Historical Geography of the United States.* New York: Harcourt, Brace & World, 1948.

Bryan, Alan L. "Early Man in America and the Late Pleistocene Chronology of Western Canada and Alaska." *Current Anthropology* 10 (1969): 339–48.

Burnette, Robert, and John Koster. *The Road to Wounded Knee.* New York: Bantam Books, 1974.

Cadwalader, Sandra L., and Vine Deloria, Jr., eds. *The Aggressions of Civilization: Federal Indian Policy since the 1880s.* Philadelphia: Temple University Press, 1987.

Calloway, Colin G. "The Intertribal Balance of Power on the Great Plains, 1760–1850." *Journal of American Studies* 16 (1982): 25–47.

———, ed. *Our Hearts Fell to the Ground: Plains Indian Views of How the West Was Lost.* Boston: Bedford Books of St. Martin's Press, 1996.

Capps, Benjamin. *The Great Chiefs.* New York: Time-Life Books, 1975.

———. *The Indians.* New York: Time-Life Books, 1973.

Carlson, Paul H. "Indian Agriculture, Changing Subsistence Patterns, and the Environment on the Southern Great Plains." *Agricultural History* 66 (spring, 1992): 52–60.

Carter, Sarah. *Lost Harvests: Prairie Indian Reserve Farmers and Government Policy.* Montreal: McGill-Queen's University Press, 1990.

Carver, Jonathan. *The Journals of Jonathan Carver and Related Documents, 1766–1770.* Edited by John Parker. St. Paul: Minnesota Historical Society Press, 1976.

Catlin, George. *Letters and Notes on the Manners, Customs, and Conditions of North American Indians.* 2 vols. Introduction by Marjorie Halpin. New York: Dover, 1973.

Ceram, C. W. *The First American: A Story of North American Archaeology.* New York: Harcourt Brace Jovanovich, 1971.

Chapman, Abraham, ed. *Literature of the American Indians: Views and Interpretations.* New York: New American Library, 1975.

Chávez, Fray Angélico. "Poke–Yemo's Representative and the Pueblo Revolt of 1680." *New Mexico Historical Review* 42 (1967): 85–126.

Chipman, Donald E. *Spanish Texas, 1519–1821.* Austin: University of Texas Press, 1992.

Chittenden, Hiram Martin. *The American Fur Trade of the Far West.* 3 vols. New York: F. P. Harper, 1902.

Clark, William P. *The Indian Sign Language.* Philadelphia: L. R. Hamersly & Co., 1885.

Clifton, James A., ed. *Being and Becoming Indian: Biographical Studies of North American Frontiers.* Chicago: Dorsey Press, 1989.

Clinton, Robert N., et al. *American Indian Law: Cases and Materials.* 3d ed. Charlottesville, Va.: The Michie Company, 1991.

Cohen, Felix. *Handbook of Federal Indian Law.* Albuquerque: University of New Mexico Press, 1942.

Cohen, Felix S. "Original Indian Title." *Minnesota Law Review* 32 (December, 1947): 28–59.

Colby, L. W. "The Sioux Indian War of 1890–91." *Transactions and Reports of the Nebraska State Historical Society* 3 (1892): 180.

Cornell, Stephen. *Return of the Native: American Indian Political Resurgence.* New York: Oxford University Press, 1988.

Crimmins, Martin L., ed. "Shafter's Exploration of West Texas." *West Texas Historical Association Year Book* 9 (1933): 82–96.

Critchfield, Howard J. *General Climatology.* 3d ed. Englewood Cliffs, N.J.: Prentice-Hall, 1966.

Crouse, Nellis M. *La Verendrye: Fur Trader and Explorer*. Ithaca, N.Y.: Cornell University Press, 1966.

Daugherty, Capt. W. E. "The Recent Messiah Craze." *Journal of the Military Service Institute of the United States* 12 (1891): 577.

Davis, Theodore R. "The Buffalo Range." *Harper's Magazine* 38 (1869): 147–63.

D'Elia, Donald J. "The Argument over Civilian or Military Indian Control." *Historian* 24 (1961–62): 207–25.

Deloria, Vine, Jr. *Behind the Trail of Broken Treaties: An Indian Declaration of Independence*. New York: Dell, 1974.

———. *Custer Died for Your Sins: An Indian Manifesto*. New York: Macmillan, 1969.

———, ed. *American Indian Policy in the 20th Century*. Norman: University of Oklahoma Press, 1985.

Deloria, Vine, Jr., and Clifford M. Lytle. *American Indians, American Justice*. Austin: University of Texas Press, 1983.

DeMallie, Raymond J. "The Lakota Ghost Dance: An Ethnohistorical Account." *Pacific Historical Review* 51 (1982): 385–405.

DeMaille, Raymond J., and Alfonso Ortiz, eds. *North American Indian Anthropology: Essays on Society and Culture*. Norman: University of Oklahoma Press, 1994.

DeMaille, Raymond J., and Douglas R. Parks, eds. *Sioux Indian Religion: Tradition and Innovation*. Norman: University of Oklahoma Press, 1987.

Denhardt, Robert Moorman. *The Horse of the Americas*. Norman: University of Oklahoma Press, 1947.

Denig, Edwin Thompson. *Five Indian Tribes of the Upper Missouri: Sioux, Arickaras, Assiniboines, Crees, Crows*. Edited with an introduction by John C. Ewers. Norman: University of Oklahoma Press, 1961.

Dixon, Roland. "Some Aspects of the American Shaman." *Journal of American Folk-Lore* 21 (1908): 1–12.

Dobak, William A. "Killing the Canadian Buffalo, 1821–1881." *Western Historical Quarterly* 27 (spring, 1996): 33–52.

Dobie, J. Frank. "Indian Horses and Horsemanship." *Southwest Review* 35 (autumn, 1950): 265–75.

———. *The Mustangs*. Boston: Little, Brown and Company, 1952.

Dobyns, Henry F. "Estimating Aboriginal American Population: An Appraisal of Techniques with a New Hemisphere Estimate." *Current Anthropology* 7 (1966): 395–416.

Dobyns, Henry F., with William R. Swagerty. *Their Numbers Became Thinned: Native American Population Dynamics in Eastern North America*. Knoxville: University of Tennessee Press, 1983.

Dodge, Richard Irving. *The Hunting Grounds of the Great West*. London: Chatto & Windus, 1878.

———. *Thirty-three Years among Our Wild Indians*. New York: Anchor House, 1959.

Driver, Harold E. *Indians of North America*. Chicago: University of Chicago Press, 1961.

Driver, Harold E., and A. L. Kroeber. "Quantitative Expression of Cultural Relationships." *University of California Publications in American Archeology and Ethnology* 31 (1932): 211–56.

Driver, Harold E., and James L. Coffin. *Classification and Development of North American Indian Cultures: A Statistical Analysis of the Driver-Massey Sample.* Philadelphia: Transactions of the American Philosophical Society, n.s., 65, pt. 3, 1975.

Eastman, Charles A. *From the Deep Woods to Civilization.* 1936. Reprint, Lincoln: University of Nebraska Press, 1977.

Eggan, Fred. *The American Indian: Perspectives for the Study of Social Change.* Cambridge: Cambridge University Press, 1966.

———, ed. *Social Anthropology of North American Tribes.* 2d ed. Chicago: University of Chicago Press, 1955.

Elam, Earl H. "The Origins and Identity of the Wichita." *Kansas Quarterly* 3 (fall, 1971): 13–20.

Erickson, Erik Homburger. "Observations on Sioux Education." *Journal of Psychology* 7 (1939): 101–56.

Ewers, John C. *The Blackfeet: Raiders of the Northwestern Plains.* Norman: University of Oklahoma Press, 1958.

———. "Contraceptive Charms among the Plains Indians." *Plains Anthropologist* 15 (1970): 216–18.

———. *Indian Life on the Upper Missouri.* Norman: University of Oklahoma Press, 1968.

———. "The Influence of Epidemics on the Indian Populations and Cultures of Texas." *Plains Anthropologist* 18 (1973): 104–15.

———. "Intertribal Warfare as the Precursor of Indian-White Warfare on the Northern Great Plains." *Western Historical Quarterly* 6 (1975): 397–410.

———. *Plains Indian History and Culture: Essays on Continuity and Change.* Norman: University of Oklahoma Press, 1997.

———. *Plains Indian Painting: A Description of an Aboriginal American Art.* Stanford, Calif.: Stanford University Press, 1939.

———. *Plains Indian Sculpture: A Traditional Art from America's Heartland.* Washington, D.C.: Smithsonian Institution Press, 1986.

———. "When Red and White Men Met." *Western Historical Quarterly* 2 (1971): 133–50.

Fagan, Brian M. *Ancient North America: The Archaeology of a Continent.* Rev. ed. New York: Thames and Hudson, 1995.

Farb, Peter. *Man's Rise to Civilization: The Cultural Ascent of the Indians of North America.* Rev. 2d ed. New York: Penguin Books, 1978.

Fenneman, Nevin M. *Physiography of Western United States.* New York: McGraw-Hill, 1931.

Fitzgerald, Michael Oren. *Yellowtail, Crow Medicine Man and Sun Dance Chief: An Autobiography.* Norman: University of Oklahoma Press, 1991.

Fixico, Donald L. *Termination and Relocation: Federal Indian Policy, 1945–1960.* Albuquerque: University of New Mexico Press, 1986.

Fleming, Walter C. "Native American Literature Comes of Age." *Montana: The Magazine of Western History* 42 (spring, 1992): 73–76.

Fleming, Walter C., and John G. Watts, eds. *Visions of an Enduring People: Introduction to Native American Studies.* Dubuque, Iowa: Kendall/Hunt, 1994.

Flores, Dan L. "Bison Ecology and Bison Diplomacy: The Southern Plains from 1800 to 1850." *Journal of American History* 78 (September, 1991): 465–85.

———. "The Ecology of the Red River in 1806: Peter Custis and Early Southwestern Natural History." *Southwestern Historical Quarterly* 88 (July, 1984): 1–42.

———, ed. *Journal of an Indian Trader: Anthony Glass and the Texas Trading Frontier, 1790–1810*. College Station: Texas A & M University Press, 1985.

———, ed. *Jefferson and Southwestern Exploration: The Freeman & Custis Accounts of the Red River Expedition of 1806*. Norman: University of Oklahoma Press, 1984.

Forbes, Jack D. *Apache Navaho and Spaniard*. Norman: University of Oklahoma Press, 1960.

Forsyth, George A. "A Frontier Fight." *Harper's New Monthly Magazine* 91 (1895): 42–62.

Foster, Morris W. *Being Comanche: A Social History of an American Indian Community*. Tucson: University of Arizona Press, 1991.

Fowler, Loretta. *Arapahoe Politics, 1851–1978: Symbols in Crises of Authority*. Lincoln: University of Nebraska Press, 1982.

———. *Shared Symbols, Contested Meanings: Gros Ventre Culture and History, 1778–1984*. Ithaca, N.Y.: Cornell University Press, 1987.

Francis, R. Douglas. *Images of the West: Responses to the Canadian Prairies*. Saskatoon, Saskatchewan: Western Producer Prairie Books, 1989.

Frederick, Joan. "Traditional Painting in Oklahoma." *Native Peoples: The Journal of the Heard Museum* 8, no. 4 (1995): 46–51.

Frideres, James S. *Native People in Canada: Contemporary Conflicts*. 2d ed. Scarborough, Ontario: Prentice-Hall Canada, 1983.

Friesen, Gerald. *The Canadian Prairies: A History*. Lincoln: University of Nebraska Press, 1984.

Frison, George C. *Prehistoric Hunters of the High Plains*. New York: Academic Press, 1978.

Fritz, Henry E. *The Movement for Indian Assimilation, 1860–1890*. Philadelphia: University of Pennsylvania Press, 1963.

Gates, C. M., ed. *Five Fur Traders of the Northwest*. Minneapolis: University of Minnesota Press, 1933.

Gelb, Norman, ed. *Jonathan Carver's Travels through America, 1766–1768: An Eighteenth-Century Explorer's Account of Uncharted America*. New York: John Wiley & Sons, 1993.

Gibson, Arrell Morgan. *The American Indian: Prehistory to the Present*. Lexington, Mass.: D. C. Heath, 1980.

———. *Oklahoma: A History of 5 Centuries*. 2d ed. Norman: University of Oklahoma Press, 1981.

Gradwohl, David Mayer. *Prehistoric Villages in Eastern Nebraska*. Lincoln: Nebraska State Historical Society Publications in Anthropology, no. 4, 1969.

Grange, Roger T., Jr. *Pawnee and Lower Loup Pottery*. Lincoln: Nebraska State Historical Society Publications in Anthropology, no. 3., 1968.

Greeley, Horace. *An Overland Journey*. New York: C. M. Saxton, Barker and Co., 1860.

Gregg, Josiah. *Commerce on the Prairies*. Norman: Oklahoma University, 1954.

Bibliography

Grinnell, George Bird. *The Cheyenne Indians*. 2 vols. New Haven, Conn.: Yale University Press, 1923.

———. *Pawnee, Blackfoot and Cheyenne: History and Folklore of the Plains*. New York: Charles Scribner's Sons, 1961.

Hafen, LeRoy R., and W. J. Ghent. *Broken Hand: The Life of Thomas Fitzpatrick, Mountain Man, Guide and Indian Agent*. Denver: Old West Publishing, 1931.

Hagan, William T. *American Indians*. Chicago: University of Chicago Press, 1961.

———. *Indian Police and Judges: Experiments in Acculturation and Control*. New Haven, Conn.: Yale University Press, 1966.

———. *Quanah Parker, Comanche Chief*. Norman: University of Oklahoma Press, 1993.

———. *United States–Comanche Relations: The Reservation Years*. New Haven, Conn.: Yale University Press, 1976.

Haines, Francis. *The Buffalo: The Story of American Bison and their Hunters from Prehistoric Times to the Present*. New York: Thomas Y. Crowell, 1970.

———. *The Plains Indians: Their Origins, Migrations and Cultural Development*. New York: Thomas Y. Crowell, 1976.

Hammond, George P., and Agapito Rey, eds. *Narratives of the Coronado Expedition*. Albuquerque: University of New Mexico Press, 1940.

Harring, Sidney L. *Crow Dog's Case: American Indian Sovereignty, Tribal Law, and United States Law in the Nineteenth Century*. New York: Cambridge University Press, 1994.

Harrod, Howard L. *Becoming and Remaining a People: Native American Religions on the Northern Plains*. Tucson: University of Arizona Press, 1995.

Hassrick, Royal B. *The Sioux: Life and Customs of a Warrior Society*. Norman: University of Oklahoma Press, 1964.

Hennepin, Louis. *A Description of Louisiana*. March of America Facsimile Series, vol. 30. Translated by John Gilmory Shea. Ann Arbor, Mich.: University Microfilms, 1966.

Hertzberg, Hazel W. *The Search for an American Indian Identity: Modern Pan-Indian Movements*. Syracuse, N.Y.: Syracuse University Press, 1971.

Hickerson, Nancy Parrott. *The Jumanos: Hunters and Traders of the South Plains*. Austin: University of Texas Press, 1994.

———. "Jumano: The Missing Link in South Plains History." *Journal of the West* 29 (October, 1990): 5–12.

Hill, Edward E. *The Office of Indian Affairs, 1824–1880: Historical Sketches*. New York: Clearwater, 1974.

Hoebel, E. Adamson. *The Plains Indians: A Critical Bibliography*. Bloomington: Indiana University Press, 1977.

Hoig, Stan. *Tribal Wars of the Southern Plains*. Norman: University of Oklahoma Press, 1992.

Holder, Preston. *The Hoe and the Horse on the Plains: A Study of Cultural Development among North American Indians*. Lincoln: University of Nebraska Press, 1970.

Hopkins, Donald R. *Princes and Peasants: Smallpox in History*. Chicago: University of Chicago Press, 1983.

Hoxie, Frederick E. *Parading Through History: The Making of the Crow Nation in America, 1805–1935.* New York: Cambridge University Press, 1996.

Hundley, Norris, Jr. "The *Winters* Decision and Indian Water Rights: A Mystery Reexamined." *Western Historical Quarterly* 13 (January, 1982): 17–42.

———, ed. *The American Indian.* Foreword by Vine Deloria, Jr. Santa Barbara, Calif.: Clio Books, 1974.

Hyde, George E. *Indians of the High Plains: From the Prehistoric Period to the Coming of Europeans.* Norman: University of Oklahoma Press, 1959.

———. *Life of George Bent: Written from His Letters.* Edited by Savoie Lottinville. Norman: University of Oklahoma Press, 1968.

———. *The Pawnee Indians.* Norman: University of Oklahoma Press, 1974.

———. *Red Cloud's Folk: A History of the Oglala Sioux.* Norman: University of Oklahoma Press, 1937.

———. *A Sioux Chronicle.* Norman: University of Oklahoma Press, 1956.

———. *Spotted Tail's Folk: A History of the Brule Sioux.* Norman: University of Oklahoma Press, 1957.

"Indian Bow and Arrow." *Frontier Times* 8 (1930): 141–42.

Innis, Harold A. *The Fur Trade in Canada: An Introduction to Canadian Economic History.* Rev. ed. Toronto: University of Toronto Press, 1956.

Irwin, Lee. *The Dream Seekers: Native American Visionary Traditions of the Great Plains.* Foreword by Vine Deloria, Jr. Norman: University of Oklahoma Press, 1994.

Iverson, Peter. *When Indians Became Cowboys: Native Peoples and Cattle Ranching in the American West.* Norman: University of Oklahoma Press, 1994.

———, ed. *The Plains Indians of the Twentieth Century.* Norman: University of Oklahoma Press, 1985.

Jackson, Donald, ed. *The Journals of Zebulon Montgomery Pike.* 2 vols. Norman: University of Oklahoma Press, 1966.

Jacobs, Wilbur R. *Dispossessing the American Indian: Indians and Whites on the Colonial Frontier.* New York: Charles Scribner's Sons, 1972.

———. "The Tip of the Iceberg: Pre-Columbian Indian Demography and Some Implications for Revision." *William and Mary Quarterly* 3rd ser., 21 (1974): 123–32.

James, Edwin, comp. *Account of an Expedition from Pittsburgh to the Rocky Mountains, Performed in the Years 1819 and '20, by orders of the Hon. J. C. Calhoun, Sec'y of War: Under the Command of Major Stephen H. Long.* Vols. 14–17 in *Early Western Travels, 1748–1846.* 32 vols. Edited by Reuben G. Thwaites. Cleveland: Arthur Clark Co., 1905; reprint, New York: Ames Press, 1966.

Jennings, Francis. *The Invasion of America: Indians, Colonialism, and the Cant of Conquest.* Chapel Hill: University of North Carolina Press, 1975; reissued, New York: W. W. Norton, 1976.

Jennings, Jesse D., and Edward Norbeck, eds. *Prehistoric Man in the New World.* Chicago: University of Chicago Press, 1964.

Jensen, Richard E., R. Eli Paul, and John E. Carter. *Eyewitness at Wounded Knee.* Lincoln: University of Nebraska Press, 1991.

John, Elizabeth A. H. *Storms Brewed in Other Men's Worlds: The Confrontation of Indians, Spanish, and French in the Southwest, 1540–1795.* College Station: Texas A&M University Press, 1975.

Jones, David E. *Sanapia: Comanche Medicine Woman.* New York: Holt, Rinehart and Winston, 1972.

Jones, Douglas C. *The Treaty of Medicine Lodge: The Story of the Great Treaty Council as Told by Eyewitnesses.* Norman: University of Oklahoma Press, 1966.

Jorgensen, Joseph G. *The Sun Dance Religion: Power for the Powerless.* Chicago: University of Chicago Press, 1972.

Josephy, Alvin M., Jr. "By Fayre and Gentle Means: The Hudson's Bay Company and the American Indian." *American West* 9 (September, 1972): 4–11.

———. *The Indian Heritage of America.* New York: Alfred A. Knopf, 1970.

———. *Now that the Buffalo's Gone: A Study of Today's American Indians.* New York: Alfred A. Knopf, 1982.

Karlen, Arno. *Napoleon's Glands and other Ventures in Biohistory.* Boston: Little, Brown and Company, 1984.

Katz, Loren William. *Black Indians: A Hidden Heritage.* New York: Atheneum, 1986.

Kavanagh, Thomas W. *Comanche Political History: An Ethnohistorical Perspective, 1706–1875.* Lincoln: University of Nebraska Press, 1996.

Kehoe, Alice Beck. *The Ghost Dance: Ethnohistory and Revitalization.* New York: Holt, Rinehart and Winston, 1989.

———. *North American Indians: A Comprehensive Account.* 2d ed. Englewood Cliffs, N.J.: Prentice-Hall, 1991.

Keller, William. *The Nation's Advocate: Henry Marie Brackenridge and Young America.* Pittsburgh: University of Pittsburgh Press, 1956.

Kendall, George Wilkins. *Narrative of the Texan–Santa Fe Expedition.* 2 vols. London: Wiley and Putnam, 1844; facsimile, Austin: Steck, 1935.

Kennedy, Michael Stephen, ed. *The Assiniboines: From the Accounts of the Old Ones Told to First Boy (James Larpenteur Long).* Norman: University of Oklahoma Press, 1961.

Kenney, M. M. "Tribal Society among Texas Indians." *Quarterly of the Texas Historical Association* 1 (July, 1897): 26–33.

Kessell, John L. "'To See Such Marvels with My Own Eyes:' Spanish Exploration in the Western Borderlands." *Montana: The Magazine of Western History* 41 (autumn, 1991): 68–75.

Kindscher, Kelly. *Medicinal Wild Plants of the Prairie: An Ethnobotanical Guide.* Lawrence: University Press of Kansas, 1992.

Krieger, Alex D. *Culture Complexes and Chronology in North Texas with Extension of Puebloan Datings to the Mississippi Valley.* University of Texas Publication no. 4640. Austin: University of Texas Press, 1946.

Kroeber, A. L. "Native American Population." *American Anthropologist,* n.s., 36 (1934): 1–25.

Kroeber, Alfred L. *Cultural and Natural Areas of Native North America.* Berkeley: University of California Publications in American Archaeology and Ethnology, no. 38, 1939.

Kupferer, Harriet J. *Ancient Drums, Other Moccasins: Native North American Cultural Adaptation*. Englewood Cliffs, N.J.: Prentice Hall, 1988.

La Barre, Weston. *The Ghost Dance: Origins of Religion*. Garden City, N.Y.: Doubleday, 1970.

———. *The Peyote Cult*. 4th ed. New York: Archon Books, 1975.

Lancaster, Richard. *Piegan: A Look from Within at the Life, Times, and Legacy of an American Indian Tribe*. Garden City, N.Y.: Doubleday, 1966.

Larpenteur, Charles. *Forty Years a Fur Trader on the Upper Missouri: The Personal Narrative of Charles Larpenteur, 1833–1872*. Introduction by Milo Milton Quaife. Chicago: Lakeside Press, 1933.

Larson, Robert W. *Red Cloud: Warrior-Statesman of the Lakota Sioux*. Norman: University of Oklahoma Press, 1997.

Laubin, Reginald, and Gladys Laubin. *American Indian Archery*. Norman: University of Oklahoma Press, 1980.

———. *Indian Dances of North America: Their Importance to Indian Life*. Norman: University of Oklahoma Press, 1977.

———. *The Indian Tipi: Its History, Construction, and Use*. Rev. ed. Norman: University of Oklahoma Press, 1977.

Laughlin, William S., and Albert B. Harper, eds. *The First Americans: Origins, Affinities, and Adaptations*. New York: Gustav Fischer, 1979.

Leckie, William H. *The Buffalo Soldiers: A Narrative of the Negro Cavalry in the West*. Norman: University of Oklahoma Press, 1967.

———. *The Military Conquest of the Southern Plains*. Norman: University of Oklahoma Press, 1963.

Lehman, Herman. *Nine Years among the Indians, 1870–1879*. Austin: Von Boechman-Jones Co., Printers, 1927.

Leland, Joy. *Firewater Myths: North American Indian Drinking Alcohol Addiction*. New Brunswick, N.J.: Rutgers Center of Alcohol Studies, 1976.

Lemert, Edwin M. "The Use of Alcohol in Three Salish Indian Tribes." *Quarterly Journal of Studies on Alcohol* 19 (1958): 90–107.

Levine, Stuart, and Nancy Oestreich Lurie, eds. *The American Indian Today*. Rev. ed. Deland, Fla.: Everett/Edwards, 1968.

Lewis, Anna. "Du Tisne's Expedition into Oklahoma, 1719." *Chronicles of Oklahoma* 3 (December, 1925): 320–23.

———. "La Harpe's First Expedition in Oklahoma, 1718–1719." *Chronicles of Oklahoma* 2 (December, 1924): 331–49.

Lewis, Thomas H. *The Medicine Men: Oglala Sioux Ceremony and Healing*. Lincoln: University of Nebraska Press, 1992.

Linderman, Frank B. *Plenty Coups: Chief of the Crows*. Lincoln: University of Nebraska Press, 1962.

———. *Pretty-shield, Medicine Woman of the Crows*. Lincoln: University of Nebraska Press, 1972.

Littlefield, Daniel F., Jr., and James W. Parins. *A Biobibliography of Native American Writers, 1772–1924*. Metuchen, N.J.: Scarecrow Press, 1981.

Livingston, Lili Cockerille. *American Indian Ballerinas*. Norman: University of Oklahoma Press, 1997.

Lomawaima, K. Tsianina. *They Called It Prairie Light: The Story of Chilocco Indian School*. Lincoln: University of Nebraska Press, 1994.

Lowie, Robert H. "The Assiniboin." *Anthropological Papers of the American Museum of Natural History* 4 (1909): 1–270.

———. *Indians of the Plains*. Preface by Raymond J. DeMallie. Lincoln: University of Nebraska Press, 1982; American Museum of Natural History, 1954.

Luebke, Frederick C., ed. *Ethnicity on the Great Plains*. Lincoln: University of Nebraska Press, 1980.

McCann, Lloyd E. "The Grattan Massacre." *Nebraska History* 37 (1956): 1–26.

McDermott, John Francis, ed. *The Frontier Re-examined*. Urbana: University of Illinois Press, 1967.

McGaa, Ed (Eagle Man). *Mother Earth Spirituality: Native American Paths to Healing Ourselves and Our World*. New York: HarperSanFrancisco, 1990.

McGinnis, Anthony. *Counting Coup and Cutting Horses: Intertribal Warfare on the Northern Great Plains, 1783–1889*. Evergreen, Colo.: Cordillera Press, 1990.

MacGregor, Gordon. *Warriors without Weapons: A Study of the Society and Personality Development of the Pine Ridge Sioux*. Chicago: University of Chicago Press, 1946.

McHugh, Tom. *The Time of the Buffalo*. New York: Alfred A. Knopf, 1972.

McLoughlin, William. "Ghost Dance Movements: Some Thoughts on Definitions." *Ethnohistory* 37 (winter, 1990): 25–44.

McNeill, William H. *Plagues and People*. Garden City, N.Y.: Anchor Press/Doubleday, 1976.

McNickle, D'Arcy. *Native American Tribalism: Indian Survivals and Renewals*. New York: Oxford University Press, 1973.

———. *They Came Here First: The Epic of the American Indian*. Rev. ed. New York: Harper & Row, 1975.

Mails, Thomas E. *Mystic Warriors of the Plains*. Garden City, N.Y.: Doubleday, 1972.

Malone, Michael P., and Richard Roeder. *Montana: A History of Two Centuries*. Seattle: University of Washington Press, 1976.

Mandelbaum, David G. "Alcohol and Culture." *Current Anthropology* 6 (1965): 281–92.

———. *The Plains Cree: An Ethnographic, Historical, and Comparative Study*. Canadian Plains Studies no. 9. Regina: Canadian Plains Research Center, 1979.

Marcy, Randolph B. *Thirty Years of Army Life on the Border*. New York: Harper & Brothers, 1866.

Margry, Pierre, ed. *Decouvertes et Etablissements des Francais dans l'Ouest et dans le Sud de l'Amerique Septentrionale, 1614–1754*. 6 vols. Paris: 1879–1888; reprint, New York: AMS Press, 1974.

Marquis, Thomas B., ed. *Wooden Leg: A Warrior Who Fought Custer*. Lincoln: University of Nebraska Press, 1962.

Martin, Calvin. *Keepers of the Game: Indian-Animal Relations and the Fur Trade*. Berkeley: University of California Press, 1978.

———, ed. *The American Indian and the Problem of History*. New York: Oxford University Press, 1987.

Martin, Paul S. "The Discovery of America." *Science* 179 (1973): 969–74.

Mathews, John Joseph. *The Osages: Children of the Middle Waters*. Norman: University of Oklahoma Press, 1961.

Maurer, Evan M., ed. *Visions of the People: A Pictorial History of Plains Indian Life*. Seattle: University of Washington Press, 1992.

Maximilian, Alexander Philip, Prince of Wied-Neuwied. *Travels in the Interior of North America, 1832–1834*. Vols. 22–24 in *Early Western Travels, 1748–1846*. 32 vols. Edited by Rueben G. Thwaites. Cleveland: Arthur Clark Co., 1905; reprint, New York: Ames Press, 1966.

Meredith, Howard. *Dancing on Common Ground: Tribal Cultures and Alliances on the Southern Plains*. Lawrence: University Press of Kansas, 1995.

Meriam, Lewis, et al. *The Problem of Indian Administration*. Baltimore, Md.: Johns Hopkins Press, 1928.

Meyer, Roy W. *History of the Santee Sioux*. Lincoln: University of Nebraska Press, 1967.

Miles, Nelson A. *Personal Recollections and Observations of General Nelson A. Miles*. Chicago: Werner, 1896.

Milloy, John S. *The Plains Cree: Trade, Diplomacy and War, 1790–1870*. Manitoba: University of Manitoba Press, 1988.

Montgomery, Henry W. "Remains of Prehistoric Man in the Dakotas." *American Anthropologist* 8, no. 4 (1906): 640–51.

Moore, John H., ed. *The Political Economy of North American Indians*. Norman: University of Oklahoma Press, 1993.

Moquin, Wayne, with Charles Van Doren, eds. *Great Documents in American Indian History*. New York: Praeger, 1973.

Morrison, R. Bruce, and C. Roderick Wilson, eds. *Native Peoples: The Canadian Experience*. Toronto: McClelland and Stewart, 1986.

Morton, Edward D. *To Touch the Wind: An Introduction to Native American Philosophy & Beliefs*. Dubuque, Iowa: Kendall/Hunt, 1988.

Morton, W. L. *Manitoba: A History*. Toronto: University of Toronto Press, 1957.

Mowrey, Daniel P., and Paul H. Carlson. "The Native Grasslands of the High Plains of West Texas: Past, Present, Future." *West Texas Historical Association Year Book* 63 (1987): 24–41.

Nabokov, Peter. *Two Leggings: The Making of a Crow Warrior*. New York: Thomas Y. Crowell, 1967.

———, ed. *Native American Testimony: A Chronicle of Indian-White Relations from Prophecy to the Present, 1492–1992*. Foreword by Vine Deloria, Jr. New York: Viking, 1991.

Nasatier, A. P., ed. *Before Lewis and Clark: Documents Illustrating the History of the Missouri*. 2 vols. St. Louis: St. Louis Historical Documents Foundation, 1952.

Neighbours, Kenneth F. "Robert S. Neighbors and the Founding of the Texas Indian Reservations." *West Texas Historical Association Year Book* 31 (1955): 65–74.

Neihardt, John G., ed. *Black Elk Speaks: Being the Life Story of a Holy Man of the Oglala Sioux*. Introduction by Vine Deloria, Jr. Lincoln: University of Nebraska Press, 1979.

Newcomb, W. W., Jr. *The Indians of Texas: Prehistoric to Modern Times*. Austin: University of Texas Press, 1961.

Nichols, Roger L. *General Henry Atkinson: A Western Military Career*. Norman: University of Oklahoma Press, 1965.

———, ed. *The Missouri Expedition of 1818–1820: The Journal of Surgeon John Gale with Related Documents*. Norman: University of Oklahoma Press, 1969.

Nichols, Roger L., and Patrick L. Holley. *Stephen Long and American Frontier Exploration*. Newark: University of Delaware Press, 1980.

Niethammer, Carolyn. *Daughters of the Earth*. New York: Macmillan, 1977.

Norall, Frank. *Bourgmont: Explorer of the Missouri, 1689–1725*. Lincoln: University of Nebraska Press, 1988.

Noyes, Stanley. *Los Comanches: The Horse People, 1751–1845*. Albuquerque: University of New Mexico Press, 1993.

Nuttall, Thomas. *A Journal of Travels into the Arkansas Territory during the Year 1819*. Edited by Savoie Lottenville. Norman: University of Oklahoma Press, 1980.

Nye, Wilbur S. "The Annual Sun Dance of the Kiowa Indians." *Chronicles of Oklahoma* 12 (September, 1934): 340–58.

———. *Bad Medicine and Good: Tales of the Kiowas*. Norman: University of Oklahoma Press, 1962.

———. *Carbine and Lance: The Story of Old Fort Sill*. Norman: University of Oklahoma Press, 1938.

Oerlemans, J., and C. J. van der Veen. *Ice Sheets and Climate*. Dordrecht, The Netherlands: D. Reidel, 1989.

Oliver, Symmes C. *Ecology and Cultural Continuity as Contributing Factors in the Social Organization of the Plains Indians*. Berkeley: University of California Publications in American Archaeology and Ethnology 48, No. 1, 1962.

Owsley, Douglas W., and Richard L. Jantz, eds. *Skeletal Biology in the Great Plains: Migration, Warfare, Health, and Subsistence*. Washington, D.C.: Smithsonian Institution Press, 1994.

Parfit, Michael. "Powwow: A Gathering of the Tribes." *National Geographic* 185 (June, 1994): 88–113.

Parman, Donald L. *Indians and the American West in the Twentieth Century*. Bloomington: Indiana University Press, 1994.

Pauketat, Timothy R. *The Ascent of Chiefs: Cahokia and Mississippian Politics in Native North America*. Tuscaloosa: University of Alabama Press, 1994.

Philp, Kenneth R. *John Collier's Crusade for Indian Reform, 1920–1954*. Tucson: University of Arizona Press, 1977.

Powell, Peter J. *Peoples of the Sacred Mountain*. 2 vols. New York: Harper & Row, 1981.

Pratt, Richard Henry. *Battlefield and Classroom: Four Decades with the American Indian, 1867–1904*. Edited by Robert M. Utley. New Haven, Conn.: Yale University Press, 1964.

Prist, Loring Benson. *Uncle Sam's Step-children: The Reformation of United States Indian Policy, 1865–1887*. Lincoln: University of Nebraska Press, 1975 (1942).

Prucha, Francis Paul. *American Indian Policy in Crisis: Christian Reformers and the Indian, 1865–1900*. Norman: University of Oklahoma Press, 1976.

———. *American Indian Policy in the Formative Years: The Indian Trade and Intercourse Acts, 1790–1834*. Lincoln: University of Nebraska Press, 1970 (1962).

————. "American Indian Policy in the Twentieth Century." *Western Historical Quarterly* 15 (January, 1984): 5–18.

————. "Indian Removal and the Great American Desert." *Indiana Magazine of History* 59 (1963): 299–322.

————. *The Sword of the Republic: The United States Army on the Frontier, 1783–1846*. New York: Macmillan, 1969.

————, ed. *Documents of United States Indian Policy*. 2d ed. Lincoln: University of Nebraska Press, 1990.

Quimby, George Irving. *Indian Culture and European Trade Goods*. Madison: University of Wisconsin Press, 1966.

Ransom, Jay Ellis. "The Big Horn Medicine Wheel: An American Stonehenge?" *American West* 8 (March, 1971): 16–17, 62–64.

Rathjen, Frederick W. *The Texas Panhandle Frontier*. Austin: University of Texas Press, 1973.

Ray, Arthur J. *Indians in the Fur Trade: Their Role as Trappers, Hunters, and Middlemen in the Lands Southwest of Hudson Bay, 1660–1870*. Toronto: University of Toronto Press, 1974.

Renaud, E. B. "Prehistoric Cultures of the Cimarron Valley, Northeastern New Mexico and Western Oklahoma." *Colorado Scientific Society Proceedings* 12, no. 5 (1930): 122–35.

Richardson, Rupert N. *The Comanche Barrier to South Plains Settlement*. Glendale, Calif.: William D. Clark, 1933.

————. "The Culture of the Comanche Indians." *Texas Archeological and Paleontological Society Bulletin* 1 (1929): 58–73.

Richardson, Rupert N., Adrian Anderson, and Ernest Wallace. *Texas: The Lone Star State*. 7th ed. Upper Saddle River, N.J.: Prentice Hall, 1997.

Rister, Carl Coke. "Indians as Buffalo Hunters." *Frontier Times* 5 (September, 1928): 456, 494–95.

————. "The Significance of the Jacksboro Indian Affair of 1871." *Southwestern Historical Quarterly* 29 (1926): 181–200.

Robinson, Elwyn B. *History of North Dakota*. Lincoln: University of Nebraska Press, 1966.

Roe, Frank Gilbert. *The Indian and the Horse*. Norman: University of Oklahoma Press, 1955.

Rollings, Willard H. *The Osage: An Ethnohistorical Study of Hegemony on the Prairie-Plains*. Columbia: University of Missouri Press, 1992.

Ronda, James P. *Lewis and Clark among the Indians*. Lincoln: University of Nebraska Press, 1984.

Roscoe, Will. "'That is My Road': The Life and Times of a Crow Berdache." *Montana: The Magazine of Western History* 40 (winter, 1990): 46–55.

Russell, Don. "How Many Indians Were Killed? White Man versus Red Man: The Facts and the Legend." *American West* 10 (July, 1973): 42–47, 61–63.

Samek, Hana. *The Blackfoot Confederacy, 1880–1920: A Comparative Study of Canadian and U.S. Indian Policy*. Albuquerque: University of New Mexico Press, 1987.

Sánchez, José María. "A Trip to Texas in 1828." Translated by Carlos E. Casteñeda. *Southwestern Historical Quarterly* 29 (April, 1926): 249–88.

Sandoz, Mari. *Cheyenne Autumn*. New York: McGraw-Hill, 1953.

Satz, Ronald N. *American Indian Policy in the Jacksonian Era*. Lincoln: University of Nebraska Press, 1975.

Savage, Henry, Jr. *Discovering America, 1700–1875*. New York: Harper & Row, 1979.

Schell, Herbert S. *History of South Dakota*. Lincoln: University of Nebraska Press, 1961.

Schlesier, Karl H., ed. *Plains Indians, A.D. 500–1500: The Archaeological Past of Historic Groups*. Norman: University of Oklahoma Press, 1994.

Schusky, Ernest L. *The Forgotten Sioux: An Ethnohistory of the Lower Brule Reservation*. Chicago: Nelson-Hall, 1975.

Secoy, Frank Raymond. *Changing Military Patterns on the Great Plains (17th Century through Early 19th Century)*. Locust Valley, N.Y.: J. J. Augustin, 1953.

Shantz. H. L. "The Natural Vegetation of the Great Plains Region." *Annals of the Association of American Geographers* 13, no. 2 (1923): 81–107.

Slotkin, J. S. *The Peyote Religion*. Glencoe, Ill.: Free Press, 1956.

Smith, Ralph D. "The Comanche Bridge between Oklahoma and Mexico, 1843–1844." *Chronicles of Oklahoma* 39 (spring, 1961): 54–69.

————, ed. "Account of the Journey of Benard de la Harpe: Discovery Made by Him of Several Nations Situated in the West." *Southwestern Historical Quarterly* 62 (July, 1958): 75–86; (October, 1958): 246–59; (January, 1959): 371–85; (April, 1959): 525–41.

Smithwick, Noah. *The Evolution of a State, or Recollections of Old Texas Days*. Austin, Tex.: compiled by his daughter, Norma Smithwick Donaldson, 1900.

Snow, Dean R. *The Archaeology of North America*. New York: Viking Press, 1976.

————. *Native American Prehistory: A Critical Bibliography*. Bloomington: Indiana University Press, 1979.

Spencer, Robert S., Jesse D. Jennings, et al. *The Native Americans: Ethnology and Backgrounds of the North American Indians*. 2nd ed. New York: Harper & Row, 1977.

Spier, Leslie. "The Sun Dance of the Plains Indians: Its Development and Diffusion." *Anthropological Papers of the American Museum of Natural History* 16 (1921): 433–527.

Standing Bear, Luther. *My People the Sioux*. Boston: Houghton Mifflin, 1928.

Stannard, David E. *American Holocaust: The Conquest of the New World*. New York: Oxford University Press, 1992.

Stark, Michael. "Blackwater Draw: An Archaeological Cornucopia." *Southwest Heritage* 5 (summer, 1975): 38–41.

Stewart, Omer C. *Peyote Religion: A History*. Norman: University of Oklahoma Press, 1987.

Stewart, T. D. *The People of America*. New York: Charles Scribner's Sons, 1973.

Studer, Floyd V. "Archeology of the Texas Panhandle." *Panhandle-Plains Historical Review* 27 (1955): 87–95.

Sundstrom, Linea. "Smallpox Used Them Up: References to Epidemic Disease in Northern Plains Winter Counts, 1714–1920." *Ethnohistory* 44 (spring, 1997): 305–44.

Sutton, Imre. *Irredeemable America: The Indians' Estate and Land Claims*. Albuquerque: University of New Mexico Press, 1985.

Swagerty, Jacqueline Peterson. "The Fruits of a Vivid Historical Imagination."
Chronicle of Higher Education 37 (September 26, 1990): B2—B3.

Swagerty, W. R., ed. *Scholars and the Indian Experience: Critical Reviews of Recent
Writing in the Social Sciences*. Bloomington: Indiana University Press, 1984.

"Systematic Discrimination in the Indian Claims Commission: The Burden of Proof
in Redressing Historical Wrongs." *Iowa Law Review* 57 (June, 1972): 1300–19.

Szabo, Joyce M. *Howling Wolf and the History of Ledger Art*. Albuquerque: University
of New Mexico Press, 1994.

Tanner, Ogden. *The Canadians*. Alexandria, Va.: Time-Life Books, 1977.

Taylor, A. A. "The Medicine Lodge Peace Council." *Chronicles of Oklahoma* 2 (June,
1924): 98–118.

Thistle, Paul C. *Indian-European Trade Relations in the Lower Saskatchewan River
Region to 1840*. Winnipeg: University of Manitoba Press, 1988.

Thomas, Alfred Barnaby, ed. *After Coronado: Spanish Exploration Northeast of New
Mexico, 1696–1727*. Norman: University of Oklahoma Press, 1935.

Thompson, David. *David Thompson's Narrative*. Edited by J. B. Tyrell. New York:
Greenwood Press, 1968 (1916).

Thornton, Russell. *American Indian Holocaust and Survival: A Population History
since 1492*. Norman: University of Oklahoma Press, 1987.

———. *We Shall Live Again: The 1870 and 1890 Ghost Dance Movements as
Demographic Revitalization*. Cambridge: Cambridge University Press, 1986.

Thornton, Russell, Gary D. Sandefur, and Harold G. Rasmick. *The Urbanization of
American Indians: A Critical Bibliography*. Bloomington: Indiana University
Press, 1982.

Thwaites, Rueben G., ed. *Original Journals of the Lewis and Clark Expedition*. 2 vols.
New York: Antiquarian Press, 1959.

Tibbles, Thomas Henry. *Buckskin and Blanket Days*. Garden City, N.Y.: Doubleday,
1957.

Trafzer, Clifford E., ed. *American Indian Identity: Today's Changing Perspectives*.
Sacramento, Calif.: Sierra Oaks, 1985.

Trigger, Bruce G. "Early Native North American Responses to European Contact:
Romantic versus Rationalistic Interpretations." *Journal of American History* 77
(March, 1991): 1195–1215.

Tyler, Daniel, ed. *Red Men and Hat-Wearers: Viewpoints in Indian History*. Fort
Collins: Papers from the Colorado State Conference on Indian History, 1974.

Underhill, Lonnie E., and Daniel F. Littlefield, eds. *Hamlin Garland's Observations
on the American Indian*. Tucson: University of Arizona Press, 1976.

Underhill, Ruth Murray. *Red Man's America: A History of Indians in the United
States*. Rev. ed. Chicago: University of Chicago Press, 1971.

Unrau, William E. *Mixed-Bloods and Tribal Dissolution: Charles Curtis and the Quest
for Indian Identity*. Lawrence: University Press of Kansas, 1989.

Utley, Robert M. *Cavalier in Buckskin: George Armstong Custer and the Western
Military Frontier*. Norman: University of Oklahoma Press, 1988.

———. *Frontier Regulars: The United States Army and the Indian, 1866–1891*. New
York: Macmillan, 1973.

———. *Frontiersmen in Blue: The United States Army and the Indian, 1848–1865*.
New York: Macmillan, 1967.

———. *The Indian Frontier of the American West, 1846–1890*. Albuquerque: University of New Mexico Press, 1984.

———. *The Lance and the Shield: The Life and Times of Sitting Bull*. New York: Henry Holt, 1993.

———. *The Last Days of the Sioux Nation*. New Haven, Conn.: Yale University Press, 1963.

———. "Origins of the Great Sioux War: The Brown-Anderson Controversy Revisited." *Montana: The Magazine of Western History* 42 (autumn, 1992): 48–52.

Van Kirk, Silvia. *Many Tender Ties: Women in Fur-Trade Society, 1670–1870*. Norman: University of Oklahoma Press, 1980.

Vickers, Chris, and Ralph Bird. "A Copper Trade Object from the Headwaters Lakes Aspect of Manitoba." *American Antiquity* 15, no. 2 (1949): 157–60.

Viola, Herman J. *Ben Nighthorse Campbell: An American Warrior*. New York: Orion Books, 1993.

Vogel, Virgil J. *American Indian Medicine*. Norman: University of Oklahoma Press, 1970.

Walker, J. R. "The Sun Dance and other Ceremonies of the Oglala Division of the Teton Dakota." *Anthropological Papers of the American Museum of Natural History* 16 (1917): 51–221.

Walker, James R. *Lakota Society*. Edited by Raymond J. DeMallie. Lincoln: University of Nebraska Press, 1982.

Wallace, Ernest. "The Great Spirit Did Not Put You Here to Steal Our Land." *Studies in History* 6 (1976): 11–26.

———. *Ranald S. Mackenzie on the Texas Frontier*. Lubbock: West Texas Museum Association, 1964.

Wallace, Ernest, and Adrian Anderson. "R. S. Mackenzie: The Raid into Mexico in 1873." *Arizona and the West* 7 (summer, 1965): 105–26.

Wallace, Ernest, and E. Adamson Hoebel. *The Comanches: Lords of the South Plains*. Norman: University of Oklahoma Press, 1952.

Washburn, Wilcomb E. *The Indian in America*. New York: Harper & Row, Publishers, 1975.

Webb, Walter Prescott. *The Great Plains*. New York: Grosset & Dunlap, 1931.

Weber, David J. *The Spanish Frontier in North America*. New Haven, Conn.: Yale University Press, 1992.

Weddle, Robert S. *The San Saba Mission: Spanish Pivot in Texas*. Austin: University of Texas Press, 1964.

Wedel, Waldo. *Prehistoric Man on the Great Plains*. Norman: University of Oklahoma Press, 1961.

Weeks, Philip. *Farewell, My Nation: The American Indian and the United States, 1820–1890*. Arlington Heights, Ill.: Harlan Davidson, 1990.

Wellman, Paul I. *Death on the Prairie*. New York: Macmillan, 1934.

Wessel, Thomas R. "Market Economy and Changing Subsistence Patterns: A Comment." *Agricultural History* 66 (spring, 1992): 61–65.

Whisenhunt, Donald W., ed. *Texas: A Sesquicentennial Celebration*. Austin, Tex.: Eakin Press, 1984.

White, Richard. *The Middle Ground: Indians, Empires, and Republics in the Great Lakes Region, 1650–1815*. Cambridge: Cambridge University Press, 1991.

———. "The Winning of the West: The Expansion of the Sioux in the Eighteenth and Nineteenth Centuries." *Journal of American History* 65 (September, 1978): 319–43.

Will, George F. "An Unusual Group of Mounds in North Dakota." *American Anthropologist* 23, no. 2 (1921): 175–79.

Willey, Gordon R. *An Introduction to American Archaeology.* 2 vols. Englewood Cliffs, N.J.: Prentice-Hall, 1966.

Williamson, Ray A. *Living the Sky: The Cosmos of the American Indian.* Norman: University of Oklahoma Press, 1984.

Wilson, George L. *Agriculture of the Hidatsa: An Indian Interpretation.* Minneapolis: University of Minnesota Studies in the Social Sciences, no. 9, 1917.

Wilson, Gilbert L. "The Horse and the Dog in Hidatsa Culture." *Anthropological Papers of the American Museum of Natural History* 15 (1924): 127–311.

Wissler, Clark. *The American Indian.* 3rd ed. New York: Oxford University Press, 1938.

———. *Indians of the United States: Four Centuries of their History and Culture.* Garden City, N.Y.: Doubleday, Doran & Company, 1948.

———. "The Influence of the Horse in the Development of Plains Culture." *American Anthropologist* 16 (1914): 1–25.

———. "Material Culture of the Blackfoot Indians." *Anthropological Papers of the American Museum of Natural History* 5 (1910): 1–175.

———. "Material Culture of the North American Indians." *American Anthropologist* 16 (1914): 477–505.

———. *North American Indians of the Plains.* 3rd ed. New York: American Museum of Natural History, 1948.

———. *Population Changes among the Northern Plains Indians.* Yale University Publications in Anthropology, 1938; reprinted, New Haven, Conn.: Human Relations Area Files Press, 1970.

———. *Societies and Ceremonial Associations in the Oglala Division of the Teton-Dakota.* New York: American Museum of Natural History, 1912.

———. *Societies of the Plains Indians.* New York: American Museum of Natural History, 1916. AMS Reprint, 1975.

Worcester, Donald E. "Spanish Horses among the Plains Tribes." *Pacific Historical Review* 14 (1945): 409–17.

———. "The Spread of Spanish Horses in the Southwest." *New Mexico Historical Review* 19 (1944): 225–32.

Worster, Donald. *Under Western Skies: Nature and History in the American West.* New York: Oxford University Press, 1992.

Wright, J. F. C. *Saskatchewan: The History of a Province.* Saskatoon, Saskatchewan: McClellan and Stewart, 1955.

Wright, Peter M. "The Pursuit of Dull Knife from Fort Reno." *Chronicles of Oklahoma* 46 (1968): 141–54.

Young Bear, Severt, and R. D. Theisz. *Standing in the Light: A Lakota Way of Seeing.* Lincoln: University of Nebraska Press, 1994.

Zavala, Adina de. "Religious Beliefs of the Tejas or Hasinias Indians." *Publications of the Texas Folklore Society* 1 (1916): 39–43.

Index

Holmes, 132; and Treaty of Medicine Lodge, 155, 156; and tribal alliances, 135; and vision quest, 117

concentration policy, 147

Conquering Bear (Lakota), 86; and Grattan affair, 43

contraries, 78

converging columns: army use of, 156–57; in Sioux war of 1876, 161

Cordero (Comanche), 130

corn: as basic crop, 55; and desert cultures, 24; and Mississippians, 26; and Pawnees, 29; and "three sisters," 24; varieties of, 55

Coronado, Francisco Vásquez de, 8, 29

cosmological system, 111

cotton, 24

cottonwood, 12, 14

Council Bluffs, 130, 131

Council House: massacre at, 135

Council of 44, 73

councils: among Comanches, 73; as governing units, 73–74; rituals of, 137–39; types of, 73

coup, 46–47

coureurs de bois, 124, 128

Court of Claims, 188

Court of Indian Offenses, 174

courtship, 87

coyotes, 16

cradle board, 83

Crazy Horse (Lakota), 70; as charismatic leader, 146; Great Sioux Reservation, 161; raiding of, 155; and Sioux war of 1868, 160; and Sioux war of 1876, 161; and Treaty of Fort Laramie (1868), 155; vision quest of, 86

creator force. See Holy One Above

Crees, 4

Crook, Gen. George: and Great Sioux Reservation, 177; and Poncas, 173; and Standing Bear v. Crook, 173

Crooked Neck (Cheyenne), 89

crops, 54–55

Cross Timbers, 2

Crow Creek Reservation: and allotment, 178; and Indian Reorganization Act, 187

Crow Dog (Lakota): heads agency

police, 174; kills Spotted Tail, 174; and polygyny, 88; visits Carlisle, 166

Crow Fair, 191

Crow Reservation, 178, 187

Crows, 1, 2, 47; acquire horses, 36; aid federal troops, 146; coup-counting of, 46; descent system of, 69; and horses, 37, 145; "in-law" taboos of, 89; kinship terms of, 69; language of, 7; migration route of, 33; and Piegans, 48; reservation of, 171; separate from Hidatsas, 33, 37; shifting alliances of, 134; and Shoshonis, 33; and smallpox, 132; tobacco planting of, 115; and vision quest, 117

Cuerno Verde (Comanche), 127

cultural revival, 183; and powwows, 190–91; and reservation dances, 169–70; and world wars, 166

culture area, 6

Curtis, Charles (Kansa-Osage), 191

Custer, Lt. Col. George A., 173; death of, 160; and Washita campaign, 157

Custer, S.Dak., 189

Custer expedition: to Black Hills, 161

Cut Nose (Arapaho), 147

Cut Nose (Santee), 149

Dakotas, 34; language of, 7. See also Santees; Yanktonais; Yanktons

dances, 169; and powwows, 190–91

Daugherty, Capt. William E., 180

Dawes, Henry L., 175

Dawes Act, 175; and allotment process, 177; and President Grover Cleveland, 176; results of, 177; terms of, 176. See also General Allotment Act of 1887

Deadwood, S.Dak., 174

death: traditions associated with, 107–108

deer, 21, 55

demography, 8. See also populations

Department of Interior, 152–53

descent systems, 68–69

Dhegiha speakers, 30; patrilineal clans of, 69

diseases, 132–33; and bison, 19; and health care, 190; impact of, 78–79; on modern reservations, 190; on northern plains, 129

Plenty Coups (Crow), 49, 50; and warfare, 45
political leadership, 71
polygyny, 88–89
Poncas, 5, 173; and Grass Dance, 169; language of, 7; migration route of, 30; moieties of, 68; and nomadism, 53; population of, 8, 80
Poor Bear (Kiowa Apache), 151; signs Treaty of Medicine Lodge, 155
Poor Wolf, 139
populations: and plains tribes, 8–12
Poverty Point, 23
Powder River, 12, 151; and bison, 142
Powder River Country: as "unceded Indian territory," 155
powwows, 190–91, 193
prairie dogs, 16
Pratt, Capt. Richard H., 166
pregnancy, 83
Pretty Bull (Crow), 155
Pretty Shield (Crow), 50; as healer, 81; and old ways, 166–67; and reservation life, 168; and warfare, 48
priests, 165; and spiritual practices, 116; and tribal rituals, 74–75. *See also* shamans
prior appropriation, 185
pronghorns, 55; hunting of, by Paleo-Indians, 17; Indian use of, 17; use of, in bows, 61–62
puberty: boys at, 85–86; girls at, 86; rites of, 85–86; and vision quest, 85–86
Pueblo people, 27, 31
Pueblo Revolt, 36
Pueblo villages: Apache attacks on, 31; and plains trade, 124
Pulitzer Prize, 192
pumpkins, 26

Quaker Peace Policy. *See* Grant's Peace Policy
Quanah, 104; and allotment, 178; as charismatic leader, 146; as "chief," 132; and Ghost Dance, 179; as Indian holdout, 159; leads raids, 160; as peyote cultist, 179; and polygyny, 88; takes Parker name, 178; and Treaty of Medicine Lodge, 156
Quapaws, 5; language of, 7; as marginal

Plains Indians, 6; migration route of, 30
Querechos, 31

raccoons, 14–15
raids, 144; end of, 164; purpose of, 45
railroads, 161, 171; extension of, 142; interference of, 179; and plains warfare, 144
Rainy Mountain, 112
rancherias, 32
ranchers, 171
rationing program, 185
Rawhide Buttes, 13
recreations, 107
Red Bed Plains, 13
red catlinite. *See* catlinite
Red Cloud (Lakota), 99; and agent struggles, 172; as charismatic leader, 146; and Peace Commission, 154, 155; signs Treaty of Fort Laramie (1868), 155; and Sioux war of 1866–68, 151; visits Carlisle, 166; and wagon box fight, 152
Red Dog (Lakota), 166
Red Feather (Assiniboin), 87
Red Middle Voice (Santee), 148
red pipestone. *See* catlinite
Red Power movement, 188–89
Red River (Canada), 12, 32; and Metis, 5
Red River (Tex.), 3, 13; and Pawnees, 29; and warfare, 148
Red River War, 159–60
Reifel, Ben (Lakota), 194; as U.S. congressman, 191
religious practices, 114. *See also* spiritual activities
Republican River, 12; and battle of Beecher's Island, 145, 156
"reserved" water right, 185
Rides on Clouds (Cheyenne), 139
Rio Grande, 1, 2; and brushland, 13; and Lipans, 32; and Pueblos, 27
riparian rights, 185
Rising Sun (Comanche), 151
River Crows, 2, 68
Rocky Boy's Reservation, 178
Rocky Mountains, 2, 6; and glaciers, 20; as western border, 1
Rolling Plains, 13